CRITICAL
INSIGHTS

Alice Munro

CRITICAL INSIGHTS

Alice Munro

Editor
Charles E. May
California State University, Long Beach

SALEM PRESS
A Division of EBSCO Publishing
Ipswich, Massachusetts

Cover Photo: © Paul Hawthorne/AP/Corbis

Editor's text © 2013 by Charles E. May

∞ The paper used in these volumes conforms to the American National Standard for Permanence of Paper for Printed Library Materials, Z39.48-1992 (R1997).

Library of Congress Cataloging-in-Publication Data
Alice Munro / editor, Charles E. May.
    p. cm. -- (Critical insights)
  Includes bibliographical references and index.
  ISBN 978-1-4298-3722-4 (hardcover) -- ISBN 978-1-4298-3770-5 (ebook) 1. Munro, Alice--Criticism and interpretation. I. May, Charles E. (Charles Edward), 1941-
  PR9199.3.M8Z54 2013
  813'.54--dc23
                              2012019661

PRINTED IN THE UNITED STATES OF AMERICA

Contents

Resources

About This Volume

Charles E. May

With remarkable unanimity, reviewers, critics, and fellow authors agree that Alice Munro is the best short-story writer in the world today. Robert Thacker, who has done a marvelous job in this volume of analyzing and synthesizing the vast amount of criticism that has illuminated the complex fiction of Alice Munro, quite rightly points out that throughout her distinguished career, Munro has stayed out of the limelight of the literary world and the morass of social debate, instead doing what she loves most and does best—writing.

Many of the critics cited here by Thacker, and most of the reviewers summarized by him in his authoritative biography, frequently justify their praise of Munro's fiction by arguing that the numerous characters and complexity of plot in her stories, especially her most recent ones, make them somehow novelistic. Yet Munro has always insisted that she does not write as a novelist does, that when she is writing a short story she gets a kind of tension she needs, like pulling on a rope attached to some definite place, whereas with a novel everything goes "flabby." Characters and events do not really matter in her stories, she says, for they are subordinated to an overall climate or mood. Munro's best work is usually about the hidden story of emotion and the secret life, communicated by atmosphere and tone. Her greatest stories simply do not communicate as novels do.

As Ailsa Cox points out in her discussion of Munro's last book, *Too Much Happiness* (2009), the author, who recently celebrated her eightieth birthday, has more than once threatened to give up writing. However, since the publication of *Too Much Happiness*, she has published four new stories. As I try to explain in my own essay in this book, these four stories demonstrate that the brilliance of Alice Munro's work derives not from any "novelistic" qualities but rather from their embodiment of the short story's singular method of exploring universal reality. The true power of her stories lies in what can only happen in the imagination, where, as Munro wisely knows, paradoxes abound: truth can develop out of lies, reality can derive from fantasy, and good can result from bad.

Timothy McIntyre suggests in his examination of Munro's Scots Protestant cultural background that her fictional exploration of the complex relationship between everyday reality and imaginative artifice developed, ironically, out of growing up in a culture in which reading and writing were more tolerated than celebrated. McIntyre reminds us that although writing was the only thing Munro wanted to do, it was something she was unable to explain or justify to her family. Fortunately, although her love of literature was not actively fostered by her parents, neither was it strongly discouraged, for her father harbored a secret wish to write and her mother was drawn to the theatrical. Forced to leave school for financial reasons, Munro got married and had little time to read and write while performing the domestic chores of wife and mother; fortunately, however, her husband was liberated and educated enough to believe that his wife's creative efforts were worthwhile. As McIntyre notes, one does not have to be familiar with the lower-class Scots Irish inhabitants of southwestern Ontario in the mid-twentieth century to appreciate Munro's work. Indeed, as many of the essays in this volume suggest, it is her love and knowledge of literature—storytelling, narrative technique, metaphor making, classical myths, fantasies, and fairy tales—that provide the most illuminating context for her brilliant fiction.

In a preface to *The View from Castle Rock* (2006), arguably the most intimate book she has ever written, Munro says that when she was in her mid-sixties and beginning to put together research about her family, she was also writing a "special set of stories" that she did not include in her previous four books of fiction, for although they were not memoirs, they were closer to her own life than other stories she had written. All the stories in this "special set," which appear in the second section of *The View from Castle Rock*, point to Munro's life devoted to being a writer. As a young woman in "Lying under the Apple Tree," she has secret poetic ideas about looking up through apple blossoms, which has an irresistible formality for her, like kneeling in church. After an interruption of what was almost her first sexual encounter, Munro says that over the next few years, sardonic, ferocious men in books, like Heathcliff and Rhett Butler, became her only lovers. In "Hired Girl," when Munro, seventeen, takes a summer job with a family, she has erotic and romantic fantasies about them and the glamorous people who visit them. When the summer is over, the husband gives her a copy of Isak Dinesen's *Seven Gothic Tales* (1934), and as soon as she begins to read, she loses herself in the book, believing that this gift of literature has always belonged to her. These are Alice Munro's most personal stories, portraits of the artist as a young woman.

Medrie Purdham's discussion of *Lives of Girls and Women* (1971), Munro's only novel and the closest thing to a *Künstlerroman* she has ever written, convincingly shows how, in spite of the ostensible realism of her early fiction, an important context of Munro's work is a classical literary tradition, not a tradition of simple mimesis. When Del's mother, Addie, dips her pen into her Laocoon inkwell, she provides a striking metaphor of Munro the artist dipping her own pen into the classical fount of Greek, Roman, and Christian mythos. Likewise, Purdham suggests that Del (and therefore Munro), drawn as she is to the formality of rituals and rites and the metaphorical nature of Christian narratives, is more interested in the aesthetics of religion than its ethics and more fascinated by the theatrical than the theological. Similarly, David Peck shows how in the stories of Flo and Rose in *The Beggar Maid* (1979), Munro explores the relationship between real life and role-playing, suggesting that as characters get caught up in pretense and become what they play, they not only discover who they are but also create their own identity. Mark Levene discusses the importance of metaphor in Munro's stories in *The Progress of Love* (1986), which in its exploration of the relationship between surface and depth is, like theater, another literary means by which one thing "stands in" for another in order to reveal its significant identity. And Naomi Morgenstern applies a sophisticated aspect of psychoanalysis to Munro's fiction to discuss the story "Trespasses" as an exploration of the importance of storytelling and role-playing as keys to the ultimate secret of identity, the age-old oedipal question: who am I?

Philip Coleman persuasively argues that Munro pushes her focus on the literary means that characters use to create their identities even further in *Friend of My Youth* (1990), by developing the self-reflexive narrative method of using short stories to think about the existential and emotional importance of narrative in human life. Coleman notes that although Munro has not discussed theoretical aspects of her fiction in discursive form, she reflects on narrative in her fictional work. Although Munro is concerned with the issues that confront women, Coleman reminds us, she is not what one would call a feminist writer. Although she is concerned with the social life of small-town Ontario, she is not what one would call a regional writer. Rather, as Coleman points out, Munro most often turns to literature to make sense of the self and the world in which one lives. As evidence of Munro's focus on the language of literature to discover the nature of human reality, J. R. (Tim) Struthers tackles the complexity of Munro's best-known and most analyzed story, "Meneseteung," paying particular attention to the nature of metaphor and the multilayered contexts that create the significance of the story.

Probing the often-theatrical complexity of what Munro's characters try to conceal in her turning-point collection, *Open Secrets* (1994), Michael Toolan argues that even as her stories take on the ambition of novels in their psychological depth and complexity of plot, they continue to be built on the basic characteristics of the short-story form: brevity, density, and intensity. Jeff Birkenstein approaches the issue of whether Munro's stories primarily exhibit the characteristics of short stories or the qualities of novels by examining the relationship between stories in Munro's *The Love of a Good Woman* (1998). Synthesizing the thematic issue of a community of women with the generic issue of the linked nature of the stories, Birkenstein argues that the book gains synergistic significance from its intratextual connections.

Like Birkenstein, Michael Trussler also approaches the stories in a single Munro collection as thematically linked in a cycle. The characters in *Runaway* (2004), Trussler argues, use various kinds of representation and discourse, such as letters, stories, and visual art, as means of providing shape for their lives. He says these stories are deeply interested in how human beings depend on narrative to shape their experience of time and offset the frailties of memory. David Crouse would agree, arguing that Munro's stories in *Hateship, Friendship, Courtship, Loveship, Marriage* (2001) are untraditional narratives that take as their subject matter how narrative is used to discover the self and shape identity. Crouse says that even as Munro explores traditional realistic modes of narrative, she has much in common with metafictional writers of the 1960s. Indeed, he argues that one of Munro's great strengths is her combination of these two elements, which she thematizes in her stories as the conflict between reality and meta-reality, between the actual and the artifice.

Caitlin Charman raises the issue of the realistic versus the universal nature of Munro's stories by discussing place in Munro's memoir-stories in *The View from Castle Rock*. Charman points out that the natural world in Munro's stories actually derives more from textual representations than from actual experiences. She convincingly shows that although Munro's use of place is never a simple matter of romantic idealization, there is no doubt that the context of her natural world is more literary than geographical. This creation of an imaginary landscape is also an important part of Carol Beran's comparison and contrast of Margaret Atwood's "Wilderness Tips" with Munro's "White Dump." Beran shows how Munro uses literary contexts from fairy tales, Christian and classical mythology, and the works of other writers to create an imaginary landscape. Arguing that Munro's geographical world is the result of intertextuality and the author's creation of this landscape, Beran demonstrates that to designate Munro's work as regional and realistic is an oversimplification of her fictional world. Finally, in her discussion of Munro's "late style" in her last book, *Too Much Happiness*, Ailsa Cox focuses on how Munro deals with what it means to grow older, especially if one is a woman, drawn to the past in order to create a narrative that makes sense of one's life. Cox thus shows how Munro's most recent stories continue to deal with the dynamics of the fiction-making process and the past as a fiction.

Although in the last forty years the short story has been characterized first by experimentation and then by attenuation, Alice Munro has continued to go her own way, so confident of the nature of the short story and her control of the form that she need not observe any trends or imitate any precursors. Munro found her own unique narrative rhythm early in her career and has continued to control it consummately. Just as literature has always nourished her, she has made a lasting contribution to literature. As she once said in an interview, "Oh, writing makes my life possible, it always has."

CAREER, LIFE, AND INFLUENCE

On Alice Munro

Charles E. May

Book publishers usually consider short stories to be the work of the beginner, MFA finger exercises they reluctantly agree to publish only if they can guarantee on the flyleaf that the writer is "currently working on a novel." This commercial capitulation to the fact that most readers prefer novels to short stories, along with the assumption that a single large work of fiction is more important than a collection of small ones, is so powerful and pervasive that few writers are able to resist it. That Alice Munro, who has been able to resist it for twelve collections of short stories, has become one of the most highly praised writers of the twenty-first century should therefore go a long way toward redeeming the neglected short form. Decades ago, when her only novel, *Lives of Girls and Women* (1971), was called "only a collection of short stories" by one reviewer, Munro was not bothered, saying she did not feel that a novel was any step up from a short story. To her credit, she has never wavered in that judgment.

In a story entitled "Fiction" in her collection *Too Much Happiness* (2009), Munro cannot resist a wily jab at all those critics who have trivialized the short story as a genre and chided her for not writing something more serious, namely a novel. The central character in "Fiction" buys a book written by a woman she has met briefly at a party. When she opens it, she is disappointed to find out it is a collection of short stories, not a novel: "It seems to diminish the book's authority, making the author seem like somebody who is just hanging on to the gates of Literature, rather than safely settled inside" (52). Having punctuated a distinguished career of numerous awards by winning the Man Booker International Prize for Lifetime Achievement in 2009, Munro must have had a sly smile on her face when she wrote those words.

Munro once said that she originally planned to write a few short stories in order to get some practice and then to start writing novels, but "I got used to writing stories, so I saw my material that way" (Rothstein).

She knows that the short story's way of seeing "reality" is different from the novel's way and seems to agree with Frank O'Connor's famous suggestion that the short story deals not, as the novel does, with problems of the moment, but rather with the profound and common interests of life. Her best work is always about something more enigmatic, unspeakable, and universal than a social or surface story generated by characters and plot.

The two most compelling constraints on the short story that differentiate its characteristic method of defining reality from that of the novel are its genetic heritage in myth and its generic quality of shortness. As anthropologist Mircea Eliade has suggested, myth narrates "all the primordial events in consequence of which man became what he is today. . . . Myth teaches him the primordial stories that have constituted him existentially" (11–12). Because the short story has always remained close to its origins in myth and folklore, at its most characteristic, it focuses more on universal existential reality than on the particularized social reality that the novel has always made its own. Moreover, the short story's historical tendency to structure itself along thematic lines rather than on the mimetic replication of everyday social experience is inherently related to the form's shortness. The focus on what constitutes human life existentially, instead of what delimits human experience in a physical and social context, forces the short-story form to cohere around an aesthetic patterned unity rather than a temporal plot. As Alice Munro well knows, the short story's complexity is due not to how extensively it explores human reality but to how intensively. A Munro story is deceptive; it may at first reading seem novelistic, but it lulls the reader into a false sense of security in which time appears to stretch out comfortably like everyday reality, only to suddenly turn and tighten so intensely that the reader is left breathless.

Between the 2009 publication of *Too Much Happiness* and the summer of 2011, Alice Munro published four new stories in the *New Yorker* and *Harper's*. As is characteristic of the short story in general and Alice Munro's work in particular, these stories thematically develop universal human complexities rather than particular realistic characters and events. They belie the common critical judgment that Alice Munro's stories are brilliant because they are "novelistic," revealing that, on the contrary, they are complex precisely because they embody the short story's unique way of exploring universal reality.

"Corrie"

The fact that Munro's story "Corrie" covers a time period of over twenty years caters to the critical assumption that the development of characters over time is a novelistic notion. However, despite this temporal span, it is a classic short story, with all the virtues of that form subtly displayed. In "Corrie," there is no development over time, which is exactly the universal theme that this short story about adultery and deception explores.

At the beginning of the story, the two main characters—Corrie, twenty-six, who always seems to be laughing or "on the verge of laughing," and Howard Ritchie, religious and "already equipped with a wife and a young family"—begin an affair (Munro, "Corrie" 95). The third major character, although seldom seen, is Sadie Wolfe, the wolf in sheep's clothing or the sheep in wolf's clothing, depending on how you read her catalyst role in the story. When Ritchie tells Corrie that he has received a blackmail letter from Sadie threatening to expose the affair to his wife, she agrees to pay the blackmail. She will give the money to Ritchie twice yearly, and he in turn will place it in a post-office box in Sadie's name.

After these arrangements are made and the affair continues, the story shifts to focus on Corrie. Her father dies, and his shoe factory is taken over by a large firm that promises to keep it running. When the company closes the factory, Corrie decides to turn it into a museum that exhibits shoemaking tools; after the company razes the building, she takes over an old library in town. If "Corrie" were a novel, these two ventures might seem mere plot elements. However, Corrie's remark to Ritchie, "You'd think my place were a shrine the way you carry on"

(98), announces the story's central theme of preserving time, which is reaffirmed by the seemingly random detail that the most prominent business in the town is a furniture store "where the same tables and sofas sat forever in the windows, and the doors seemed never to be open" (97).

Time seems similarly stopped and dust laden for Corrie, while off-screen, Ritchie engages in everyday activities with his family. When Sadie Wolfe dies and Corrie goes to the reception following the funeral, she meets the woman for whom Sadie worked, who tells Corrie how much Sadie's children, and later grandchildren, loved her and how she kept her illness to herself. It is at this point that Munro, in classic short-story fashion, begins to tighten the tension. Corrie begins to compose a letter to Ritchie, telling him that the days of the blackmail are over, wondering if he will hear about Sadie's death before he gets it. However, she then asks herself whether Ritchie has looked in the post-office box to see if the August blackmail payment has been picked up, for she knows that Sadie would have been too ill to retrieve it.

When she awakes the next morning, Corrie realizes that there was never a post-office box, and that Ritchie kept the money for family trips and everyday expenses. Corrie now tries to get used to this "current reality" and is surprised to discover that she is capable of shaping another reality. If Ritchie does not know that Sadie is dead, he will "just expect things to go on as usual." Corrie thinks she could say something that would destroy them, but she knows that "what they had—what they have—demands payment" and that she is the one who can "afford to pay." The last sentence of the story—"When she goes down to the kitchen again she goes gingerly, making everything fit into its proper place" (101)—is a meaningful, self-reflexive ending to a story in which, indeed, as is appropriate for the short-story form, everything does fit in its proper place.

If "Corrie" were a novel about a real-life situation, the reader might ask, Why does Corrie tolerate Ritchie all these years? What kind of experience do they have together? Why does Corrie not find herself a good man? Why does she not leave him when she discovers his deception? But the story is not about such issues. Corrie is not a "real" person in a realistic novel; she is a paradigm of a woman having an affair. Ritchie is not a cad in a domestic melodrama; he is a paradigmatic married man having an affair. Munro's story is about the affair as a universal, classic phenomenon that survives on secrecy and time, played out in two different modes: one in which life is statically preserved unchanged, the other moving on offscreen in a routine, temporal fashion.

The complexity of Munro's short story is nothing like the complexity of a novel. In a novel, we are interested in particular people in a particular situation at a particular time and place. We make judgments on those people as if they were real people. But "Corrie" does not lead us to make those kinds of judgments; instead, it asks us to contemplate not a particular affair but the quintessential meaning of *affair*. And an affair, Munro suggests, is about secrecy, sacrifice, selfishness, retribution, and stasis. This story does not embody a novelistic complexity about the evolution of experience over time; rather, it features a short-story complexity about the revelation of a secret that has sustained a situation enacted in two radically different frameworks of time. We only have to stand back a bit and watch this static universal drama embody its dusty secrets.

"Axis"

Read as a realistic or novelistic story, "Axis" seems simple and straightforward, recounting the experiences of two particular young women at a given place and time. Thematically, however, the story is about a universal reality that constitutes human beings existentially: not merely the experience of what has happened, but the primordial experience of what might have been. The story begins by locating two young farm girls, Grace and Avie, fifty years in the past, waiting for a bus to take them home from college for summer vacation. Grace is fair and voluptuous; Avie is lively and challenging. While Avie wants to have sex with her boyfriend, Hugo, because she thinks it will make him manlier,

Grace keeps her virginity intact in order to keep her boyfriend, Royce, interested in her.

During the summer, when Royce visits Grace on her parents' farm, he passes through the town where Avie lives and sees her on the street, looking so lively and pretty that he has the urge to get off the bus and not get on again. He knows, however, that doing so will land him in a lot of trouble. Royce is not in love with Grace; he is primarily interested in getting her into bed. One day, she finally seems willing, and they become "far enough advanced" in her bedroom not to hear her parents drive up. Grace's mother is shocked when she discovers them, but Royce tells her to shut up, gets dressed, and leaves. Grace asks him to take her with him, but he acts as if he did not hear her. On the road, Royce sees a tower of ancient-looking rock, which he later learns is the edge of the Niagara Escarpment. Captivated, he decides to forgo philosophy and political science and take up geology. Later, he tells people how the sight of the escarpment turned his life around and only vaguely remembers that he had been there to see a girl. In the fall, when Avie, who is now pregnant, comes to school to pick up some books, she encounters a young classmate who has sent Grace letters but has heard nothing from her. The classmate tells Avie, "Somebody said she had colitis. That's when you get all swollen, isn't it? That would be miserable" (Munro, "Axis" 68).

When the story shifts to the present, fifty years later, Avie, widowed and in her late sixties, is on the train to visit one of her six grown children and runs into Royce, who is now retired and has never married. When he tells her about seeing her on the street that day, looking so "irresistible" he wanted to get off the bus, Avie keeps repeating, "I never knew." If she had known, Royce asks her, would she have agreed to meet him, even with the "complications that would have caused"? "Without hesitation," Avie says yes. When he indifferently responds, "So it's a good thing? That we didn't make contact" (68), Avie does not even try for an answer. In a story about the passage of time, in which what might have happened seems more important than what did, it is thematically significant that Royce says, "Water under the bridge" (69).

The universal theme of "Axis" turns, as it were, on the implications of the title, the usual dictionary definition of which is a straight line through a body on which the body turns. The axis mundi would, therefore, be the center of the world. The "profound and common interest of life," the myth that constitutes human beings existentially, in this story might be expressed by the clichéd title of a long-running American television soap opera that began in 1956, *As the World Turns*. Although we usually think of an axis in spatial terms, the main point of an axis is that motion takes place in time. Geology, Royce's professional passion, is, of course, concerned with spatial layers that reflect temporal events. Several times in Munro's story, if the world spinning on the axis of time could possibly stop, the lives of the characters would be changed, but of course it cannot. Although "Axis" is a story about two particular young women and the events that happened to them fifty years ago, one primordial aspect of time that interests Munro here is that as we look back on the past, we consider not only what happened but also what might have happened. What if Royce had gotten off the bus that day when he saw Avie on the street? What if Grace's mother had not come into her room that day? What if Royce had not run away and accidentally discovered the Niagara Escarpment?

As in all great short stories, details in "Axis" are not random verisimilitude but intentional thematic motifs. Grace's colitis ("when you get all swollen") suggests that Grace's mother did not come into the room soon enough, that Grace got pregnant. But we know nothing of what happened to Grace after that event fifty years ago; we only know that she remained haunted by a dream Avie once had about a discarded child, which we may now suspect reflects Grace's own discarded child. "Axis" is the story of Avie—the life she might have lived, the life she did live, and the eruptions in the spatial axis of time that might have made a difference. Munro's story suggests that although we are temporally caught up in the turn of time, we are trapped like fossils in the layers of the past.

"Pride"

Although the male narrator (never named) of "Pride" is not a highly educated man, he is given to intellectual pondering. For example, in the first few paragraphs of the story, he divides people into two types: those who prove themselves to be hearty and jovial regardless of their mistakes, claiming they would not want to live any place but where they live, and those who do not get away from where they live, although others might wish for their own sake that they had. The narrator adds metaphorically, "Whatever hole they started digging for themselves when they were young . . . they kept right on at it, digging away" (Munro, "Pride" 59).

The narrator tells the story of Oneida, the daughter of a wealthy banker, a private-school student whose mother died when she was in her teens. He also tells the backstory of her father's investment in a scheme for which he extorted funds from the bank. When the schemers skip town with the money, the father is demoted to a small bank in a village six miles away. This introduces the first reference in the story to the title, "Pride"; the narrator says that the father could have refused the demotion, but "pride, as it was thought, chose otherwise. Pride chose that he be driven every morning those six miles to sit behind a partial wall of cheap varnished boards, no proper office at all. There he sat and did nothing until it was time for him to be driven home" (60).

Because the narrator has a harelip, he is exempted from service in World War II and feels cut off from men his own age, although he says that this is nothing new. However, he says, he does not miss "the brief swagger of walking off to war" (62); nor does he miss having a father (who died before he even saw him) or a girlfriend. He contentedly spends time listening to the radio and going to movies with his mother.

When the narrator's mother and Oneida's father die, she comes to ask his advice about selling her house. Although he cautions her against it, she sells it anyway but comes to regret her action, eventually moving into the apartment building that is later built on the site of the house. The narrator begins to spend time with Oneida in the 1950s, inviting her to watch his new television. Because meeting new people is an ordeal for him, they seldom go out. He says that all his school years were spent getting used to what he is like, and he considers it a triumph of sorts to have managed that feat and to know that he could stay where he is and make a living without having to continually break new people in to the way he looks.

When the narrator becomes ill, Oneida settles into his mother's bedroom to care for him, and he comes to depend on her, "feeling like a small child again." However, he is embarrassed that she cares for his intimate hygiene needs, feeling that she is able to do so because the way he looks makes him a "neuter to her, or an unfortunate child" (64). When Oneida wants to move in with him permanently, suggesting, "We could live together like brother and sister and look after each other like brother and sister," the narrator feels "angry, scared, appalled" (65). To escape this dilemma, he sells his house and finds an apartment in the building where Oneida lives. Realizing that he has lived in the town long enough to become accepted, he thinks, "Just living long enough wipes out the problems. Puts you in a select club. No matter what your disabilities may have been, just living till now wipes them out, to a good measure" (66). When Oneida shows up at his house while he is packing to move, suddenly she laughs and points out the window to a birdbath that seems full of black-and-white birds, splashing in the water. However, they are not birds but a group of young skunks, which the narrator also thinks are beautiful. The story ends with a tableau of the two watching the skunks.

If "Pride" were a novel, we would not expect it to have any universal thematic significance; we would accept it as a realistic slice of life, chronicling the culture of a small Canadian town and how a young man with a harelip and a young woman fared there. However, because it is a short story, especially a short story by Alice Munro, we expect it to explore a universal theme beyond the particular events and unique characters involved. Just as the narrator's opening rumination that "good use can be made of everything, if you are willing" suggests some general significance, so also does the culminating metaphoric scene in which small skunks are playing in a birdbath. The fact that skunks, usually thought to be repulsive, smelly creatures, here look beautiful and seem "proud" of themselves makes us reflect back on the references to pride throughout the story.

Three people illustrate pride in this story: Oneida's father, who has so much dignity that even after having been brought low by a scandal, he holds his head up high; Oneida, who, because of her wealthy up-bringing and "fair dazzle of skin and hair," stirs awe and admiration in all those around her; and the narrator, stricken at birth by a cleft lip, who must develop pride in himself by his own efforts and attitude. Of the two types of people the narrator thinks about at the opening of the story, he seems to be an example of the first: someone who has every-thing against him but who turns out fine, lives out his life in his home-town, and proclaims that he would never want to live anyplace else. Oneida seems to be the latter type; she never gets away from the town, but the narrator, among others, thinks that for her own sake, she should have. She digs a hole for herself and never gets out of it.

If this were a novel, although one might understand why the nar-rator and Oneida do not get together when they are young, one might wonder why they do not develop a mutually dependent relationship when they are older. The mystery of Munro's story is not why these two people fail to get together but why people ever get together at all. The universal thematic question the story raises is, if one has pride in oneself, then does one even need another person? With pride, a person can live a satisfactory life no matter what impediment or shortcomings or bad luck he or she might have. The secret of the narrator's success is that he accepts himself for who he is, does not feel sorry for himself, does not need someone to provide him with a good image of himself.

The final scene of the baby skunks splashing in the water as if they were little birds is a metaphor of the narrator's life. Although he may have been repulsive to those around him, he has accepted himself with self-pride and acts as if he were not a pariah. This does not suggest arrogance but rather acknowledgment. The narrator describes the little skunks walking across the lawn "as if they were proud of themselves." Oneida's face, even though it has grown older, looks "dazzled" when she sees the skunks; she says only, "Have you ever seen such a sight?" And he says, "No. Never." The narrator is glad that neither says anything more to spoil a moment when the potentially ugly is transformed into the beautiful. Thus, the story ends with the line "We were as glad as we could be" (67). If this were a realistic novel, we might question whether the narrator's life has really been satisfying, might characterize him as an outcast victim of social prejudice. But if nothing in the story suggests that he is lonely or self-pitying or deprived, either sexually or emotionally, who are we to say he must have been unhappy? Does one have to love someone to be happy? Does one have to experience sex to live a good life? Does one have to have children to be fulfilled? Obviously, in Munro's story, the answer to all these questions is no.

"Gravel"

Beginning with the sentence "At that time we were living beside a gravel pit," Munro immediately locates "Gravel" in the past and accounts for its title in symbolic space (65). The central event in the story takes place when the narrator is about five, after her mother has left her insurance-salesman husband in search of a freer, more bohemian life, taking the narrator and her sister Caro, age nine, with her to live in a trailer with an amateur actor named Neal. When rain fills up the gravel pit near the trailer, Caro instructs the narrator to run back to the trailer to tell Neal and her mother that their dog Blitzee has fallen in the water and that she has jumped in to save her. The narrator runs to the trailer, but sits down outside before going in. When she does go in and the mother tries to get Neal to go to the gravel pit, he refuses; as a result, Caro drowns.

In the final section of the story, when the adult narrator learns that Neal is living near where she teaches at a university, her partner, Ruthann, convinces her that she should go see him in order to help rout her demons. Neal tells the narrator that he was stoned at the time of the drowning and is not a swimmer and thus would also have drowned if he had tried to save Caro. When she asks him what he thinks Caro had in mind on that day, Neal says that it does not matter, and that she should not waste her time feeling guilty for not hurrying to tell them.

A summary of the plot of "Gravel" seems sufficient to establish that on the surface, it is a story of a tragic childhood event for which the narrator still harbors some sense of responsibility and guilt. However, trying to determine guilt for Caro's death oversimplifies the mystery of the story. Like most great short-story writers, Alice Munro knows that short stories are not mere realistic accounts, but rather hold together by means of a universal theme.

At the very beginning of the story, the narrator says, "I barely remember that life. That is, I remember some parts of it clearly, but without the links you need to form a proper picture" (65). The universal problem the story raises is that we usually remember the past in isolated moments but have difficulty remembering what relationship one event has to another. One tells a story in order to try to understand the links, the motivation, the causes. This need to know, to be sure of the connection of events in the misty, disconnected past, is buttressed by the theme of solidity and security versus instability and uncertainty, which is repeated throughout "Gravel." The gravel pit symbolically embodies this split between what is solid and what is uncertain: "The pit was shallow enough to lead you to think that there might have been some other intention for it—foundations for a house, maybe, that never made it any further" (65).

After the mother leaves her husband, she is happy to have exchanged her solidly established house for Neal's transient trailer. The father is an insurance salesman who sells people security against the future; Neal, on the other hand, with his concern about the atomic bomb, thinks there may be no future. "His philosophy, as he put it later, was to welcome whatever happened. Everything is a gift. We give and we take" (65). Neal accepts uncertainty. Meanwhile, Caro desires stability. When Neal asks Caro what would happen if they all disappeared and Blitzee had to fend for herself, Caro says that she is not going to disappear; she is always going to look after her dog. The narrator feels caught between stability and instability, between things that exist solidly in the world and things that are so unstable they simply disappear. Indeed, after Caro drowns, Neal does in fact disappear.

This stability/instability theme is reinforced throughout the story by the theme of "acting like an actor." The mother dresses like an actress and leaves her husband for an actor because she wants to "really" live; this reflects the ambiguity between what is "real" life and what is play or pretend life. Neal acts like an actor, drifting, floating, subsuming himself rather than asserting himself as an individual: "He had performed as part of the chorus in 'Oedipus Rex.' He had liked that—the giving yourself over, blending with others" (65). The relationship between the solidity/instability theme and the acting/actor theme is also reflected when Neal is asked to play Banquo in *Macbeth*: "Sometimes they make Banquo's ghost visible, sometimes not. This time they wanted a visible version and Neal was the right size. An excellent size. A solid ghost" (65). After Caro's death, Neal writes a letter saying "that since he did not intend to act as a father it would be better for him to bow out at the start" (69).

When the narrator recalls sitting down outside the trailer rather than immediately knocking on the door, she says, "I know this because it's a fact. I don't know, however, what my plan was or what I was thinking. I was waiting, maybe, for the next act in Caro's drama" (68). And indeed, her helplessness, her failure to act quickly, is a result of her not knowing what her "role" is in a drama that is not of her own making. From the time Caro instructs the narrator to go to the trailer and tell Neal and her mother, the narrator has no secure memory that the events happened, were about to happen, might have happened, or are what she imagined happened:

In my mind I can see her picking up Blitzee and tossing her, though Blitzee was trying to hang on to her coat. Then backing up, Caro backing up to take a run at the water. Running, jumping, all of a sudden hurling herself at the water. But I can't recall the sound of the splashes as they, one after the other, hit the water. Not a little splash or a big one. Perhaps I had turned toward the trailer by then—I must have done so. (68)

When the adult narrator meets Neal at the end of the story, he is still the voice of one who accepts life as it comes and refuses to feel responsibility about the past. His view about why Caro did what she did is that it does not matter: "'The thing is to be happy,' he says. 'No matter what. Just try that. You can. It gets to be easier and easier. It's nothing to do with circumstances. You wouldn't believe how good it is. Accept everything and then tragedy disappears. Or tragedy lightens, anyway, and you're just there, going along easy in the world.'" Although the narrator understands Neal's advice, she cannot follow it: "I see what he meant. It really is the right thing to do. But, in my mind, Caro keeps running at the water and throwing herself, as if in triumph, and I'm still caught, waiting for her to explain to me, waiting for the splash" (70).

It is obviously true that if one accepts everything that happens, tragedy disappears. For example, if Oedipus had been able to accept the fact that he accidentally killed his own father and married his mother unawares, there would be no tragedy. If Ahab had been able to accept his first mate Starbuck's advice that the whale was just a dumb brute, there would be no epic *Moby-Dick*. If Hamlet had been able to just go back to school and forget his doubts about his father's death, the rottenness in Denmark would not have mattered. If Gatsby could just forget about Daisy, the word *great* would have no meaning in that book. If Kurtz would just get out of the jungle, there would be no *Heart of Darkness*. Indeed, if these characters could be less than heroically human, there would be no great literature. To be a human being in the world is to live in doubt and fear and trembling, not knowing why others do what they do, not knowing what really happened in the past, not always being able to get on with one's life. And thus, like the narrator of "Gravel," human beings are caught waiting for an explanation, always waiting for the concrete confirmation of the splash.

One of the main reasons reviewers and other critics have tried to justify the complexity of Alice Munro's stories by arguing that they are "novelistic" is the assumption that because the short story tells a story, it must therefore be read by following the rules of reading temporal narrative—that is, by focusing on plot, character, context, and ideology. However, the short story as practiced by Munro and other great short-story writers does not depend on such conventional elements of the novel; rather, it depends on some unspeakable universal significance explored and communicated by the reiteration of themes through aesthetic patterns. Munro has said that when she reads a story, she does not take it up at the beginning and follow it like a road "with views and neat diversions along the way." Rather, for her, reading a story is like moving through a house, making connections between one enclosed space and another. Consequently, Munro declares, "When I write a story I want to make a certain kind of structure, and I know the feeling I want to get from being inside that structure" ("What Is Real?" 224). When Geoff Hancock asked her if the meaning of a story is more important to her than the event, she replied, "What happens as event doesn't really much matter. When the event becomes the thing that matters, the story isn't working too well" (Munro, "Interview" 81).

Daniel Menaker, editor in chief at Random House, has suggested that although somebody reading Munro might get the feeling that she is trying to "help you get at some true emotional psychological insight," that insight goes beyond the individual and "takes the form of a kind of philosophical surrender to the unknowability of people's motives and characters, a dark existential uncertainty about what makes people tick" (qtd. in Edemariam 20). The secret of Alice Munro's short stories is that she is able to suggest universal, unspoken human desires by describing what seems to be ordinary, everyday reality. Her stories are complex and powerful, not so much because of what happens in them, but because of what cannot happen except in the mysterious human imagination.

Works Cited

Edemariam, Aida. "Profile: Alice Munro." *Guardian* 4 Oct. 2003: 20.

Eliade, Mircea. *Myth and Reality*. Trans. Willard R. Trask. Prospect Heights, IL: Waveland, 1998.

Munro, Alice. "Axis." *New Yorker* 31 Jan. 2011: 63–69.

_____. "Corrie." *New Yorker* 11 Oct. 2010: 95–101.

_____. "Gravel." *New Yorker* 27 June 2011: 64–70.

_____. "An Interview with Alice Munro." By Geoff Hancock. *Canadian Fiction Magazine* 43 (1982): 74–114.

_____. "Pride." *Harper's* Apr. 2011: 59–67.

_____. *Too Much Happiness*. New York: Knopf, 2009.

_____. "What Is Real?" *Making It New: Contemporary Canadian Stories*. Ed. John Metcalf. Toronto: Methuen, 1982. 223–26.

O'Connor, Frank. *The Lonely Voice: A Study of the Short Story*. Cleveland: World, 1963.

Rothstein, Mervyn. "Canada's Alice Munro Finds Excitement in Short-Story Form." *New York Times* 10 Nov. 1986: C17.

Biography of Alice Munro _____

Charles E. May

Alice Munro has always been dedicated to her writing. She was making up stories as soon as she started school, composing poetry when she was eleven, planning a novel when she was in high school, and writing short stories seriously when she was eighteen. Now that she is universally acclaimed as the greatest short-story writer in the world, she continues to be absorbed by her lifelong passion: writing brilliant, complex stories about the mysterious secrets of the human heart. When asked in 2006 what she loved about writing, she replied, "It just seems to me to be the best thing you can do with your life . . . tackling the experience of being alive as best you can" (Kennedy).

Alice Ann Laidlaw was born on July 10, 1931, to Robert Laidlaw and Anne Clarke Chamney Laidlaw on a fox farm near Wingham, Ontario, a small town about 125 miles northwest of Toronto. Whereas Robert Laidlaw, descended from Scots Presbyterians, was reserved and timid—what he once called a family characteristic—Anne Clarke Chamney came from an Anglican Irish family and was somewhat more gregarious and outgoing. Moreover, whereas Robert Laidlaw seemed to hold to the prevailing social suspicion of overachievers of small-town Ontario (best expressed by the title of one of Munro's early books, *Who Do You Think You Are?*), Anne Clarke Chamney, an educated schoolteacher chafing against the poverty of her childhood, had high ambitions for herself and her children.

Munro enjoyed the privileges of being an only child until about age five, when, in rapid succession, her brother Bill and sister Sheila were born and she was enrolled in the somewhat harsh environment of Lower Town School in 1937. After two years, her mother managed to get her into Wingham Public School, attended by a more educated class, but Alice felt no less an outsider there than at Lower Town. However, she was a good student, winning scholastic achievement prizes and making her theatrically inclined mother proud by getting parts in school plays. As she grew older, Alice aligned herself with her father's policy of self-deprecation and rebelled against her mother's sometimes embarrassing self-assertion, creating a conflict between her need to fit in and her desire to assert her independence. She admitted later that, although she identified with her father, it was her mother who most influenced her decision to become an author.

Munro's mother was diagnosed with Parkinson's disease when Alice was about twelve years old. Being the oldest daughter, she had to take over the traditional female roles of the house, a responsibility that was alleviated somewhat by the arrival of her paternal grandmother and her great-aunt. They took it upon themselves to train Alice to become a farmer's wife by teaching her knitting and sewing, neither of which she excelled at. What she did do well, although she had to practice in secret, was read and write. One book that had a powerful effect on her was L. M. Montgomery's *Emily of New Moon* (1923), about a young girl who wants to become a writer. But the most important literary influence on her youth was Emily Brontë's *Wuthering Heights* (1847), which Munro said she read constantly for four or five years. Throughout high school, she worked on planning her own imitation of *Wuthering Heights*, a novel entitled *Charlotte Muir*.

After World War II, when the family's fur business began to decline and Robert Laidlaw had to take a job as a night watchman at a foundry, Munro realized that if she were to attend university, she would have to find ways to fund her education herself. In the summer of 1948, she worked as a maid for a family in a wealthy neighborhood of Toronto, but she knew that the real financial solution for her was to win scholarships. Although she secured several small grants that enabled her to enroll at the University of Western Ontario in London, Ontario, she sometimes had to resort to selling her blood to pay her expenses. She also earned some money by working in the university library and the London public library, a job that had the fringe benefit of feeding her reading hunger.

Because her real goal of studying literature and writing fiction was not considered a viable, or even respectable, means for a young woman to earn a living, Munro enrolled in the journalism program at Western and switched to an English honors program in her second year. She tried her hand at writing commercial fiction for *True Confessions* magazine to earn some money, but with no success. Her first published story, entitled "The Dimensions of a Shadow," appeared in the April 1950 issue of the Western student publication *Folio*. Coincidentally, the man who would become her second husband twenty-six years later, a senior named Gerald Fremlin, also had a piece in this issue of *Folio* and was much impressed with her work, becoming the first of many readers to compare Munro to the great Russian short-story master Anton Chekhov.

However, Alice met the man who became her first husband, James Munro, during her second year at university, and he was as different from Munro as her parents had been from each other. Whereas he came from a well-to-do family and was conventionally proper, she came from a poor farm family and affected flashy, unconventional dress. His career aim was to become an executive of Eaton's department store, while Alice, who had no intention of becoming a conventional wife, wanted to live the somewhat bohemian life of a writer.

After two years at university, Munro's scholarship money ran out, and she certainly did not want to return to Wingham and take over the role of caring for her family. Fortunately, Jim Munro approved of her desire to become a writer. They were married on December 29, 1951, at the home of her parents and almost immediately left on the train for Vancouver, where Jim took a job at Eaton's and Alice worked part time in the public library. Two years later, their daughter Sheila was born on October 9, 1953. Two years after that, a second daughter, Catherine, was born, but she lived only two days. Jenny was born on June 4, 1957. Munro has admitted that although she is glad that her children were born when they were, if she had had a choice in the matter, she would probably not have had them at all (Beyersbergen). Although this admission may seem somewhat callous, it simply reflects that during this period of time, there was no real choice for a woman but to be a housewife and mother. Alice Munro, on the other hand, was driven strongly by her lifelong desire to be a writer.

During the early years of her marriage, Munro struggled to find the time to write while doing domestic chores. She finally sold her first commercial story, entitled "A Basket of Strawberries," in 1953 to the magazine *Mayfair*. After that, she continued to sell one or two stories each year, some of them heavily influenced by such Southern US women writers as Eudora Welty, Flannery O'Connor, and Carson McCullers. However, after the death of her mother in 1959, Munro began to draw more on her own experience for her writing. Most critics agree that her story "The Peace of Utrecht" is an important milestone in the transformation of her personal experiences into fiction. By 1961, though, she was discouraged, especially in her efforts to write a novel.

Munro's breakthrough came from a decision by her husband to quit his job at Eaton's department store and strike out with a business of his own. In 1963, the family moved to Victoria and opened a bookstore they named Munro's Books. By focusing her attention on working in the bookstore, thus releasing herself from the pressure of trying to write a novel, Munro began to write more stories. However, her life changed in another direction when Jim decided to buy a large house, which Munro hated because of the showy, high-class style it seemed to demand of her. Munro marks the move to the big house as the beginning of the breakup of her marriage. She was thirty-five when their daughter Andrea was born, still working in the bookstore and trying to maintain the huge house in the style that Jim desired.

Munro got her first big publishing break in 1967, when an editor at Canada's Ryerson Press asked her to pull together a collection of stories. She polished the stories she had been writing for the past fourteen years and wrote three new ones: "Postcard," "Walker Brothers Cowboy," and "Images." The result was her first book of fifteen stories, *Dance of the Happy Shades*, published in 1968. Although it won the Governor General's Award, the book did not sell well. Canadian newspapers simply announced that a "shy housewife" and "mother of three" had won an award (Thacker 197).

The closest Munro ever came to writing a conventional novel was her second book, *Lives of Girls and Women,* published in 1971. Although she had been mulling over the material in this book for a number of years, she wrote draft after draft almost daily for a year on a makeshift table in her laundry room. Winning the Canadian Booksellers Award in 1971–72 and named as an alternate for the Book-of-the-Month-Club in both Canada and the United States, *Lives of Girls and Women* sold better than *Dance of the Happy Shades*, and it was the last time Munro would allow herself to become stymied trying to write a novel.

Although Munro's conviction that these first two books covered all the material she possessed threw her into another dry period, she forged ahead with the stories that were published in her third book, *Something I've Been Meaning to Tell You* (1974). After her separation from her husband while she was completing this book, she took on several short-term teaching jobs: first a summer session at Notre Dame University in Nelson, British Columbia, then a part-time position at York University in Toronto in the fall, after which she accepted a writer-in-residence position at Western University for 1974–75. In 1974, her old college classmate Gerry Fremlin happened to hear a radio interview in which she mentioned that she was separated from her husband. Fremlin invited her out for a drink, and less than a year later, she moved into his family home with him in Clinton.

Munro's fourth book, *Who Do You Think You Are?* (1978), released in the United States and Great Britain under the title *The Beggar Maid: Stories of Flo and Rose* (1979), was her greatest success to date. It received enthusiastic reviews, was short-listed for the British Booker Prize, and won the Governor General's Award, thus establishing her as a major writer. She finally took on an agent, Virginia Barber of New York, who sold her story "Royal Beatings" to the *New Yorker*, leading to a long-running first-refusal contract with the magazine.

In the late 1970s, Munro worked on stories that were later published in *The Moons of Jupiter* (1982) while traveling rather extensively in the United States, Australia (where she was a writer in residence at the University of Queensland), and China (where, with six other Canadian writers, she was a guest of the Chinese Writers Association). When *The Moons of Jupiter* was released in the United States in 1983, it earned a review on the front page of the *New York Times Book Review* and sold remarkably well for a short-story collection—almost three times the number of copies that *The Beggar Maid* had sold.

Four years later, Munro published her sixth book, *The Progress of Love* (1986), for which she won her third Governor General's Award and the first Marian Engel Award for a "distinguished and continuing body of work." After an exhausting and personally unpleasant promotional tour for *The Progress of Love,* Munro was confident enough of her success that she could openly express her distaste for such tours, insisting she would never do another one. When her next book, *Friend of My Youth*, was published in 1990, she refused to go on tours and severely restricted the number of interviews she would give. *Friend of My Youth* won the Trillium Award for best book of the year published in Ontario. By this time, Munro's work was selling well in Canada and the United States, especially for collections of literary short stories.

In the 1990s, Alice Munro was continually feted as one of the best fiction writers in the world, and certainly the best short-story writer. Writer Cynthia Ozick dubbed her "our Chekhov." She and Fremlin bought a condo on Vancouver Island and divided their time between it and their home in Clinton, Ontario. During this decade, Munro experienced some health problems that necessitated heart-bypass surgery, but she did not seem to slow down appreciably. She won a number of important awards during this period, including the Order of Ontario and the $50,000 Lannan Foundation Literary Prize.

The fact that *Open Secrets* (1994) spent some time on the *New York Times* best-seller list further demonstrates the remarkable ability of Alice Munro to create complex literary short stories that can find a large audience. Another indication of her widespread recognition was the release of a volume of *Selected Stories* at this time. She also became the first non-American to receive the PEN/Malamud Award.

Munro continued to devote herself to her work, publishing the long story "The Love of a Good Woman" in the *New Yorker* in December 1996. It was selected for the *O. Henry Prize Stories* collection for that year and became the title story of her eighth collection, published in 1998. Munro won the National Book Critics Circle Award (the first native-born Canadian to do so) and the Giller Prize for *The Love of a Good Woman*. In 2001, she won the $30,000 Rea Short Story Award for Lifetime Achievement.

Munro's book *Hateship, Friendship, Courtship, Loveship, Marriage* was published in 2001, followed three years later by *Runaway* (2004) and only two years after that by *The View from Castle Rock* (2006), her most autobiographical collection to date. In 2009, she made a passing reference in an interview to having been diagnosed with cancer but said that it had been successfully treated. Also in 2009, Munro won the Man Booker International Prize and published the collection *Too Much Happiness*. Several new stories subsequently appeared in *Harper's* and the *New Yorker*, where it was announced that a new collection would be released in 2012. Having celebrated her eightieth birthday in July 2011, Alice Munro continues to maintain her claim, in the words of fellow author Jonathan Franzen, to being "the best fiction writer now working in North America."

Works Cited

Beyersbergen, Joanna. "No Bitterness or Anxiety for Writers." *London Free Press* 22 June 1974: 70.

Franzen, Jonathan. "Alice's Wonderland." *New York Times Book Review* 14 Nov. 2004: 1.

Kennedy, Janice. "Canadian Literary Icon Opens Up." *Ottawa Citizen* 1 Apr. 2006: K3.

Thacker, Robert. *Alice Munro: Writing Her Lives; A Biography*. Toronto: McClelland, 2011.

CRITICAL
CONTEXTS

Alice Munro: Critical Reception _____

Robert Thacker

Early in 2008, while reviewing William Trevor's *Cheating at Canasta* (2007) in the *New York Review of Books*, Claire Messud made an apt observation. She noted that Trevor's books had been praised in the same pages by a long list of "distinguished" reviewers, whom she names, and then asked, "But when did William Trevor—or, for that matter, his fellow contemporary master of the short story form, Alice Munro, the pair of them sharing of the laurels of Chekhov . . . —last spark a controversy, let alone incite a debate?" (20). Regarding Munro, Messud's point is ultimately fair enough, although it is possible to counter it by citing attempts to ban her putative novel *Lives of Girls and Women* (1971) in parts of Ontario in the 1970s as controversial, or by so seeing her decisions to pull *Who Do You Think You Are?* (1978) from the press for restructuring just before publication and, later, to follow her editor to a new publisher with an almost-finished book in hand. More recently, Munro criticized and refused permission to quote from archived letters to a particular critic, who, for her part, published her book without the quotations with wounded protest. Most recently, Munro caused small stirs when she announced in 2006 that she might well give up writing altogether and, in 2009, that she had had cancer (see Thacker, *Alice Munro: Writing* 333–36, 348–50, 418–22, 532, 549–50; McCaig, *Reading* ix–xiv).

That these small controversies escaped Messud's notice is no surprise, since from the beginning of her career, Munro the person has largely stayed out of the limelight. Instead, she just writes. Munro has written out of her own life and her own place; she writes of being alive, of just being a human being, wondering, trying to understand and maintain. She avoids politics, personalities, lessons—the stuff of controversy. And she has achieved the reputation she has—a large one, as befits a winner of the 2009 Man Booker International Prize—by writing only short stories. As such, Munro's critical reception has been one of steady, persistent growth since she published her first book, *Dance of the Happy Shades*, in 1968. Made up of stories written over a fifteen-year span, that book won Canada's highest literary award; it was followed in 1971 by *Lives*, a book that quickly became something of a feminist cri de coeur. After another collection of stories appeared in 1974, Munro hired a New York agent, Virginia Barber, who both placed her stories in commercial magazines, most notably the *New Yorker*, and brought Munro's next book, *Who Do You Think You Are? / The Beggar Maid* (1979), to Alfred A. Knopf. There have been nine collections since, with another announced for fall 2012. Her *Selected Stories* appeared in 1996; an Everyman's Library selection, *Carried Away*, was published in 2006; and her stories continue to appear in the *New Yorker* and in *Harper's*. Munro writes on, reviewers' superlatives abound, and critical analyses have increased to a level befitting Munro's major-author status. In 2005, my extended biography written with Munro's cooperation, *Alice Munro: Writing Her Lives*, was published, with an updated paperback appearing in 2011. And in 2007, Carol Mazur and Cathy Moulder's massive *Alice Munro: An Annotated Bibliography of Works and Criticism* supplanted earlier attempts at bibliography. The *MLA International Bibliography* lists almost two hundred entries focused on Munro's work published since the mid-1990s.

Throughout the growth of Munro's reputation, reviewers and critics have consistently struggled to define and articulate just how she does what she does in her stories. E. D. Blodgett writes that Munro is a writer whom readers see "endeavoring to locate the meaning that unifies, and yet always wary of it"; hers is an art of "accommodating contradictions" (*Alice* 68, 126). Ildikó de Papp Carrington sees Munro in the same fashion, as an author who tries to "control the uncontrollable." Louis K. MacKendrick maintains that it "is quite hopeless and redundant to expect an Alice Munro story to surrender a clear, indisputable, and singular 'meaning'" (*Some Other Reality* 26). Katherine J. Mayberry asserts that, for Munro, "to tell is at best to revise, but never to perfectly revive" (540) and that a Munro story "virtually defies plot summary" (532). And Helen Hoy quotes Munro in a 1987 interview in which she said that in each story she is seeking "an admission of chaos" because "a belief in progress is unfounded"; as she told another interviewer, "It doesn't make much difference . . . how [a heroine] ends up at all. Because we finally end up dead." Thus, Hoy asserts, "Munro both captures life's capriciousness and requires a simultaneous acceptance of conflicting perspectives on reality" ("Alice" 17, 18, 20). That said and admitted, Magdalene Redekop offers what is perhaps the great fact of Munro's most effective and affective art: that each of us as readers perceives "the story Alice Munro is telling *me*," that the "pleasure of reading Alice Munro is, in the final analysis, that we catch ourselves in the act of looking" (*Mothers* x, 3). She looks at the way life is and, at the same time, recognizes in postmodern ways the inability of any narrative version of events to really reconstruct a central occurrence in a character's life. Again and again in her stories, Munro shows us, as she writes in "White Dump," "the way the skin of the moment can break open" (*Progress* 308).

While Munro began publishing stories and having them read on the Canadian Broadcasting Corporation (CBC) during the 1950s, and she made several appearances in the *Montrealer* in the early 1960s, her critical reception really begins with the publication of *Dance of the Happy Shades* (1968). It vaulted Munro to the forefront of Canada's leading writers and, through the singular nature and quality of the praise it received—one reviewer spoke of "the breadth and depth of humanity in the woman herself, and the beauty—the almost terrifying beauty—she commands in expressing it" (qtd. in Thacker, *Alice Munro: Writing* 193)—Munro was launched. Such reaction continued, amplified and made more acute, with the publication of *Lives of Girls and Women* in 1971 in Canada and its appearance from McGraw-Hill in the United States the following year. Taken together, the reviews that these and subsequent books received are an apt beginning of Munro's critical reception, and summary overviews of them, gauged to Munro's biography, are available throughout my *Alice Munro: Writing Her Lives*.

Separate from newspaper and broadcast reviews, and from various pieces with broader treatment in the literary press, the first critical article on Munro's fiction was a thematic study of "unconsummated relationships" that appeared in early 1972 in *World Literature Written in English* (Dahlie, "Unconsummated"). It was followed in 1975 by two pieces by J. R. (Tim) Struthers, one on Munro and the American South, the other on Munro and James Joyce in *Lives*. These two critics were the vanguard, and were followed throughout the 1970s by others focusing increased critical attention on Munro as the decade passed, with articles in such journals as *Canadian Literature* (Conron, Bailey), the *Journal of Canadian Fiction* (Martin, "Alice Munro and James Joyce"), *Modern Fiction Studies* (Macdonald, "Madman"), *Mosaic* (Dawson), *Open Letter* (New), *Studies in Canadian Literature* (Macdonald, "Structure"), and *Studies in Short Fiction* (Monaghan). At the same time, Munro was considered very much a part of book-length studies aimed at treating Canadian fiction as an entity (Blodgett, "Prisms"; Moss; Packer). Also during the 1970s, much critical work was being done in graduate theses. Initial critical impetuses were identification and connection, the treatment of central matters in the fiction, and making connections between Munro and others; critics also focused on her work amid what were then being seen as "Canadian" considerations, given the nationalist fervor of the decade in English-speaking Canada and its concomitant concern with the growth of a definable Canadian literature. In keeping with this, Dahlie returned to Munro in 1978 with an overview essay, "The Fiction of Alice Munro," published in the American magazine *Ploughshares* to accompany one of Munro's stories, "Characters" (never republished in a collection). There, he writes, both accurately and presciently, that Munro's "fiction is rooted tangibly in the social realism of the rural and small town world of her own experience, but it insistently explores what lies beyond the bounds of empirical reality" (56–57). So it was then with Munro, so it is still.

By this time, Munro had made her first appearances in the *New Yorker*, so the interest of the editors of *Ploughshares*—like the interest of the editors of *Modern Fiction Studies* and *Studies in Short Fiction*, already noted, in the 1970s—suggests a salient fact: the growth of Munro's critical reputation during that decade was a two-tracked affair. While certainly seen at home as primarily, even quintessentially, a Canadian writer, Munro has from the early 1970s on attracted her critics irrespective of nationalist considerations, and perhaps even despite them. Munro writes of life, not nations, and for her as a Canadian writer this fact has proved at times a bit vexing at home because of how she is read abroad, most especially in the United States.

Early in 1980, Helen Hoy published "'Dull, Simple, Amazing and Unfathomable': Paradox and Double Vision in Alice Munro's Fiction," a singular essay that directs critical attention away from thematics and toward language, structure, and style in Munro's stories. "Verbal paradox . . . particularly cryptic oxymoron, remains a more distinctive feature of Munro's style, and . . . functions particularly as a means of definition, of zeroing in on the individual qualities of an emotion or moment" (106). Frequently cited since, Hoy's essay proved prescient in directing critical attention to the textures of Munro's well-wrought stories, which critics began exploring in earnest during the 1980s. The first book devoted to Munro, *Probable Fictions: Alice Munro's Narrative Acts* (1983), edited by Louis K. MacKendrick, offers nine essays by various hands, plus an interview with Munro by Struthers; each essay, seen now, has proved influential in shaping subsequent scholarship, having been frequently noted and responded to since.

In 1984, three indicative publications appeared: another collection of essays devoted to Munro, *The Art of Alice Munro: Saying the Unsayable*, edited by Judith Maclean Miller; the first single-authored book-length study, B. Pfaus's *Alice Munro*; and my own annotated bibliography of Munro in the fifth volume of *The Annotated Bibliography of Canada's Major Authors*. Taken together, following after *Probable Fictions* and with the realization that Munro's then-just-published *The*

Moons of Jupiter (1982) revealed the author herself to be still ascendant, these demonstrate an accelerating critical interest in Munro's work. The Miller volume, a collection of presentations and an interview from the first Alice Munro conference held at the University of Waterloo in 1982, demonstrates this most especially (see Thacker, "Conferring").

While Pfaus's book is technically the first single-authored critical book to be published on Munro, its brevity and many weaknesses are such that it has exerted almost no influence in Munro studies. Nothing of the sort can be said of the ten such volumes published between 1987, when W. R. Martin's *Alice Munro: Paradox and Parallel* was published, and 1994, when Ajay Heble's *The Tumble of Reason: Alice Munro's Discourse of Absence* appeared. More than this, during the same period, essays continued; a brief, though very fine, biography by Catherine Sheldrick Ross appeared; and Coral Ann Howells, who would later publish what is still perhaps the best single-authored book on Munro, offered an extended consideration of Munro in her *Private and Fictional Words: Canadian Women Novelists of the 1970s and 1980s* (1987). Looking back at this outpouring now, the critical books of sustaining influence have been Carrington's *Controlling the Uncontrollable* (1989), Redekop's *Mothers and Other Clowns* (1992), and, largely because of its theoretical inflections (which engage and extend Blodgett's in his *Alice Munro*, 1988), Heble's *The Tumble of Reason*. Yet two of the books published among the ten appearing between 1987 and 1994, Neil K. Besner's *Introducing Alice Munro's Lives of Girls and Women* (1990) and Louis K. MacKendrick's *Some Other Reality: Alice Munro's Something I've Been Meaning to Tell You* (1993), demonstrate abundantly that Munro's art, one of always pushing the limitations of the short story, is not well served by the critical form of the single-author extended critical overview. On the contrary, in short critical volumes of about one hundred pages each, both sharply focused on the aesthetic and biographical contexts defined by a single Munro collection, Besner and MacKendrick demonstrate that she is an artist whose variegated stories ever and always elude broad overview. In fact, Munro's critical reception has demonstrated that her work is best understood at the level of the single story or by considering a small group of stories.[1]

As it happened, in 1991 and again in 1998, I surveyed Munro criticism in two omnibus review essays published in the *Journal of Canadian Studies* (Thacker, "Go Ask Alice" and "What's 'Material'"). My treatment included the ten critical books noted above and others that treated Munro as one of several authors in other contexts; in the 1998 essay, I also surveyed the critical articles. Given the availability of these essays, there seems little point in rehearsing my assessments again here, so I refer readers to them. That said, I would also point readers toward Coral Ann Howells's final chapter in her *Alice Munro*, also published in 1998, in which she offers differing views on much of the same critical writing (137–53).

Also in 1998, I edited a special issue of *Essays on Canadian Writing* devoted to Munro, entitled "Alice Munro, Writing On. . . ." A year later, it was republished as a book, retitled *The Rest of the Story: Critical Essays on Alice Munro* (1999); it is in the latter form that it is most often noted. Following after *Probable Fictions* and *The Art of Alice Munro*, *The Rest of the Story* again demonstrates that the best critical approach to Munro's art is by way of the single story. More than that, it also demonstrates that individual stories in each collection seem to draw repeated critical analyses. "Royal Beatings" (1977), "The Moons of Jupiter" (1978), "The Progress of Love" (1985), "Meneseteung" (1988), "Carried Away" (1991), "Vandals" (1993), "The Love of a Good Woman" (1996), "The Children Stay" (1997), and "Save the Reaper" (1998) seem to have continued to garner the most attention, most especially "Meneseteung" and "The Love of a Good Woman."

Throughout the 1990s and leading up to the publication of *The Rest of the Story,* individual critics—some with previous writing on Munro, some not—published essays that were broadly general in analyzing the bases of Munro's art, as well as ones that were sharply focused on a single telling story. Katherine J. Mayberry did this in 1992 by focusing on "Hard-Luck Stories" (1982) from *Moons*, while in the same year, Pam Houston offered an early and almost immediately influential reading of "Meneseteung." Taking that story into her classroom, Houston contextualizes it within the work of numerous other renowned short-story writers, and within narrative theory, asserting,

> What is true is untrue, what is untrue is true. We have an hysterical bleeding woman inside an admittedly fictitious account, written by a narrator who doesn't even know her name. We have a distortion of reality within a distortion of reality, within a story that is also a poem, and sometimes a river. Nothing here will stay still long enough to mean just one thing. (90)

Also keeping close to Munro's latest stories was Ildikó de Papp Carrington, who followed her 1989 book with several articles on stories from Munro's most recent works during the next decade. Firmly grounded in Munro's techniques and always attuned to telling details, Carrington's essays persuade by their precision and well-informed research.

The work of these and other critics during the 1990s demonstrates that critical analyses of Munro's stories were being driven in part by her own publications during this period. Beginning with *Friend of My Youth* (1990) and continuing through the increasingly complex stories in *Open Secrets* (1994) and *The Love of a Good Woman* (1998), with her status well established, Munro seemed to immediately draw critics intent on discerning the complexities of her work and probing new directions there. Nathalie Foy, for instance, writes that the "stories in *Open Secrets* hang together precisely because they are not continuous but layered. Some layers remain forever parallel, and some intersect in the weird geometry of this collection" (153). This notion of layering in Munro's work—spatially, geographically, historically, and especially chronologically—has drawn and continues to draw critical analysis. Writing about the same time as Foy, Charles Forceville and Coral Ann

Howells ("Intimate") examine Munro's layerings in persuasive ways that both acknowledge and extend our understanding of the relation between space and time in her stories. In the same way, critics turned attention to previously unexamined aspects of Munro's art: Robert Lecker extended John Weaver's earlier examination of Munro's telling of Ontario's history by looking at the economic and social history told in "Carried Away," while Magdalene Redekop ("Alice Munro") and Christopher E. Gittings began the discussion of Munro's use of her Scots ancestors that has continued through the present, especially in Munro's *The View from Castle Rock* (2006) (see also Karl Miller).

During the 1990s too, articles began appearing that, whatever their interest in Munro, seemed much more intent on demonstrating ways in which her stories confirm the writings of various literary theorists (see for example Garson, "Synecdoche"). Yet some critics, much less concerned with seeing Munro's stories as confirmation of secondary writing on theory, argued instead that her stories are themselves inherently theoretical, in that they demonstrate the limitations of narrative completeness. Mark Nunes, for instance, writes in "Postmodern 'Piercing': Alice Munro's Contingent Ontologies," an important essay, that Munro "defies [the] margins of 'Postmodernism' while raising the same challenges of a determination, overflow, and the denial of totalizing narrative. Her writing, as she has noted, captures the 'funny jumps' of living: bumps that unsettle the narrative frame" (11). Complementing this view, in a powerful essay that has much to say about Munro's writing generally and *The Progress of Love* (1986) through *The Love of a Good Woman* particularly, Mark Levene writes, "In the most obvious sense, Munro is a regional writer, but her regionalism, like her overt realism, is densely ambiguous not because she is really writing about covert biblical or Freudian realms, but because no world is intact, or can be assumed to be whole or predictable, to be knowable" (845).

From the early years of her critical reception, Munro has attracted commentators who have written personally about her work with an eye toward focusing on the intimate communion they feel when reading

Munro's stories (see Wallace). Avowedly nonacademic, such writers are bent on defining, as Redekop wrote, "the story Alice Munro is telling *me*." In 1998, Judith Maclean Miller, who edited *The Art of Alice Munro*, published the first of three such essays in the *Antigonish Review*; they are singular and complementary pieces. The first of these, "An Inner Bell That Rings: The Craft of Alice Munro," looks closely at published interviews with Munro and connects her work to the Canadian photographer Freeman Paterson's reverence for, and understanding of, the surfaces he photographed. In the same way, Munro "shows us not a pre-chosen, fixed, un-changing way of writing or seeing, but a deep integrity which insists on finding its way into whatever is interesting, especially what is not well understood, or talked about, to find the angle of vision from which it can be experienced, and then to find a way to construct that" (175–76). The second essay, largely a review of *Friend of My Youth*, bears attention also, but the third, "Deconstructing Silence: The Mystery of Alice Munro," offers a sharp and precise reading of "Save the Reaper" that wholly demonstrates Munro's making of mystery there. Miller writes, "These are stories about strange deaths, sinister people, darkness, and also about story, about mystery, creating without ever saying so a new genre, another way to write about the unsolved, the unspoken. About what is said. Or not said" (51). Miller's impulse here, and in the creative nonfictional form she uses to express that impulse, has become frequent in the past decade or so; it has turned up in issues of the *Writer's Chronicle*, published by and for those involved in creative writing programs, where there have been articles titled "How to Write like Alice Munro" and "Rhyming Action in Alice Munro's Short Stories," both how-to essays (Aubrey, Bucholt). And younger writers have come to Munro for inspiration and the shared fellowship of being writers together (Strayed), while others, also fiction writers, have sharply probed her stories with a deep sense of shared endeavor (Glover).

As this suggests, it is possible to see Munro's critical reception at the end of the twentieth century as engaged in several separate fields. She was inspiring fellow writers, both at home and abroad. Equally, Munro was still a key presence in questions surrounding Canadian literature; in 2001, for instance, Gerald Lynch's excellent *The One and the Many: English-Canadian Short Story Cycles* saw "the masterful *Who Do You Think You Are?*" as central in "the continuum of Canadian short story cycles" (159). And owing largely to her work's ongoing presence in the *New Yorker*—by the end of 2001, she had published forty stories there, and in 2004, its editors would publish three of her stories in a single issue—Munro was established as a looming literary presence. As such, during the decade that followed, criticism and single volumes devoted to Munro increased in both frequency and extent.

In June 2000, the Canadian writer John Metcalf published an essay in the Toronto *National Post* entitled "Canada's Successful Writers Must Rely on Blessings from US First," a piece that he had originally called "Who Reads Alice Munro?" Intended to be contentious, Metcalf's point was that Munro's reputation was determined outside of Canada, not within. He hit his mark at home. The essay's publication brought a flurry of letters to the editor, including one from Munro herself and another from Douglas Gibson, her editor at McClelland & Stewart. Munro disputed the interpretations of one of the essayists Metcalf mentions, JoAnn McCaig, who had published an article in *The Rest of the Story* on Munro's correspondence with Virginia Barber, her agent, found in the Munro archive at the University of Calgary (see Thacker, "Canadian"). For her part, McCaig also wrote to defend what she was doing. After some delay caused by Munro's refusal to allow her to quote from her letters in the Calgary archive, McCaig published *Reading In: Alice Munro's Archives* (2002). Focused on what is available in the archive, rather than on Munro's fiction, the book is more a meditation on the uses of evidence than any real critical or biographical analysis. Infused with inappropriate theoretical analyses, avoiding historical and biographical contexts, and defiantly iconoclastic in its cultural-studies approach to the Munro archive, *Reading In* is just not a very good book. Even so, McCaig has at least done what only a very few Munro critics have: she has read and used the available archival sources. My own essays and biography have attempted to demonstrate this ongoing necessity in critical work on Munro, but there is still a very great deal yet to do. Would that more critics would stir themselves to actually use this invaluable resource (see Thacker, "Mapping").

The frequency and number of critical articles on Munro published since 2000 certainly suggest that the continued interest in her work shows no sign of abating. Of particular note have been several influence studies, in which critics have variously focused on a wide range of classical and mythological allusions (Stich, "Letting Go" and "Munro's Grail Quest"), *Sir Gawain and the Green Knight* (Luft), Charlotte Brontë and Henry James (Garson, "Alice"), or Virginia Woolf (Lilienfeld). These analyses have been offered with detailed and often compelling arguments. Munro's relation to the short story as a form—what Adrian Hunter in a masterful analysis calls a "minor literature"—has received close attention; recognizing that Munro is writing within a generic continuum and that her uses of history have played a critically significant role in her work's development, Hunter argues that her "interrogative stories dramatise an interdiction against all kinds of summary statement" ("Story" 237; see also May). Hunter is a critic whose essays on Munro have each been significant, with another published in 2010 on Munro's use of her ancestor James Hogg's *The Private Memoirs and Confessions of a Justified Sinner* (1824) in "A Wilderness Station" (1992). In this essay, he argues that Hogg and Munro both write "stories that refuse to take possession of their subjects" ("Taking Possession" 127).

Another notable Munro critic who has emerged during the early twenty-first century is Robert McGill, who has published a succession of essays on "Vandals," "Something I've Been Meaning to Tell You" (1974), "Material" (1973), and the adaptation of Munro's "The Bear Came over the Mountain" (1999–2000) into Sarah Polley's feature film *Away from Her* (2007). The latter two articles are especially good, with "'Daringly Out in the Public Eye': Alice Munro and the Ethics of

Writing Back" of special note. In it, McGill offers what is probably the best analysis of the oft-analyzed story "Material," which he calls "a metafiction about the ethics of writing fiction": it "considers the relationship between ethical writing and ethical living and what the criteria for each might be" (875).[2] In his essay on adaptation, McGill positions Polley's film in relation to both the dominant discourses on Canadian writing and, more effectively, the effects of Munro's story and especially her overall aesthetic of indeterminacy ("No Nation").

The first decade of the twenty-first century has also seen publication of a succession of Munro tribute volumes. In 2003–4, *Open Letter* published papers from an Alice Munro conference held in May 2003 at the University of Orléans, "L'écriture du secret / Writing Secrets" (Ventura and Condé). Similarly, *Reading Alice Munro in Italy* (2008) is based on another gathering held in May 2007 in Siena, "Alice Munro: The Art of the Short Story / L'arte del racconto" (Balestra et al.). Each volume is a valuable record of how Munro's work is seen in Europe, although each includes North American critics. In *Open Letter*, Coral Ann Howells, in one of the strongest essays in the volume, concludes by wondering if Munro's stories are "like houses that we enter, as she once suggested . . . , or are they like floating bridges, unstable structures thrown out over dark spaces where we can see stars reflected from above, but not the secrets hidden beneath the surface of the water?" ("Telling" 52). Another singular piece is the dialogue between Donna Bennett and Russell Morton Brown, two interwoven papers given together at the conference in back-and-forth style. There, while discussing Munro's use of time in "Save the Reaper," Bennett asserts that "perhaps no other Canadian writer so often makes use of counterfactual statements and of past perfect and conditional perfect tenses" (192). And concluding a discussion of "The Love of a Good Woman," Brown says of Enid at the end of that mysterious story, "It is no longer guilty secrets that intrigue her; she is now preoccupied with those secrets that open one heart to another. Munro does not permit the readers to do more than speculate on how that plot will unfold" (206).

Like most conference volumes, this one is uneven, but taken together, its essays reveal the broad and extremely high critical stature accorded Munro's art. Again and again, her critics confirm an assertion made by coeditor Héliane Ventura: "To look at a Munro landscape or to read a Munro text is not to participate in the decoding of photographic realism. It is to take part in an archaeological process which consists of recovering traces that have been destroyed" (Ventura and Condé 256). In the same way, *Reading Alice Munro in Italy* offers a succession of readings on individual stories, with forays into broader matters; there is also an especially good piece by Susanna Basso on translating Munro's work into Italian.

Five more recent Munro volumes are notable. Ailsa Cox's *Alice Munro* is a brief introduction published in the British series Writers and Their Work in 2004. It is current on both Munro's fiction and its criticism, and offers a sharply focused and detailed appreciation that displays eminent good sense throughout. Munro's work demonstrates, Cox writes, that "nothing defeats mortality, but fiction can suspend time for a while" (85). "But in every story, finally, words fail. There is always something which has to be left out, and can only be approximated through imagery and paradox" (97). Another brief single-authored book appeared in 2009, *Daughters and Mothers in Alice Munro's Later Stories* by Deborah Heller, who also has an excellent essay on *Friend of My Youth* in *The Rest of the Story*. This book, not much more than an essay, considers Munro's recent use of the perennial mother-daughter relation in "My Mother's Dream," "Family Furnishings," and the Juliet triptych in *Runaway*. The *Virginia Quarterly Review* published "Ordinary Outsiders: A Symposium on Alice Munro," another tribute from various hands, in 2006. It includes a biographical critical overview by Marcela Valdes; appreciations by Munro's editors, her agent, other writers, and friends; and the revised version of Munro's memoir story "Home" (1974), which was included in *The View from Castle Rock*. A special issue of *Eureka Studies in Teaching Short Fiction* devoted to Munro's work, also published in 2006, demonstrates a wide range of interest in teaching Munro's stories and their broad appeal. In 2009, Harold Bloom included Munro in his Bloom's Modern Critical Views series, republishing ten critical essays and sections from books (most mentioned here). In his brief introduction, Bloom says he only managed to read Munro's *Selected Stories* himself, but from that he places Munro in the second tier of "major artists of short fiction of the twentieth century." She does not, however, make his top ten, which includes Henry James, Anton Chekhov, Franz Kafka, James Joyce, and Ernest Hemingway, among others—all men (1).

In an important, though contentious, recent article, "The Problem with Alice Munro," Philip Marchand argues that her "problem" is that "she has been so true to the world she has chosen to depict." Marchand continues:

> The horizons in this world are uniformly low, due partly to the absence of characters whose education, experience and character might enable them to expand those horizons. Instead, it's a standoff between her hicks and her smarties. Her intellectuals have no heft and are riddled with egotism; her men of God are pale reflections of their Victorian predecessors. Her heroines, who are a combination of hick and smarty, who only want to be allowed to go off somewhere and study Greek, like Del Jordan's mother and Juliet Henderson, are as passive and helpless in the face of the world's unfriendliness as Munro's adolescent girls are helpless in the face of sexual urgency. (13–14)

Munro's great talent notwithstanding, we critics should not, Marchand argues, "shirk the issue of the sad paltriness of her world," challenging, "Did the limitations of her world have to correlate so closely to the limitations of her art?" (14). Marchand's essay is less compelling than it is indicative of just where Munro criticism is now: by trying to approach Munro's oeuvre whole, he offers salient and broad commentary on her material, some of it quite good, but he ultimately fails to convince that his objections are any more than niggling preference.

The essay may also indicate the presence, at least in Canada, of some weariness over Munro's familiar material, her approaches to it, and especially her dominating presence. Here, too, *niggling* is an apt word.

By contrast, and certainly consistently enough to see a trend, Munro's critics during the last half-dozen years have quite narrowed their focus, limiting their treatment most often to a single story and, more specifically, to questions of narrative structure within that story. Caitlin J. Charman does this in her examination of "Fits" (1986), Ryan Melsom does the same for "Labor Day Dinner," and most impressively, Timothy McIntyre offers an extremely close, detailed, and thorough analysis of "The Moons of Jupiter." Each critic also synthesizes previous commentary in ways suggesting that the reading offered is fairly complete. Two other stories, "Meneseteung" and "The Love of a Good Woman," have continued to draw detailed interest in extensive ways. Taking up the latter story in the *Journal of Narrative Theory*, John Gerlach builds on the work of previous critics to argue that the story's open ending is a "charged incompleteness" that is

> particularly tantalizing and distinctive among open endings. . . . In this story, ultimate issues, good and evil, confession and repression are stunningly irresolvable. . . . Munro has teased us with very traditional expectations: she has written in the mode of realism, not as a self-conscious, mocking postmodern. She has teased us with variable types of closure in the various sections of the story. (154)

Detailing this in the story, Gerlach almost exclaims, "We've been teased in every way possible; the rhythm of delay with stunning penultimate climaxes surely must resolve itself. But it doesn't" (155; see also Carrington, "Don't"; Duffy, "Dark"; McCombs; and Ross, "Too Many").

But if "The Love of a Good Woman" has attracted considerable sustained analysis, the story that continues as a paradigmatic text, given the sustained attention it has drawn, is "Meneseteung." Two essays published in 2010—by Tracy Ware and Dennis Duffy, both in the same critical book on historical fiction—demonstrate this unequivocally, and their work is supplemented by another essay by Douglas Glover. Ware, a critic who reads criticism carefully, completely, and very thoughtfully, creates what might be called a deep synthesis of criticism already published on "Meneseteung" and links it to broader theories on the uses of historical fact in fiction. Ware writes that at one point, "Munro is less skeptical of history than of the ethics of 'historiographic metafiction.' What right does she have to supplement history with concerns of a later day? How can she know that she is not doing exactly that, despite her best intentions?" (76). Drawing on these distinctions and especially on his sharp synthesis of others' analyses, Ware convincingly argues that with the story, Munro "aligned her resistance to any ideological program with the skepticism at the core of much historical fiction" (77). Duffy, for his part, roots "Meneseteung" deeply in what he calls "the Munro Tract"—her home place in Huron County, Ontario—and draws persuasively on Munro's biography and her use of prototypes for the protagonist, Almeda Roth. He argues that "the story's fictional weight rests instead upon the foundations that its narrative mode composes, a way of storytelling reminiscent of the devices of orality." In so doing, Munro "has produced a story that appears to follow the agenda set by the traditional, continuous, and pointed historical novel but which finally slams through those guardrails, crosses the median, and drives away in the other direction of the postmodern, de-centred, and diffuse fiction familiar to us now" (210–11).[3]

But if the scholarly bases of Ware's and Duffy's essays are impressive in their deep syntheses—and they very much are—Douglas Glover reminds critics in his "The Mind of Alice Munro" that in "Meneseteung," it is all about the primary text itself:

> She uses resonating structures so that various parts of the text echo off each other. She uses a complex point of view structure to create variety and contrast in the types of text threaded through the narrative (and thus

a variety of perspectives). She dances with time. She creates action, conflict, and emotion even in those parts of the story that are not directly relating plot. (31)

Glover argues, "Munro seems to realize that the inner life of a man or a woman is also a text, that in our secret hearts we are talking to ourselves, muttering, declaiming; at its deepest point this is our experience of experience" (35). Concluding, Glover cites what is perhaps the most-quoted line from "Meneseteung": its penultimate image of the narrator, and by extension Munro herself, engaged in research "in the hope of seeing this trickle in time, making a connection, rescuing one thing from the rubbish" (Munro, *Friend* 73). He then asserts that "there is this allegorical element in everything Alice Munro writes; she is always teaching readers how to read her stories as she writes them; there are always connections to be made" (Glover 37). So there are, always and ever, as we read her stories and we hear the stories Alice Munro is telling each of us. So her critics have realized from our first readings, and so we continue to do now. Not controversial, but human. Profound. Alice Munro, "our Chekhov." Better, our Alice Munro.

Notes

1. This is a point I first asserted in "What's 'Material'" (208). There have been no single-authored volumes focused on the fiction since Howells's, save a faulty "appreciation" by an ill-informed American reader, Brad Hooper, and a fine small book by Ailsa Cox in a British series that introduces writers to students. Another scholarly volume, by Isla Duncan, was published in November 2011.

2. Despite its many strengths, I nonetheless notice an important weakness in McGill's essay: he neglects to mention Louis K. MacKendrick's *Some Other Reality*, which covers many of the same considerations of this important story; this is hardly justified.

3. Another essay that might have been mentioned regarding "Meneseteung" is Naomi Morgenstern's "The Baby or the Violin?," which reads the story in concert with "My Mother's Dream" (1998), concentrating on the ethics of feminism and paying special attention to Almeda's dream in the story. Driven by an apparent desire to demonstrate that Munro actualizes literary theory in her stories, Morgenstern offers readings of Munro's stories that are ultimately unsatisfactory.

Works Cited

Aubrey, Kim. "How to Write Like Alice Munro." *Writer's Chronicle* 38.1 (2005): 12–15.

Bailey, Nancy I. "The Masculine Image in *Lives of Girls and Women*." *Canadian Literature* 80 (1979): 113–18, 120.

Balestra, Gianfranca, et al., eds. *Reading Alice Munro in Italy*. Toronto: Frank Iacobucci Centre for Italian Canadian Studies, 2008.

Bennett, Donna. "Open. Secret. Telling Time in Alice Munro's Fiction." Ventura and Condé 185–209.

Besner, Neil K. *Introducing Alice Munro's Lives of Girls and Women: A Reader's Guide*. Toronto: ECW, 1990.

Blodgett, E. D. *Alice Munro*. Boston: Twayne, 1988.

_____. "Prisms and Arcs: Structures in Hébert and Munro." *Figures in a Ground: Canadian Essays on Modern Literature Collected in Honor of Sheila Watson*. Ed. Diane Bessai and David Jackel. Saskatoon, SK: Western Producer Prairie, 1978. 99–121.

Bloom, Harold, ed. *Alice Munro*. New York: Chelsea House, 2009.

Brown, Russell Morton. "Open Secrets? Alice Munro and the Mystery Story." Ventura and Condé 185–209.

Bucholt, Maggie. "Rhyming Action in Alice Munro's Short Stories." *Writer's Chronicle* 39.6 (2007): 46–54.

Carrington, Ildikó de Papp. *Controlling the Uncontrollable: The Fiction of Alice Munro*. DeKalb: Northern Illinois UP, 1989.

_____. "'Don't Tell (on) Daddy': Narrative Complexity in Alice Munro's 'The Love of a Good Woman.'" *Studies in Short Fiction* 34.2 (1997): 159–70.

_____. "Other Rooms, Other Texts, Other Selves: Alice Munro's 'Sunday Afternoon' and 'Hired Girl.'" *Journal of the Short Story in English* 30 (1998): 2–8.

_____. "Recasting the Orpheus Myth: Alice Munro's 'The Children Stay' and Jean Anouilh's *Eurydice*." Thacker, *Rest of the Story* 191–203.

_____. "Talking Dirty: Alice Munro's 'Open Secrets' and John Steinbeck's *Of Mice and Men*." *Studies in Short Fiction* 31.4 (1994): 595–606.

_____. "What's in a Title? Alice Munro's 'Carried Away.'" *Studies in Short Fiction* 30.4 (1993): 555–64.

_____. "Where Are You, Mother? Alice Munro's 'Save the Reaper.'" *Canadian Literature* 173 (2002): 34–51.

Charman, Caitlin J. "There's Got to Be Some Wrenching and Slashing: Horror and Retrospection in Alice Munro's 'Fits.'" *Canadian Literature* 191 (2006): 13–30.

Conron, Brandon. "Munro's Wonderland." *Canadian Literature* 78 (1978): 109–23.

Cox, Ailsa. *Alice Munro*. Tavistock, Eng.: Northcote, 2004.

Dahlie, Hallvard. "The Fiction of Alice Munro." *Ploughshares* 4.3 (1978): 56–71.

_____. "Unconsummated Relationships: Isolation and Rejection in Alice Munro's Stories." *World Literature Written in English* 11.1 (1972): 43–48.

Dawson, Anthony B. "Coming of Age in Canada." *Mosaic* 11.3 (1978): 47–62.

Duffy, Dennis. "'A Dark Sort of Mirror': 'The Love of a Good Woman' as Pauline Poetic." Thacker, *Rest of the Story* 169–90.

_____. "Too Little Geography; Too Much History: Writing the Balance in 'Meneseteung.'" *National Plots: Historical Fiction and Changing Ideas of Canada*. Ed. Andrea Cabajsky and Brett Josef Grubisic. Waterloo, ON: Wilfrid Laurier UP, 2010. 197–213.

Duncan, Isla. *Alice Munro's Narrative Art*. New York: Palgrave, 2011.

Eureka Studies in Teaching Short Fiction 6.2 (2006). Spec. issue on Alice Munro.

Forceville, Charles. "Alice Munro's Layered Structures." *Shades of Empire in Colonial and Post-Colonial Literatures*. Ed. C. C. Barfoot and Theo d'Haen. Amsterdam: Rodopi, 1993. 301–10.

Foy, Nathalie. "'Darkness Collecting': Reading 'Vandals' as a Coda to *Open Secrets*." Thacker, *Rest of the Story* 147–68.

Garson, Marjorie. "Alice Munro and Charlotte Brontë." *University of Toronto Quarterly* 69.4 (2000): 783–825.

_____. "Synecdoche and the Munrovian Sublime: Parts and Wholes in *Lives of Girls and Women*." *English Studies in Canada* 20.4 (1994): 413–29.

Gerlach, John. "To Close or Not to Close: Alice Munro's 'The Love of a Good Woman.'" *Journal of Narrative Theory* 37.1 (2007): 146–58.

Gittings, Christopher E. "Constructing a Scots-Canadian Ground: Family History and Cultural Translation in Alice Munro." *Studies in Short Fiction* 34.1 (1997): 27–37.

Glover, Douglas. "The Mind of Alice Munro." *Canadian Notes and Queries* 79 (2010): 30–31.

Heble, Ajay. *The Tumble of Reason: Alice Munro's Discourse of Absence*. Toronto: U of Toronto P, 1994.

Heller, Deborah. *Daughters and Mothers in Alice Munro's Later Stories*. Seattle: Workwomans, 2009.

Hooper, Brad. *The Fiction of Alice Munro: An Appreciation*. Westport, CT: Praeger, 2008.

Houston, Pam. "A Hopeful Sign: The Making of Metonymic Meaning in Munro's 'Meneseteung.'" *Kenyon Review* 14.4 (1992): 79–92.

Howells, Coral Ann. *Alice Munro*. Manchester: Manchester UP, 1998.

_____. "Intimate Dislocations: Buried History and Geography in Alice Munro's Sowesto Stories." *British Journal of Canadian Studies* 14.1 (1999): 7–16.

_____. *Private and Fictional Words: Canadian Women Novelists of the 1970s and 1980s*. London: Methuen, 1987.

_____. "The Telling of Secrets/The Secrets of Telling: An Overview of Alice Munro's Enigma Variations from *Dance of the Happy Shades* to *Hateship, Friendship, Courtship, Loveship, Marriage*." Ventura and Condé 39–54.

Hoy, Helen. "Alice Munro: 'Unforgettable, Indigestible Messages.'" *Journal of Canadian Studies* 26.1 (1991): 5–21.

_____. "'Dull, Simple, Amazing and Unfathomable': Paradox and Double Vision in Alice Munro's Fiction." *Studies in Canadian Literature* 5.1 (1980): 100–115.

Hunter, Adrian. "Story into History: Alice Munro's Minor Literature." *English* 53.207 (2004): 219–38.

_____. "Taking Possession: Alice Munro's 'A Wilderness Station' and James Hogg's *Justified Sinner*." *Studies in Canadian Literature* 35.2 (2010): 114–28.

Lecker, Robert. "Machines, Readers, Gardens: Alice Munro's 'Carried Away.'" Thacker, *Rest of the Story* 103–27.

Levene, Mark. "'It Was about Vanishing': A Glimpse of Alice Munro's Stories." *University of Toronto Quarterly* 68.4 (1999): 841–60.

Lilienfeld, Jane. "'Something I've Been Meaning to Tell You': Alice Munro as Unlikely Heir to Virginia Woolf." *Virginia Woolf out of Bounds*. Ed. Jessica Berman and Jane Goldman. New York: Pace UP, 2001. 92–96.

Luft, Joanna. "Boxed In: Alice Munro's 'Wenlock Edge' and *Sir Gawain and the Green Knight*." *Studies in Canadian Literature* 35.1 (2010): 103–26.

Lynch, Gerald. *The One and the Many: English-Canadian Short Story Cycles*. Toronto: U of Toronto P, 2001.

Macdonald, Rae McCarthy. "A Madman Loose in the World: The Vision of Alice Munro." *Modern Fiction Studies* 22.3 (1976): 365–74.

_____. "Structure and Detail in *Lives of Girls and Women*." *Studies in Canadian Literature* 3.2 (1978): 199–200.

MacKendrick, Louis K., ed. *Probable Fictions: Alice Munro's Narrative Acts*. Downsview, ON: ECW, 1983.

_____. *Some Other Reality: Alice Munro's* Something I've Been Meaning to Tell You. Toronto: ECW, 1993.

Marchand, Philip. "The Problem with Alice Munro." *Canadian Notes and Queries* 72 (2007): 10–15.

Martin, W. R. "Alice Munro and James Joyce." *Journal of Canadian Fiction* 24 (1979): 120–26.

_____. *Alice Munro: Paradox and Parallel*. Edmonton: U of Alberta P, 1987.

May, Charles E. "Why Does Alice Munro Write Short Stories?" *Wascana Review* 38.1 (2003): 16–28.

Mayberry, Katherine J. "'Every Last Thing . . . Everlasting': Alice Munro and the Limits of Narrative." *Studies in Short Fiction* 29.4 (1992): 531–41.

Mazur, Carol, and Cathy Moulder, ed. *Alice Munro: An Annotated Bibliography of Works and Criticism*. Lanham, MD: Scarecrow, 2007.

McCaig, JoAnn. "Alice Munro's Agency: The Virginia Barber Correspondence, 1976–83." Thacker, *Rest of the Story* 81–102.

_____. *Reading In: Alice Munro's Archives*. Waterloo, ON: Wilfrid Laurier UP, 2002.

McCombs, Judith. "Searching Bluebeard's Chambers: Grimm, Gothic, and Bible Mysteries in Alice Munro's 'The Love of a Good Woman.'" *American Review of Canadian Studies* 30.3 (2000): 327–48.

McGill, Robert. "'Daringly Out in the Public Eye': Alice Munro and the Ethics of Writing Back." *University of Toronto Quarterly* 76.3 (2007): 874–89.

_____. "No Nation but Adaptation: 'The Bear Came over the Mountain,' *Away from Her*, and What It Means to Be Faithful." *Canadian Literature* 197 (2008): 98–111.

_____. "Somewhere I've Been Meaning to Tell You: Alice Munro's Fiction of Distance." *Journal of Commonwealth Literature* 37.1 (2002): 9–29.

_____. "Where Do You Think You Are? Alice Munro's Open Houses." *Mosaic* 35.4 (2002): 103–19.

McIntyre, Timothy. "'The Way the Stars Really Do Come Out at Night': The Trick of Representation in Alice Munro's 'The Moons of Jupiter.'" *Canadian Literature* 200 (2009): 73–88.

Melsom, Ryan. "Roberta's Raspberry Bombe and Critical Indifference in Alice Munro's 'Labor Day Dinner.'" *Studies in Canadian Literature* 34.1 (2009): 142–59.

Messud, Claire. "Signs of Struggle." Rev. of *Cheating at Canasta*, by William Trevor. *New York Review of Books* 14 Feb. 2008: 20–22.

Metcalf, John. "Canada's Successful Writers Must Rely on Blessings from US First." *National Post* 17 June 2000: E4–5.

Miller, Judith Maclean, ed. *The Art of Alice Munro: Saying the Unsayable; Papers from the Waterloo Conference.* Waterloo, ON: U of Waterloo P, 1984.

_____. "Deconstructing Silence: The Mystery of Alice Munro." *Antigonish Review* 129 (2002): 43–52.

_____. "An Inner Bell that Rings: The Craft of Alice Munro." *Antigonish Review* 115 (1998): 157–76.

_____. "On Looking into Rifts and Crannies: Alice Munro's *Friend of My Youth.*" *Antigonish Review* 120 (2000): 205–26.

Miller, Karl. "The Passion of Alice Laidlaw." *Changing English* 14.1 (2007): 17–22.

Monaghan, David. "Confinement and Escape in Alice Munro's 'The Flats Road.'" *Studies in Short Fiction* 14.2 (1977): 165–68.

Morgenstern, Naomi. "The Baby or the Violin? Ethics and Femininity in the Fiction of Alice Munro." *Literature Interpretation Theory* 14.2 (2003): 69–97.

Moss, John. *Sex and Violence in the Canadian Novel: The Ancestral Present.* Toronto: McClelland, 1977.

Munro, Alice. *Friend of My Youth.* Toronto: McClelland, 1990.

_____. *The Progress of Love.* Toronto: McClelland, 1986.

New, W. H. "Pronouns and Prepositions: Alice Munro's Stories." *Open Letter* 3.5 (1976): 40–49.

Nunes, Mark. "Postmodern 'Piercing': Alice Munro's Contingent Ontologies." *Studies in Short Fiction* 34.1 (1997): 11–26.

"Ordinary Outsiders: A Symposium on Alice Munro." *Virginia Quarterly Review* 82.3 (2006): 80–128.

Packer, Miriam. "*Lives of Girls and Women*: A Creative Search for Completion." *Here and Now: A Critical Anthology.* Ed. John Moss. Toronto: NC, 1978. 134–44.

Pfaus, B. *Alice Munro.* Ottawa: Golden Dog, 1984.

Redekop, Magdalene. "Alice Munro and the Scottish Nostalgic Grotesque." Thacker, *Rest of the Story* 21–43.

_____. *Mothers and Other Clowns: The Stories of Alice Munro.* London: Routledge, 1992.

Ross, Catherine Sheldrick. *Alice Munro: A Double Life.* Toronto: ECW, 1992.

_____. "'Too Many Things': Reading Alice Munro's 'The Love of a Good Woman.'" *University of Toronto Quarterly* 71.3 (2002): 785–811.

Stich, K. P. "Letting Go with the Mind: Dionysus and Medusa in Alice Munro's 'Meneseteung.'" *Canadian Literature* 169 (2001): 106–25.

_____. "Munro's Grail Quest: The Progress of Logos." *Studies in Canadian Literature* 32.1 (2007): 120–40.

Strayed, Cheryl. "Munro Country." *Missouri Review* 32.2 (2009): 96–108.

Struthers, J. R. (Tim). "Alice Munro and the American South." *Canadian Review of American Studies* 6 (1975): 196–204.

_____. "Reality and Ordering: The Growth of a Young Artist in *Lives of Girls and Women*." *Essays on Canadian Writing* 3 (1975): 32–46.

Thacker, Robert. "Alice Munro: An Annotated Bibliography." *The Annotated Bibliography of Canada's Major Authors*. Ed. Robert Lecker and Jack David. Vol. 5. Toronto: ECW, 1984. 354–414.

_____. *Alice Munro: Writing Her Lives; A Biography*. Rev. ed. Toronto: Emblem, 2011.

_____. "Canadian Literature's 'America.'" *Essays on Canadian Writing* 71 (2000): 128–39.

_____. "Conferring Munro." *Essays on Canadian Writing* 34 (1987): 162–69.

_____. "Go Ask Alice: The Progress of Munro Criticism." *Journal of Canadian Studies* 26.2 (1991): 156–69.

_____. "Mapping Munro: Reading the 'Clues.'" *Dominant Impressions: Essays on the Canadian Short Story*. Ed. Gerald Lynch and Angela Arnold Robbeson. Ottawa: U of Ottawa P, 1999. 127–35.

_____, ed. *The Rest of the Story: Critical Essays on Alice Munro*. Toronto: ECW, 1999.

_____. "What's 'Material'? The Progress of Munro Criticism, Part 2." *Journal of Canadian Studies* 33.2 (1998): 196–210.

Ventura, Héliane, and Mary Condé, eds. *Open Letter* 11.9 (2003), 12.1 (2004). Spec. issue on Alice Munro.

Wallace, Bronwen. "Women's Lives: Alice Munro." *The Human Elements: Critical Essays*. Ed. David Helwig. Ottawa: Oberon, 1978. 52–66.

Ware, Tracy. "'And They May Get It Wrong, After All': Reading Alice Munro's 'Meneseteung.'" *National Plots: Historical Fiction and Changing Ideas of Canada*. Ed. Andrea Cabajsky and Brett Josef Grubisic. Waterloo, ON: Wilfrid Laurier UP, 2010. 67–79.

Doing Her Duty and Writing Her Life: Alice Munro's Cultural and Historical Context _____

Timothy McIntyre

As a writer, and perhaps just as a person, Alice Munro is strongly tied to a particular place and culture. Small-town, rural southwestern Ontario and its inhabitants, particularly as they were in the 1930s and 1940s when she was growing up there, loom large in her imagination. Her writing, however, resonates far beyond this context. With her 2009 Man Booker International Prize win and her status as "perennial contender" for the Nobel Prize in Literature (Flood), Munro has established herself as one of the major writers of fiction in the late twentieth and early twenty-first centuries. Yet this rise to the upper echelons of the literary world was hardly overnight. Munro spent much of the 1950s and 1960s publishing her fiction in magazines but having, by her own account, "absolutely no status as a writer," even if the quality of her fiction, according to Robert Thacker, "was becoming increasingly well known to the small coterie of people who watched alertly for emerging Canadian writers" (191–92). Only in 1968, with the publication of her first book, *Dance of the Happy Shades*, did Munro become well known in the literary world to more than a handful of keen observers. This particular trajectory of Munro's career—from being "the least praised good writer in Canada," according to literary journalist Robert Fulford (qtd. in Thacker 167), to reaching the highest echelon of literary success in first Canada and then the world—is inextricably linked to her cultural heritage, her personal circumstances, and the political and economic contexts that shaped the publishing and literary worlds in the post–World War II era.

Cultural Inheritance

Alice Munro was born Alice Ann Laidlaw on July 10, 1931, in Wingham, a small town in southwestern Ontario, Canada. She was the first of three children. Her younger brother, William George, was born

---

in 1936, and for almost the first five years of her life, Munro was a beloved only child. In these early years, her family ran a fox farm on the edge of Lower Wingham, or Lower Town, an area separate from Wingham proper and populated by people of decidedly lesser means. As was the case for most of rural southwestern Ontario, the majority of the population was composed of Irish Anglicans, Scots Presbyterians, and other Protestant sects. Robert Thacker describes them as "people for whom virtue came from hard work, who often felt guilt, who were quick to remember a slight but would seldom recall a compliment" (44). Catholics were in the minority of the population, and relations between the two groups were hostile. Indeed, Munro, a Protestant in the cultural if not religious sense, has written that sectarian school-yard fights were common: "People were Catholics or fundamentalist Protestants, honor-bound to molest each other" (qtd. in Thacker 56). In one of her early stories, "Walker Brothers Cowboy," Nora Cronin, the father's Catholic female friend and apparent one-time love interest, appears to the child protagonist almost as a sort of exotic Other. The child observes a picture of the Virgin Mary, "Jesus' mother—I know that much," before recalling a half-understood phrase her grandmother and aunt used to refer to Catholics: "*So-and-so digs with the wrong foot*" (Munro, *Dance* 14).

Munro's childhood and adolescence in Huron County had a profound effect on her writing in terms of both content and style. Collections such as *Dance of the Happy Shades*, *Lives of Girls and Women* (1971), and *Who Do You Think You Are?* (1978) explore with painstaking clarity the circumstances of small-town and rural Ontario, particularly from the point of view of the lower-middle class. Munro writes of this time and place with a "spare lucid style" and "command of detail" that "have given her fiction a precision which is one of her most distinctive accomplishments" (Hoy). Gothic themes of madness, decay, melodramatic violence, and the grotesque frequently coexist with her almost documentary realism. Such instances include the "Gothic mother" with her debilitating illness in "The Peace of Utrecht" (*Dance*

195), Almeda Roth's uncanny encounter with the grotesque figure of the drunken woman in "Meneseteung" (*Friend* 64–67), and the shocking violence in the life and death of Mr. Tyde in "Royal Beatings" (*Who* 7–8), to name only a few. These elements, too, reflect her upbringing, according to Munro: "The part of the country I come from is absolutely Gothic" (qtd. in Gibson 248). Thacker's examination of Wingham's newspaper headlines from the 1930s and 1940s, such as "Howick Baby Scalded to Death," "Hand Nearly Severed," and "Lamb Born with 7 Legs and 2 Tails," testifies to this southern Ontario Gothic sensibility in the culture (45). Many of Munro's stories also concern deeply personal facets of her life. "The Ottawa Valley" draws heavily on her relationship with her mother and her dawning childhood realization of her mother's Parkinson's disease, while "Home" clearly deals with the circumstances of her father's death from heart disease.

Like that of many, if not all, writers, Munro's work in some ways reflects her life and circumstances. "I write about where I am in life," she has said (qtd. in Thacker 431). Her Huron County past has been, and continues to be, important to her work, but she writes of other facets of her life as well. Elements of her relationships with men and her life as a writer, for example, have appeared in work as far back as "The Office," from her first book, *Dance of the Happy Shades*, and still inform her writing. Furthermore, stories such as "The Albanian Virgin," "The View from Castle Rock," and "Too Much Happiness" display Munro's ability to craft a sense of reality in contexts far removed from her own experience, such as a remote 1920s Albanian village, her own ancestors' nineteenth-century voyage from Scotland to Canada, or the life of nineteenth-century Russian mathematician and novelist Sophia Kovalevsky. In an introduction to her collection *The Moons of Jupiter*, Munro says that when one writes "a certain type of story—first-person, seemingly artless and straight-forward—people imagine that about all you did was write down everything that happened on a certain day." Yet the more personal stories "are carried inexorably away from the real," presumably by the demands of art, while stories based more on observation "lose their anecdotal edges, being invaded by familiar shapes and voices" (*Moons* xv). Munro draws on both her life and her skills as a writer to create this sense of reality, regardless of whether in any given story she leans more on what she has observed, experienced, or imagined, if those distinctions can even be maintained in writing. Bearing that in mind, throughout her career, it has nevertheless been Huron County, her past, and her cultural heritage to which Munro has returned again and again.

This cultural inheritance has proved to be rich material for Munro, despite, or perhaps because of, her ambivalence regarding the act of writing itself. In her essay "Remember Roger Mortimer," Munro paints a picture of her childhood as one in which reading and literary interests were more tolerated than celebrated: "Reading in our family was a private activity and there was nothing particularly commendable about it. It was a pesky sort of infirmity, like hay fever, to which we might be expected to succumb; anyone who managed to stay clear of it would have been the one to be congratulated. But once the addiction was established, nobody thought of interfering with it" (34). Thacker notes that in general, the Scots Irish Protestants of Huron County had "little appreciation for fiction" (377). Over the years, Munro has even experienced some hostility to her writing. Local residents occasionally took offense at elements of the stories that they felt resembled their own lives: one man "drunkenly threatened" Munro's father, Robert Laidlaw, by "walking around [Laidlaw's] house, firing a shotgun into the air" in response to Munro's 1956 story "The Time of Death," in which a toddler is accidentally scalded to death, because he felt the incident was drawn from his family history (Thacker 159). Feelings for Munro have softened considerably in the intervening decades, however, to the point even of pride at being the birthplace of such an internationally renowned writer. Wingham is now home to the Alice Munro Literary Garden, and its North Huron Museum offers a brochure called the *Self-Guided Tour of Points of Interest in the Town of Wingham Relating to Alice Munro* (Foran).

Not surprisingly, given this background, a certain ambivalence toward the value of writing is apparent in Munro's work. Ildikó de Papp Carrington suggests that for Munro's characters, "manipulating and controlling language—the imaginative act of writing itself—somehow becomes a form of shame or humiliation" (15), and she notes an interview in which Munro says that "although writing was 'the only thing' that she 'ever wanted to do,' she felt 'embarrassment' about 'doing something' that she could neither 'explain' nor 'justify' to her hardworking parents" (16). This sentiment appears perhaps most clearly in the 1974 version of "Home." The story's narrator, who seems to stand in for Munro herself, questions both her ability and her right to tell the story of her father as he approaches death, and she ascribes these doubts to "the hard voice of my upbringing telling me it is always better to dig potatoes, and feed sheep" (152). Munro's upbringing and cultural heritage, however, provided her with more than just this hard voice.

If the enjoyment of reading was not, as Munro writes in "Remember Roger Mortimer," seen as a particularly commendable activity, neither was it, like hay fever, altogether uncommon. Munro writes that because she was a voracious reader in her youth, her mother, "with a fatalistic gesture," called her "another Emma McClure!" in front of some visiting aunts. Emma McClure "was a relative . . . who lived somewhere deep in the country, where she had been reading day and night for thirty-five years, with no time to get married, learn the names of her nephews and nieces, or comb her hair when she came in to town." Though Emma must surely be somewhat of a cautionary tale, Munro writes, "They all looked at me pessimistically, but nobody took my book away" ("Remember" 34). It seems, then, that there was a place, if not a place of honor, for cultivating a life of the mind, as well as examples of such rural intellectual types around her. Munro has said that her father, Robert Laidlaw, "understood the artist in her" and was "always a reader, always a thoughtful man," who in the last years of his life "had become a writer himself" and published a novel,

The McGregors (1979), as well as "five memoirs and a short story" (Thacker 315). Though the value of fiction may have been a bit suspect in her community, and perhaps to some extent to her family and even herself, the value of reading was nevertheless recognized. Munro has noted the place in Protestant culture afforded to the power of reading; in an interview on CBC radio with Shelagh Rogers, Munro points out that John Knox's push for an educated peasantry led to the development of an intelligent community of critical readers with a suspicion of symbols but a belief in the power and value of reading (Munro, interview). Munro's willingness to commit herself to a literary life was only partially a rejection of past and community.

Education and First Publication

In 1949, Alice Munro began attending the University of Western Ontario on a two-year scholarship that only just covered her expenses, if she also worked "two library jobs and, for extra money, sold her blood for fifteen dollars a pint" (Thacker 91). Munro says she enjoyed her years at Western, enjoyed "being in that atmosphere, having all those books, not having to do any housework" (qtd. in Thacker 94), even if her desire to be a writer—"that's all I wanted," she recalls (91)—sometimes conflicted with her academic studies, though not with any major repercussions for her grades (96). These university years came at the tail end of an influx of World War II veterans: older, more mature men who "brought a will to work to the campus which eventually resulted in generally higher standards" (Talman and Talman 163). Across Ontario, these veterans came to exert a powerful influence on campus life. They "rapidly assumed positions of leadership within student institutions and associations," and because "they knew how to organize and to operate within a chain of command," they soon "came to dominate student unions and newspapers" (McKillop 554). Munro's university education took place among these serious men, before the great expansion of Ontario's postsecondary education system would bring masses of new students and change the culture of universities during the 1960s and 1970s. These postwar years also saw the "cult of domesticity" reach "new heights" in North America and a concomitant "decline in the percentage of women who sought higher education," as women faced a variety of pressures steering them toward homemaking (McKillop 555–56). Munro herself left Western after her scholarship ran out, married James Munro, and moved with him to Vancouver, where he went to work for Eaton's, at the time Canada's largest retailer. Yet it was in this university context that Munro would have her first taste of publishing success and form connections that would shape her writing career for over a decade.

Munro first made a name for herself in Western's literary community and branched out from there. Her first published story, "The Dimensions of a Shadow," appeared in 1950 in *Folio*, the University of Western Ontario's arts and literature publication. Later that year, she published two more stories in *Folio*, "Story for Sunday" and "The Widower." In 1951, quite likely due to the encouragement and example of her classmates and professors, she began corresponding with Robert Weaver and submitting stories for his consideration on his radio show, *Canadian Short Stories*, on the Canadian Broadcasting Corporation (CBC) (Thacker 109). Weaver proved to be a major figure in the development of Munro's early work, and through his efforts with the CBC, as founder of the literary journal *Tamarack Review*, and as editor of numerous anthologies, he would also be a major figure in the development and growth of Canadian literature as a whole for decades to come.

Early Career

Robert Weaver would be the first of several key individuals in Munro's career. He joined the CBC in 1948 and made it his mission as much as his job to support, encourage, and promote the writing of literature in Canada. He formed a series of radio programs that featured then-up-and-coming writers such as Munro, Margaret Atwood, and Mordecai Richler. During the 1950s and 1960s in particular, when Munro had virtually no other contacts in the Canadian literary community, Weaver regularly corresponded with her to offer his insightful criticism and steadfast encouragement—and, often, a venue for publication. Thacker describes Weaver as Munro's "literary lifeline" during those years and notes that it was Weaver who first encouraged her to submit her fiction to quality Canadian and American magazines (112–13). Munro passed almost two decades of her writing career in this fashion: writing stories, submitting them for publication, and, outside a few trusted people, like her husband, mostly keeping her literary life to herself. She had success publishing in periodicals like *Chatelaine*, the *Tamarack Review*, and the *Montrealer*, and built a solid reputation on the basis of these works.

During these years, Munro had to balance the social and domestic expectations of a housewife against her desire to write, and while this balance no doubt cost her some writing time, her conditions were not wholly inhospitable to her creative efforts. Though their marriage would ultimately end in divorce, Jim Munro, for one, valued and encouraged Munro's work. Munro has said that he, like her subsequent partner, Gerald Fremlin, who also attended Western at the same time as Munro, "believed that a woman doing really serious work, not just amusing herself, was possible" and that in her generation, "those men were not that easy to find" (qtd. in Thacker 354). Jim was a serious reader of fiction, and he and Alice Munro eventually moved from Vancouver to Victoria to open a bookstore. While writing remained essentially an individual affair for Munro, as she had few ties to the literary community and no institutional support, she was writing at a time of expanding opportunities for Canadian writers and on the cusp of a time when things would improve even more. The Massey Commission published a report in 1951 that led to a wide range of government funding opportunities for writers and other artists in Canada. The early 1950s marked the beginning of a commitment to developing a Canadian audience for fiction.

The publishing climate in Canada, however, remained difficult, particularly in some ways for Munro. While she may have indirectly benefited from government funding and the growth of Canadian culture over the 1950s, 1960s, and 1970s, she did not have much luck benefiting from them financially. Her first applications for grants from the Canada Council for the Arts and the Humanities Research Council of Canada were unsuccessful (Thacker 145–46). Moreover, such grants and government support existed largely to offset what was an otherwise difficult situation for Canadian writers. Publishing opportunities for writers within Canada at the time were relatively few. As Roy MacSkimming writes in his history of Canadian publishing, *Perilous Trade*, "There is no such language as Canadian. English Canadians share the mother tongue of the world's two largest book-exporting nations" (3). As such, even in the best of times, "Canadian publishers face a daunting dilemma"; thanks to the economies of scale enjoyed by American and British publishers, Canadian publishers, "even while publishing for a relatively small population, . . . must underprice their books to be competitive" (4). The Canadian market for homegrown fiction, and dedicated publishing companies to satisfy this niche, was still in its infancy in the 1950s.

Munro's career was further hampered by the fact that she did not produce a novel. Thacker writes, "At this time in North American publishing in general, but in Canada especially, there was a widely held prejudice against collections of short stories," and claims that "it is fair to see the almost twenty-year genesis of her first book . . . as a direct result of this attitude" (142). Munro spent years working on various drafts of novels, but none were ever finished to her satisfaction. Ryerson Press was the first press to demonstrate a genuine interest in publishing a collection of her short fiction. Neither Ryerson nor Munro, however, seemed to feel any particular urgency to push forward with a collection of short stories. Ryerson first received Munro's manuscript in 1961, but due primarily to personnel changes there, as well as to the circumstances of Munro's own life—the demands of raising young children and operating a bookstore, and perhaps her own hesitations about putting out a collection of short stories—her first book, *Dance of the Happy Shades*, did not appear until 1968 (Thacker 166, 170).

Rise to Fame

The late 1960s and early 1970s brought many changes to Munro's personal and professional life, as well as to Canadian literature and culture. *Dance of the Happy Shades* was a critical success, receiving nearly universally positive reviews and winning her the Governor General's Award. Munro's career was launched, and she became a public figure in the Canadian literary community in a way she had not been before. *Lives of Girls and Women* followed closely after, in 1971, to great success as well. *Lives* particularly resonated with the feminism of the times because of a shared interest in "exposing the power politics of gender in heterosexual relations and with women's quests to discover their individual identities by finding their voices and reclaiming their rights over their own bodies" (Howells 196–97). Though *Lives* was passed over for the Governor General's Award, successful editions were published in the United States and Great Britain, and the international exposure "fundamentally altered Munro's status" as a writer (Thacker 240). These years also coincided with an upsurge in Canadian nationalism and an increased desire for Canadians to support and develop their own distinctive culture, a context in which writers found increased support. According to Thacker, Munro "recalls the 1960s and 1970s as a period when writers in Canada supported one another freely, seeing common progress in an individual's success" (208).

Munro's disintegrating marriage finally ended in divorce in 1972, and for a few years after, she turned to funding organizations and universities in a way that she never had before. She received her first and only Canada Council grant in 1973; taught creative writing at Notre Dame University in Nelson, British Columbia, and then briefly at York University in Toronto, Ontario, in 1973 and 1974; and was the writer in residence at the University of Western Ontario in 1974–75 (Thacker

237, 238, 240, 242, 273). Writer, editor, and essayist John Metcalf was a major support to Munro in these years, offering both personal and professional advice that eased her transition (Thacker 235). However, Munro's turn to public funding and university appointments did not last long. In 1974, while still living in London, she reconnected with Gerald Fremlin, with whom she had been acquainted at Western (Thacker 288). Fremlin lived in nearby Clinton, Ontario, and in 1975, Munro moved in with him.

A New Level of Success

Thacker identifies Munro's return to southwestern Ontario in the 1970s as another major turning point in her career. Her move back to Huron County in particular put her once again "living in the midst of her material" (Thacker 378), and the "enriched awareness of her home, its culture, and her relation to it" (368) that resulted seems to have prompted a deeper and more introspective, perceptive engagement with Huron County and her own past. Stories like "Winter Wind" and "The Ottawa Valley" from *Something I've Been Meaning to Tell You* (1974), "Royal Beatings" and "Privilege" from *Who Do You Think You Are?*, and the two-part "Chaddeleys and Flemings" from *The Moons of Jupiter* (1982) demonstrate this sophistication, forming the basis upon which, in the late 1970s and early 1980s, Munro made the transition from renowned Canadian to a writer with an international reputation.

This ascent was made possible not only by the strength of her writing but also by the hard work and support of her literary agent and her editors (though, of course, it was the quality of Munro's writing that attracted them to her in the first place). Literary agent Virginia Barber had approached Munro and been hired as her representative in 1976 (Thacker 277). Barber was instrumental in securing publication for Munro in the *New Yorker*, the flagship publication for short fiction in the English language. Munro had been submitting her work to the *New Yorker* since the late 1950s, but with "the quality of her work, Virginia Barber's abilities, good timing, and a bit of luck," she finally

---

succeeded in placing her fiction there (Thacker 318). Munro went on to have a fruitful and decades-long relationship with the magazine, including a lucrative first-reading agreement (325). She developed a supportive and productive relationship with her editors there, first Charles McGrath and Daniel Menaker, then later Alice Quinn (319, 383). Barber also secured the prestigious publishing house Alfred A. Knopf as Munro's American publisher for her next book, *Who Do You Think You Are?*, which appeared in the United States as *The Beggar Maid* because, according to Munro, the publishers "felt the colloquial put-down was not familiar to Americans" ("Real Material" 29). Knopf has remained her American publisher, and Munro has worked for years with Knopf editor Ann Close (Thacker 351). For the Canadian publication of this book, Munro changed her publisher to Macmillan, where she worked with editor Douglas Gibson. He and the company as a whole supported and valued Munro's work, and, perhaps more importantly, were content to publish her as a short-story writer rather than a novelist (367).

At this point, the foundation was laid for the rest of Munro's career. She had time and space to write in Huron County, and she had a diligent agent and supportive editors at the *New Yorker*, Macmillan, and Knopf. Since then, Munro has continued to write, achieving success after success. She went on to win two more Governor General's Awards, a Trillium Book Award, two Giller Prizes, and, as mentioned, the 2009 Man Booker International Prize for Fiction, to name but a few of her numerous accolades and awards.

Success in Context

Munro's career demonstrates how writing is a social practice embedded in a particular time, place, and culture; her success has involved the support of many people and is also tied to the combination of private and state-sponsored opportunities available to her. Her career is not simply the result of some romantic notion of literary genius, in which she had only to write brilliantly and let the rest take care of itself.

Although her writing career closely coincided with the beginning and flourishing of the culture-building programs of the Canadian state, personal support and commercial book and magazine publications appear to have been most vital to her career. Munro did not draw much direct benefit from government grants or university appointments, although the benefit of such funding for the literary community as a whole was certainly important to her and a host of other writers. The CBC, and Robert Weaver in particular, played an important role in her early career, and she has occasionally written scripts for CBC radio and television over the years (Thacker 277–78, 304), but these opportunities did not further her career in the way her commercial publishing did.

To some extent, Munro's commercial publishing, as well as her disinclination to play the role of the public writer, also allowed her to stay at arm's length from some of the social and political issues that have created conflict within Canadian literature. In her introduction to *Selected Stories*, a 1996 collection drawn from her oeuvre to that point, Munro wrote, "I keep an eye on feminism and Canada and try to figure out my duty to both" (ix), but she did this duty without being particularly partisan or engaging directly in the debates of the day. Her work remained deeply personal, reflecting her life and background.

Perhaps ironically, given how intensely personal and directly tied to her own culture and past so much of her work is, Munro's writing has been able to transcend social barriers. One certainly does not have to be familiar with rural southwestern Ontario or the mores particular to its lower-class Scots Irish inhabitants of the mid-twentieth century to appreciate much of her work. Thacker, for example, details the enthusiastic response of the *New Yorker*'s editorial staff to the first batch of Munro stories given to them by Virginia Barber (320–22). One can picture in particular the sophisticated, urbane *New Yorker* editors getting excited over "Royal Beatings," a story that conjures up a rather ramshackle rural 1940s childhood for its protagonist, Rose, and includes the off-color schoolyard rhyme "Two Vancouvers fried in snot! / Two pickled arseholes in a knot!" One can assume the pleasure these editors felt did not come from the thrill of recognition, and the same is likely true of the vast majority of *New Yorker* readers. Rather, as Thacker reminds us, the power of Munro's writing comes from the fact that she "creates the very sense of being that all humans feel moving from birth to death" (18). This power entails an ability to cross social and cultural boundaries.

Though this power to create a sense of being may hold a certain universal appeal, the particular fashion in which Munro achieves this does indeed resonate with her times. Because of the strong feeling of being, because of the mimetic power of her language, and because of her focus on the personal and the everyday, Munro is often seen as a realist. Her writing, as she herself asserts, has sometimes been seen as "quaint" or "old-fashioned" (qtd. in Quinn). But Munro is not a realist in the sense of, say, nineteenth-century naturalism, with its archetypal characters, omniscient narrators, and sweeping assertions about humanity and society. Her realism comes more from the tradition of the well-wrought modernist story and the attempt to reproduce a feeling of being by tracking consciousness and all its vagaries.

Although her fiction is not simply a throwback to an earlier era of the twentieth century, it does bear some of the hallmarks of the post–World War II, post-Holocaust, postmodern era. Munro's writing displays an aversion to the artifice inherent in grand narratives as they sweep incidents into neat patterns of beginning, middle, and end, thereby giving events a coherence they lack. This aversion is perhaps most apparent in her avoidance of the novel. In a 1986 profile in *Publishers Weekly,* Munro told Beverly Slopen, "The novel has to have a coherence which I don't see anymore in the lives around me" (77). As David Crouse has observed in his reading of *Friend of My Youth* (1990), Munro even avoids and subverts that staple of the modernist short story, the epiphany: the sudden, dramatic flash of insight and self-revelation that ends stories such as James Joyce's "Araby" (1914). Many of Munro's stories avoid such dramatic moments. Some end not with an epiphany but with "many small realizations" (Crouse 57). Others end by "stacking

... short, vague events at the endings" (56) to complicate previous dramatic insights or interpretations, or by "framing" (58) the epiphany in the past and making it a moment of realization upon which the protagonist looks back. Munro thus avoids the neatness and certainty of both the tightly plotted tale and the powerful epiphany. Though far from an exemplar of postmodernism, her work embodies a certain amount of indeterminacy, mystery, and awareness of the human ability to know and understand.

Despite, then, her writing's strong ties to the past, to rural southwestern Ontario, and to her own personal life, Munro's body of work has been and continues to be at the forefront of her times. Her stories provide readers with a feeling of being that satisfies the desire for connection, yet they do so with sophistication and a dash of skepticism to prevent any too-easy identification. Since Cynthia Ozick first made the observation, it has become cliché to say that Alice Munro is "our Chekhov." In 2011, it is fast becoming cliché to assert that Munro is the living Canadian writer most likely to be read one hundred years from now.

Works Cited

Carrington, Ildikó de Papp. *Controlling the Uncontrollable: The Fiction of Alice Munro*. DeKalb: Northern Illinois UP, 1989.

Crouse, David. "Resisting Reduction: Closure in Richard Ford's *Rock Springs* and Alice Munro's *Friend of My Youth*." *Canadian Literature* 146 (1995): 51–64.

Flood, Alison. "Alice Munro Wins Man Booker International Prize." *Guardian*. Guardian News and Media, 27 May 2009. Web. 14 Sept. 2011.

Foran, Charles. "Alice in Borderland." *Walrus*. Walrus Foundation, Sept. 2009. Web. 14 Sept. 2011.

Gibson, Graeme. *Eleven Canadian Novelists*. Toronto: Anansi, 1973.

Howells, Coral Ann. "Writing by Women." *The Cambridge Companion to Canadian Literature*. Ed. Eva-Marie Kröller. Cambridge: Cambridge UP, 2004. 194–215.

Hoy, Helen. "Dull, Simple, Amazing and Unfathomable: Paradox and Double Vision in Alice Munro's Fiction." *Studies in Canadian Literature* 5.1 (1980): n. pag. Web. 14 Sept. 2011.

MacSkimming, Roy. *The Perilous Trade: Book Publishing in Canada, 1946–2006*. Toronto: McClelland, 2007.

McKillop, A. B. *Matters of Mind: The University in Ontario, 1791–1951*. Toronto: U of Toronto P, 1994.

Munro, Alice. *Dance of the Happy Shades*. Toronto: Ryerson, 1968.

_____. *Friend of My Youth*. Toronto: Penguin, 1991.

_____. "Home." *74: New Canadian Stories*. Ed. David Helwig and Joan Harcourt. Ottawa: Oberon, 1974. 142.

_____. Interview by Shelagh Rogers. *Sounds Like Canada*. CBC Radio One. 12 Oct. 2006. Radio.

_____. *The Moons of Jupiter*. Toronto: Penguin, 1995.

_____. "The Real Material: An Interview with Alice Munro." By J. R. (Tim) Struthers. *Probable Fictions: Alice Munro's Narrative Acts*. Ed. Louis K. MacKendrick. Downsview, ON: ECW, 1983. 5–36.

_____. "Remember Roger Mortimer: Dickens' *Child's History of England* Remembered." *Montrealer* Feb. 1962: 34–37.

_____. *Selected Stories*. Toronto: Penguin, 1998.

_____. *Who Do You Think You Are?* Agincourt, ON: NAL, 1979.

Quinn, Alice. "Q&A: Go Ask Alice." *New Yorker*. Condé Nast, 19 Feb. 2001. Web. 14 Sept. 2011.

Slopen, Beverly. "PW Interviews Alice Munro." *Publishers Weekly* 22 Aug. 1986: 76–77.

Talman, James, and Ruth Davis Talman. *"Western," 1873–1953, Being the History of the Origins and Development of the University of Western Ontario, during Its First Seventy-Five Years*. St. Thomas, ON: Sutherland, 1953.

Thacker, Robert. *Alice Munro: Writing Her Lives; A Biography*. Toronto: McClelland, 2005.

Seduction and Subjectivity: Psychoanalysis and the Fiction of Alice Munro _____

Naomi Morgenstern

> The problem of the other in psychoanalysis is not a problem of the outside world. . . . The problem is the reality of the other, and of his message.
>
> (Jean Laplanche)

> You are a kid that is not short of information.
>
> (Delphine to Lauren; Alice Munro, "Trespasses")

I

Alice Munro's fiction rewards psychoanalytic reading because it resists the simple application of preformed and unalterable psychoanalytic ideas. That is to say, Munro's stories do not simply await psychoanalytic decoding; instead, they sustain a dialogue with, and can be read as their own instances of, psychoanalytic inquiry. In this essay, I will explore the relevance of a particular and peculiar psychoanalytic understanding of seduction to Munro's fiction, first by introducing the concept and then by unfolding its significance in two stories by Munro: "Trespasses," from the collection *Runaway* (2004), and "Deep-Holes," from *Too Much Happiness* (2009).

In 1897, or so the story goes, Sigmund Freud abandoned his hypothesis concerning the seduction of daughters by their fathers, thereby founding psychoanalysis. Sexuality would no longer be traced to a violent imposition from the outside (Freud had believed that daughters were "seduced" by their fathers and became neurotic) but instead was to be thought of as a drive internal to each subject, a wild drive that eventually gave rise to oedipal fantasies (fathers did not seduce their daughters, but daughters fantasized about such scenes of seduction—every subject experienced his or her own Oedipus complex). Freud wrote in a letter to his good friend Wilhelm Fliess, "I will confide in you at once the great secret that has been dawning on me in the last few months. I no longer believe in my *neurotica*" (Masson 264). Freud biographer Peter Gay argues that Freud did not give up on seduction entirely, only on seduction as the general origin of all neuroses. Gay claims that Freud's recognition was liberating and allowed him to listen to his patients "more seriously," if "far less literally," than before (Gay 96).[1]

In 1987, French psychoanalyst Jean Laplanche returned to this foundational story and proposed a retheorization of seduction. For Laplanche, as indeed for Freud, sexual seduction can constitute a very wide range of behaviors, including "lived scenes in which the initiative [is] taken by the other person, who [is] most often an adult" (Laplanche and Pontalis 404). For Laplanche, however, seduction is always marked by an inequality between the subjects and a certain opacity in the communication that takes place between them. The adult "seduces" the child with signs and meanings that he or she (the adult) cannot be said to fully and consciously possess. Moreover, seduction, in Laplanche's account, is not an exceptional occurrence; it is inevitable. Without it, there would be no subjectivity, no ego, no identity. Laplanche proposes a complex theory of the "enigmatic signification" that takes place between children and adults and plays an elementary role in subject formation; it is my contention that this formative encounter with "the other's message," this initial and inevitable trauma, is also subjected to careful and compelling scrutiny in Alice Munro's short fiction.

In *New Foundations for Psychoanalysis*, Jean Laplanche proposes to look for what is foundational in the human experience. He suggests that each new child, whatever particular familial formation into which he or she is born, will inevitably confront the adult world of language and, more generally, of signification. Freud wrote that "no mortal can keep a secret. If his lips are silent, he chatters with his fingertips; betrayal oozes out of him at every pore" (*Case Histories* 114). For Laplanche, it is the closed self, not the self that is open to otherness and the outside world, that is the initial problem. How does one come to be oneself? How does one come to have borders, to live in one's own skin? There are two protagonists in this account, and if the first, the child, has not yet built an ego, the other, the adult, houses a strange relationship to her own being within her being, and this is what we call an unconscious. It is because this other protagonist has an unconscious, in Laplanche's sense, that he or she signifies enigmatically. That is to say, the child receives messages that exceed the conscious meaning attached to them by the adults, and the child is then "seduced" by these messages. Laplanche writes: "I am, then, using the term *primal seduction* to describe a fundamental situation in which an adult proffers to a child verbal, non-verbal and even behavioural signifiers which are pregnant with unconscious sexual significations. We do not have to look far to find concrete examples of what I call *enigmatic signifiers*" (*New Foundations* 126). For Laplanche, in other words, "the *enigma* is in itself a *seduction*" (128). This is important because it suggests that while sexuality cannot simply be reduced to questions of meaning and signification, it is nevertheless inseparable from such questions. Thus, Laplanche takes what once had the status of a violent imposition—a particular and perverse event of seduction—and gives it a more general standing in the form of what he calls his "general theory of seduction."

Among various types of enigmatic signifiers, Laplanche singles out for particular attention what is known as the *primal scene*. The primal scene, according to Freud, is a scene in which one witnesses or fantasizes that one witnesses one's parents having sexual intercourse. Such scenes are "uncanny," according to Freud; they "arouse anxiety," and they are often misread as scenes of violence (my father is attacking my mother) (qtd. in Laplanche, *New Foundations* 127). But for the purposes of my discussion of Munro, I want to emphasize the primal scene's significance as an encounter with the enigma of one's own origin, with the question of how one came to be. Laplanche's theory of seduction offers us a theory of what it means to be oneself, to be *a* self in the human world, a theory that is also necessarily an account of the relationship between self and other. He thus moves us beyond "a crude opposition between reality and fantasy" (*New Foundations* 122), and this I believe to be of import to any student of literature, not just those with a penchant for psychoanalysis. Every individual being, Laplanche claims, is a response to another's message, and yet it is only after such messages have become incorporated, and perhaps translated, that one can be said to have a singular (if singularly divided) being. To come into being as subjects, Laplanche provocatively contends, we must learn to misread our fundamentally decentered selves as centered individuals. Our self-sufficiency or individuality is a necessary fiction.

II

"Trespasses" is a story about a ten-year-old girl (although her age is crucially withheld for most of the narrative) who is forced into a confusing encounter with adult sexuality. In other words, Lauren is addressed, or spoken to, by the unconscious or semiconscious behaviors and secrets of the adults who make up her world. As a dependent and vulnerable child, Lauren cannot possibly ignore the signifiers that call to her and constitute the very meaning of her being, and Munro's account of this dynamic suggests that she shares Laplanche's fascination with the process whereby apparently individual subjects form themselves in relationship to the enigmatic message of the other.[2]

The opening of "Trespasses" is pointedly disorienting. We are given a collection of proper names, but we do not know how to set them in relationship to one another to form a structure, even as the characters are quite literally positioned for us:

> They drove out of town around midnight—Harry and Delphine in the front seat and Eileen and Lauren in the back. The sky was clear and the snow had slid off the trees but had not melted underneath them or on the rocks that jutted out beside the road. . . . There was a slight crackle to the snow, though the ground underneath was soft and mucky. Lauren was still wearing her pajamas under her coat, but Eileen had made her put on her boots. (Munro, *Runaway* 197)

It is, of course, significant that we do not know who these people are and how they are related to one another. Munro positions her reader to participate in Lauren's experience, as the narrative forces upon us questions that, it will turn out, have been forced upon Lauren too: Who is she? Who are these three adults? What do they have to do with her origin? How does she fit into this particular configuration? And while we do not yet know who any of these characters are, we do pick up on a trace of a maternal relation ("Eileen had made her put on her boots"), and this, too, is central to the enigma of Lauren's being. Munro is fascinated by the way in which structural familial relations crucially order our world: Are the people in the car a family? Who are the adults and who are the children? Are there, in fact, adults and children? What are the names for their relationships? Structures of familial relations have the potential to oppress, as we do not get to choose our parents, but they also generate relation and meaning and, thus, identity. They produce us as the very subjects who might wish that we had a choice. But what happens, Munro's stories often ask, when the structure that is one's family begins to give way, to reveal itself in its contingency? What kind of affective response does such a collapse produce? In "Trespasses," roles and relations reveal themselves to be provisional, and any ground for identity is thus undermined as Lauren encounters another mother and a divided or doubled origin. While a certain excitement is generated by the apparent excess of meaning available to Lauren, such encounters can also be, as Munro shows us, profoundly threatening.

Early in "Trespasses," we encounter a grotesquely comic version of the enigmatic signifier as primal scene. Lauren and her relatively worldly parents, Harry and Eileen, are newly arrived in small-town Ontario. Harry has quit his job at a magazine and purchased the weekly newspaper. He professes a certain nostalgic attachment to this place that he "remember[s] from his childhood," as "his family used to have a summer place on one of the little lakes around here, and he remembered drinking his first beer in the hotel on the main street" (Munro, *Runaway* 198). They encounter a family party: "Little girls in patent shoes and scratchy frills, a toddling baby, a teenaged boy in a suit, half-dead with embarrassment, various parents and parents of parents—a skinny and distracted old man and an old woman flopped sideways in a wheelchair and wearing a corsage. Any one of the women in their flowery dresses would have made about four of Eileen" (198–99). Harry identifies the occasion as a wedding anniversary and jovially proceeds to extend his congratulations and introduce himself as "the new fellow at the paper." He then asks "the recipe for a happy marriage," and the narrative continues:

"Momma can't talk," said one of the big women. "But let me ask Daddy." She shouted in her father's ear, "Your advice for a happy marriage?"

He wrinkled up his face roguishly.

"All-eeze keep a foot on er neck."

All the grown-ups laughed, and Harry said, "Okay. I'll just put in the paper that you always made sure to get your wife's agreement." (199)

This moment functions as a Laplanchean primal scene and as an example of an enigmatic signifier, insofar as it presents the secret of the relationship between father and mother as one of violence ("Momma can't talk," "All-eeze keep a foot on er neck"). No one knows quite how to accommodate this surprising violence—although they do not even realize that they do not know—and thus they fold it into humor. In a crucial sense, however, this scene is not for Lauren; we have no access to, or representation of, her consciousness here—although we do know that she is present and presumably taking this all in, and perhaps her consciousness is minimally registered with the phrase "all the grown-ups laughed." Lauren will become the story's center of consciousness, but at this point, the scene is recorded for Harry and Eileen and for us, the readers. In other words, Munro includes this encounter with the elderly couple to show us in formal terms that the enigmatic sexual message predates the subject.

"Trespasses" includes other primal scenes that do seem to be performed for, or addressed to, Lauren herself. We learn, for example, that her parents have always exposed their daughter to their displays of passion; she witnesses both their erotic intimacy and their theatrical arguments (Munro, *Runaway* 215, 228–30). It is often unclear, moreover, whether the intimacy and the arguments are "about" Lauren or whether they exclude her (the answer is both). Indeed, Munro's treatment of seduction in this story is given a particular twist by the open or transparent sexual behaviors favored by Lauren's parents and their peers at this historical moment, the era of sexual liberation. These parents also entertain the idea that "children and adults [can] be on equal terms" with one another (209), and thus their assumptions run entirely contrary to Laplanche's insistence that adult and child are necessarily unequal and there can never be transparency between them, since no subject is transparent to him- or herself. With "Trespasses," therefore, Munro explores some of the intimate consequences of what it means to disavow both secrecy and inequality. She depicts for us an experience of decided subjection (childhood) and a situation in which transparency can and will function as obscurity, as enigma. Lauren's very precocious knowledgeability creates for her an isolating and burdensome sense of difference: "The things that were wicked mysteries to others were not so to her and she did not know how to pretend about them. . . . it gave her a sense of embarrassment and peculiar sadness, even of deprivation. And there wasn't much she could do except remember, at school, to call Harry and Eileen Dad and Mom. That seemed to make them larger, but not so sharp" (205–6).

At the same time, and on another narrative level, Harry and Eileen have not been open with Lauren at all; they do indeed have a secret, one that Lauren eventually learns about from Harry. She discovers a box containing a baby's ashes and is told the story of her parents' first child, who died in a car accident when Eileen was pregnant with Lauren. She is then told to withhold the knowledge from her mother: "'Now,' [Harry] said. 'Now, Lauren. I could make up some kind of a lie to tell you, but I am going to tell you the truth. Because I believe that children should be told the truth. At least by the time they're your age, they should be. But in this case it has got to be a secret. Okay?'" (Munro, *Runaway* 203). Harry's partial disclosure (there is more to this story than he lets on) gives Lauren information that she does not really want to hear. Harry's story (and he is decidedly "Harry," as opposed to "Dad" or "Lauren's father") functions as a perverse invasive seduction. Even as Harry appears to play the role of the compassionate parent—"When they went out on their walks he occasionally asked her if she was worried, or sad about what he had told her. She said 'No,' in a firm, rather impatient, voice, and he said, 'Good'" (204)—his revelation cannot help but have incestuous resonances (the secret shared by the father with his daughter who is told not to tell her mother).

Harry is not the only adult with a secret to withhold in "Trespasses." He has already suggested that someone, anyone, "even that fat tough-talking waitress" at the hotel coffee shop, "could be harboring a contemporary tragedy or adventure which would make a best seller" (Munro, *Runaway* 201). And the "fat tough-talking waitress," it will turn out, does indeed harbor her own tragedy: she is the mother of the baby that Lauren's parents initially adopted. She has tracked them down, unbeknownst to them, and presumes, not surprisingly, that Lauren is the baby she gave up years before. She attempts to initiate a relationship with Lauren, who, as we know, is not aware of the past that Harry, Eileen, and Delphine share. Delphine "seduces" Lauren; she offers her food, candy, gifts, and companionship: "You don't have to bribe me to come and see you," says Lauren (209). As this seduction becomes increasingly ominous, "Trespasses" threatens to become an account of the mother-as-stalker.

The scenario of mother-as-stalker suggests a perversion that few writers would be able to discern and depict. But it is worth recalling that motherhood is never a simple fact in Munro's fiction. Motherhood is not what comes "first," not simply what is essential and established before being called into crisis.[3] Hence, it is not unimportant that

Lauren's (presumably) biological mother, Eileen, is not herself exces-sively maternal. In fact, she does not display marked maternal behavior until she finds herself in a rivalrous relationship with the other mother, Delphine (and one should note here the similarity between the names Delphine and Eileen as well as the fact that *D* comes before *E*). Lauren is always short on milk in this story, and milk, of course, signifies ma-ternal nurturance. Almost the first thing we learn about Lauren in the story is that she "made her own breakfast, usually cereal with maple syrup instead of milk. Eileen took her coffee back to bed and drank it slowly" (Munro, *Runaway* 201). And similarly, when Lauren finds herself in Delphine's meagerly furnished room, Delphine serves her lumpy hot chocolate made with water, commenting, "I guess you're used to milk" (217). Lauren is drawn to Delphine because Delphine shows profound interest in her, and Lauren does not (yet) experience this interest as a form of violation: "And she never got the feeling—as she did at home—that there was any other question behind Delphine's questions, never the feeling that if she didn't watch out she would be pried open" (211).

At first, Delphine represents, for Lauren, the possibility of an inte-riority that will be safe from, and separate from, her parents—what we might call an identity. The reader, however, is rendered uncomfortable even before Lauren herself starts to get the picture. Here is a stranger, after all, an adult bribing a child with food and gifts and asking her to share in another secret (that is, the secret of their visits, their rela-tionship). The culminating scene between Lauren and Delphine is pro-foundly disturbing for Lauren and the reader. Despite the intimations of sexual abuse, this is not how their relationship unfolds; instead, we witness a revelation and the potential establishment of a mother-child bond. Lauren herself becomes more unsettled as Delphine moves clos-er to revealing the secret of Lauren's identity—which, of course, is not actually the secret of Lauren's identity. Lauren's sense of a now-unbearable and threatening intimacy with Delphine is associated with dissolution and the coming apart of a structure, the familial structure, that produces her as "Lauren." Nothing is as it should be, as it was, and this produces nausea for Lauren. Delphine's very body becomes unbearable: "Delphine bent over. Lauren backed off, scared that the white hair, the silky flopping curtains of hair, were going to get in her mouth. If you were old enough for your hair to be white, then it shouldn't be long" (221).

The name Delphine suggests, of course, the Delphic oracle, traditionally located at the site of the navel of the earth. Delphine, we are told, "spoke about herself—her tastes, her physical workings—as about a monumental mystery, something unique and final" (Munro, *Runaway* 210).[4] But Delphi also means "womb," and thus Munro's naming invokes both enigma, mystery, and the truth or true (maternal) source in a kind of undecidable or ironic conjunction. The reader may also recall that the prototype of the psychoanalytic subject, Oedipus himself, seeks his truth from the Delphic oracle. Many of us first encounter Freud or psychoanalysis by way of the Oedipus complex, often summed up far too neatly and dismissively as "the desire to kill one's father and sleep with one's mother." A Laplanchean articulation of psychoanalysis, with its particular emphasis on seduction, works, as I have suggested, to displace the primacy of this story, or to strip away at it until a "new foundation" is revealed. And the Oedipus narrative in its most limited sense is certainly not the tale that Munro writes and rewrites. Yet perhaps one need not dismiss Oedipus quite so quickly. Oedipus's quest was just as important for Freud as was the content of his secret; indeed, Freud equated Oedipus's heroic quest for self-knowledge with "the work of a psychoanalysis" (*Interpretation* 363). But Munro's story asks what it means to know oneself if one is constituted, as Laplanche insists, by the address of others. Are we driven by a desire to encounter the very knowledge that will precipitate our dissolution or nonbeing? Moreover, Munro slyly alerts us to this oedipal intertext in another of the story's wonderful details, another replaying of the primal scene. Delphine's employer at the hotel is Mr. Palagian, and on one of her visits, Lauren witnesses Delphine's lack of deference to her boss. The minimalist Mr. Palagian makes an appearance with a wounded and bandaged foot: "Just about where his big toe must be there was a dried blood spot." Lauren asks Delphine what has happened to his foot and Delphine replies, "What foot? . . . Could be somebody stepped on it, I guess. Maybe with the heel of their shoe, eh?" (*Runaway* 216). Munro thus folds an overt oedipal reference into "Trespasses" at this point: the limp and the wounded foot signify castration, a punishing wound to the male body, even as they recall the etymology of Oedipus's name, "swollen foot." But the account of Delphine and Mr. Palagian also very nicely replays the story's first primal scene concerning the couple celebrating their sixty-fifth wedding anniversary. This time, of course, the shoe is on the other foot, so to speak; no man will be putting his foot on Delphine's neck.[5]

Laplanche's revision of Freud suggests that the child is seduced by the enigma of an adult sexuality that is opaque not merely to the child but also to the adult who is proffering the sign. As Laplanche insists, and as I have reiterated, no one, child or adult, is in full conscious possession of sexual meaning. What Laplanche may not adequately register, however, is the possibility that it is the child him- or herself who is, in some sense, the enigmatic signifier.[6] To the question "Who am I?" the answer comes back: "I am the enigma of my parents' desire." It is this deceptively simple (non)answer that Munro explores in "Trespasses." Delphine first summons Lauren to her and reveals that she has found a gold necklace, one that we later learn she has purchased for this ploy: "She opened a drawer and lifted out a gold chain. Dangling from the chain were the letters that spelled LAUREN" (*Runaway* 207). It is this necklace, and, indeed, the very word *Lauren*, that constitutes the seduction and the privileged enigmatic signifier in Munro's story. And in this sense, we might add, *everyone* "is" an enigmatic signifier: one's very name (and can one think of one's identity without one's name?) is the seductive, unreadable parental message. Munro elaborates on this quite brilliantly. We learn, with Lauren, that the first baby was also called Lauren, and thus we share in her radically disorienting sense that she may suddenly have become somebody else: "'It was me,' she said. 'Who was it if it wasn't me?'" (232). To be herself, it turns out, is to be someone else, to be divided in her very sameness: Lauren and Lauren. Harry tells her, "We called it Lauren and then we called you Lauren—I guess because it was our favorite name and also it gave us a feeling we were starting over" (232).

The story ends by circling back to the beginning, and the reader finds herself at a point just before the first paragraph. We now of course understand who is sitting in the car and why, even as we also discern that the original lack of clarity was substantial and meaningful, not incidental. Delphine has pursued Lauren with the necklace in stalker-like fashion, and Lauren has given away her secret to Eileen, trading "something private and complex" for "safety and comfort" (Munro, *Runaway* 225). Harry has been to see Delphine, and now, at midnight, all three parents are going to scatter the baby's ashes. Harry addresses Lauren with a peculiar assertion of faith in the end of secrecy and the reestablishment of familial relations; he might be said to miss the fact that this is not all up to him: "So tonight as a family, tonight while everything is all wide-open, we are going to go out and do this. And get rid of all this—misery and blame. Delphine and Eileen and me, and we want you to come with us—is that all right with you? Are you all right?" Lauren resists, saying, "I was asleep. I've got a cold," but a resigned Eileen prods her into action: "You might as well do as Harry says" (233).

"Trespasses" is a story that could be said to end with a subject witnessing her own (belated) funeral. But it is also more simply and directly a story about a ten-year-old girl necessarily participating in the mess and perversity that the adults in her life have bequeathed to her. Eileen, Delphine, and Harry attempt to scatter the baby's ashes, which simply fall at their feet. Lauren puts her hands in her pockets:

> Harry said clearly, "This is Lauren, who was our child and whom we all loved—let's all say it together." He looked at Delphine, then Eileen, and they all said, "This is Lauren," with Delphine's voice very quiet, mumbling,

and Eileen's full of strained sincerity and Harry's sonorous, presiding, deeply serious.

"And we say good-bye to her and commit her to the snow—"

At the end Eileen said hurriedly, "Forgive us our sins. Our trespasses. Forgive us our trespasses." (Munro, *Runaway* 235)

III

"Deep-Holes" begins with a description of Sally, from her own perspective, preparing for a family picnic in honor of her geologist husband's first solo publication in a prestigious journal. Sally and Alex and their three young children are going to Osler Bluffs, "because it figured largely in the article, and because Sally and the children had never been there" (Munro, *Too Much* 94). While there, nine-year-old Kent falls into one of the deep holes, breaking one leg and shattering the other. He is rescued by his father with his mother's help and spends six months at home recuperating. He finishes his schoolwork very quickly and is assigned "Extra Projects." It is at this point that Sally shares with Kent her fantasy about remote islands, "small or obscure islands nobody talked about and which were seldom if ever visited. . . . She and Kent began to collect every scrap of information they could find about these places, not allowing themselves to make anything up. And never telling Alex what they were doing" (99). These islands, I would suggest, are the inverse of the story's holes. One knows where islands end and where one might fall in; they are safe and private places. These islands represent Sally's interiority as safe from the intrusions and demands of her husband, and they also temporarily allow her to map familial relationships differently. (Later in life, Alex will ruin this fantasy for Sally, who imagines that the estranged Kent is living on one of these islands, by showing her how the internet has rendered accessible information about the most obscure of locations almost instantly.)

Kent at first appears to thrive after his accident, but he eventually drops out of university and then out of any form of relationship with his parents and his siblings. The story thus raises certain questions about what is accidental and what is determined in a life story, as when Sally learns about Kent's fall: "Sally will always believe that she knew at once, even before she heard Peter's voice she knew what had happened. If any accident happened it would not be to her six-year-old who was brave but not inventive, not a show-off. It would be to Kent" (Munro, *Too Much* 97). It also prompts us to ask about the status of events we call accidents. What caused Kent's accident? If an accident has a cause, can it still be called an accident? In "Deep-Holes," moreover, the consequences of the accident are significantly deferred, further complicating our sense of the temporality of an event.

Sometime after they lose contact with Kent, Sally and Alex get a letter telling them that he is working at a Canadian Tire store; three years later, they receive another letter from Needles, California, and "that letter, signed with love, was the last they had heard from him" (Munro, *Too Much* 103). Many years later, after Alex has died, Kent is located by his adult sister, Savanna, who spots him on the television news helping out at the scene of a dramatic fire in Toronto. Sally meets with Kent, who has changed his name to Jonah—"I thought of Lazarus," he says, "but it's too self-dramatizing" (112)—and is living his life on the fringe, outside of the institutions of private property and familial relation. He says to Sally, "My life, my life, my progress, what all I could discover about my stinking self. Purpose of me. My crap. My spirituality. My intellectuality. There isn't any inside stuff, Sally. You don't mind if I call you Sally? It just comes out easier. There is only outside, what you do, every moment of your life. Since I realized this I've been happy." Sally replies, "You are? Happy?" (113).[7] Kent/Jonah wants to know what has become of his father's money, which he seems to feel entitled to in an impersonal way. Sally thinks,

> But a cheque, she can write some sort of cheque, not an absurd one. Not too big or too small. He'll not help himself with it, of course. He'll not stop despising her, of course.
>
> Despising. No. Not the point. Nothing personal. (115)

She leaves Kent not knowing if she will ever see him again: "She had said maybe [we'll be in touch]. He hadn't corrected her" (115).

Kent turns away from his family in order to take upon himself a distinctly impersonal responsibility to all others, and the narrative conveys Sally's response to his rejection of their bond with a markedly literal description of her trip back to the subway: "Sally gets lost, then finds her way" (Munro, *Too Much* 114). But we also hear another, less literal resonance in this brief remark. "Deep-Holes" is Sally's story above all, and it is a story about the possibility of having a story or a private, inviolable self when one gives away so much of oneself to being a wife and mother. (After the children are grown, Alex notes that Sally needs something to do and asks her to be the scale model in his geological photographs, as he is retired and thus can no longer use graduate students.) But Munro regularly invites her readers to take up the story of an off-center character, thereby reminding us, both formally and with specific verbal cues, that there are multiple points of entry into her stories. So for the purposes of this discussion, I want to stay with the figure of Kent and look more closely at what happens to the young boy when he falls into the hole. I want to ask if Kent's fall coincides with his becoming subject to—being seduced by—his father's enigmatic message.

Kent's eventual rejection of his family does not appear, on the surface, to participate in a classically oedipal drama. But a careful reader will notice that a kind of oedipal tension characterizes Kent and Alex's relationship in a form that certainly predates, and perhaps even produces, the "accident." In Alex's opinion, at the time of the picnic, his son is "a sneak and a trouble-maker and the possessor of a dirty mind" (Munro, *Too Much* 95–96). After Kent has recovered from the fall and gone back to school, he is "especially courteous to his father," and this "got on Alex's nerves." "He's saying you must have loved him," Sally tries to explain, "because you rescued him." "Christ, I'd have rescued anybody," Alex replies. "Don't say that in front of him," says Sally. "Please" (100). But in one sense or another, it is already too late. Kent obviously does hear his father's message; he learns that he must owe his life to a profoundly indifferent paternal force ("I'd have rescued anybody"). Thereafter, Kent lives out his father's message with a peculiarly insistent fidelity: he, too, would rescue anybody; later, he says, "We take in anybody that comes" (111). He adopts a kind of violent position of nonviolence and non-exclusiveness that can be read as Christlike, and in so doing, he proves himself, ironically, to be a profoundly oedipal subject. Kent appears to revolt against his father and all that his father represents, while unconsciously adhering very closely to his father and quite literally living out his message, his address. In his very grandiosity, Kent is also his father all over again, and this dynamic, Munro cannily observes, is what a particular historical version of familial structure naturalizes, rather than pathologizes, as patriarchy. Munro alerts us to the social conditions that produce, if not wholly determine, what we call madness.

The grandiosity of Kent's gesture, however, also constitutes a certain misreading of his father's message, and as such, Kent's story reminds us that there is always an excess involved when it comes to being constituted by the other's words. This is the translation, if you will, and it is why one is not simply and wholly determined by the other. In other words, Kent hardly succeeds in his project of leaving relationships and the personal behind. "I don't usually try to get anywhere talking to people," he says. "I usually try to avoid personal relationships. I mean I do. I do avoid them" (Munro, *Too Much* 114). Yet his words betray more than a mere residue of desire here, and we are reminded that he is still prone to express an "almost savage" rage that compromises his claim to nonviolence (114). And, of course, the narrative also lets us know that Kent would have liked his father to have been the one to include him in his obituary: "He wondered, Had his father told them what names he wanted listed, before he died?" (106).

When the family in "Deep-Holes" first sets out on their celebratory picnic, we encounter another site at which the literal and the figurative meet: "The entrance to the woods looked quite ordinary and unthreatening. Sally understood, of course, that these woods were on top of a high bluff, and she expected a daunting look-out somewhere. She did not expect to find what had to be skirted almost immediately in front of them" (Munro, *Too Much* 94). This last sentence refers, of course, to the deep holes, but also to the unpredictability of the future—that which is "immediately in front of them"—which, ironically, may already be quasi-determined by the very personalities of the family members as well as their structural relationships to one another. "Deep-Holes" suggests, in other words, that the dangers Sally seeks to protect her family from may already be internal to the family itself; one need not go too far afield to encounter such risk.

If Jean Laplanche offers us new ways of thinking about what it means to be a subject (we are seduced into being; we are the enigmas of our parents' desire; we productively misread the unconscious signals of our fathers and mothers), Alice Munro's fiction gives us individuals who live out those ideas in singular and often haunting scenarios. Each one of us, Munro and Laplanche suggest, is a kind of translated message, a misreading with a very precarious claim on subjecthood. But Munro's words say and do more than their theoretical counterparts, and this is not only because Munro is gifted with unusual insight into the relationship between children and parents, or intimacy and violence. A successful work of literature is itself a weave or web of enigmas, and Alice Munro's skillfully crafted stories prompt us to think about our debt to such enigmatic signification even as they are submitting us to their own irresistible acts of seduction.

Notes

1. This is an extremely condensed version of a far more complicated story. See "Scene of Seduction; Theory of Seduction" in Laplanche and Pontalis, as well as Peter Gay's *Freud: A Life for Our Time*.
2. While my discussion is devoted to two stories that I will read in some detail, the set of ideas generated by a reading of Laplanche certainly applies to a wide range of Munro's stories—in fact, far too many to list. A few others to consider include "Walker Brothers Cowboy," "Privilege," "Meneseteung," "The Bear Came over the Mountain," "Chance," and "Fathers."

3. A great deal of Munro's fiction explores the complexity of the bond between mothers and children. See particularly "My Mother's Dream," in which the bond between mother and infant is constituted belatedly: "She took on loving me, because the alternative to loving was disaster" (Munro, *Love* 338).

4. With this name, one gets a hold on one of the places at which the various levels of a Munro story become apparent. In other words, every Munro story and every detail does the work of constructing a realist narrative, and yet the stories also open themselves up to a more allegorical or philosophical dimension without either becoming grandiose or losing (or appearing to compromise on) their realism.

5. A reader attuned to Munro's play with names might also pick up on Mr. Palagian's significance. Pelagius was the early Christian ascetic who argued against the doctrine of original sin. He believed instead that human beings had choice and that, therefore, they were more fully responsible for their sins, or "trespasses." Pelagius was declared a heretic by the Council of Carthage, and his doctrine of free will became known as Pelagianism. While a full unpacking of anything like the theological significance of this story is well beyond the scope of this essay, I would like to briefly suggest that the connection to the substance of the story might concern the question of the relationship between individual responsibility and complex patterns of familial/theological predetermination: original sin. I would like to add that seduction is a necessarily violent trespass on the other's interiority that also comes to constitute the other's interiority. It might, therefore, be said to be something like the psychoanalytic equivalent of original sin.

6. For an extensive literary example of this point, see Hawthorne's *The Scarlet Letter*. One encounters in Laplanche what one might call a Hawthornian theory; consider that "Pearl's inevitable tendency to hover about the enigma of the scarlet letter seemed an innate quality of her being" (Hawthorne 123). And Hawthorne would have us understand that Pearl is the "living hieroglyphic" (140), the letter itself: "But it was a remarkable attribute of this garb, and indeed, of the child's whole appearance, that it irresistibly and inevitably reminded the beholder of the token which Hester Prynne was doomed to wear upon her bosom. It was the scarlet letter in another form; the scarlet letter endowed with life!" (70).

7. As I have already suggested, names are often condensed and intertextual sites in a Munro story. In other words, they generate for the attentive reader a kind of web of significance, seeming to quote and rewrite other, often literary, sources. "Kent," for example, invokes Shakespeare's *King Lear* and the subject who remains loyal to his deluded king—and, as I hope my discussion shows, the name Kent is at once the wrong name and precisely the right name for Munro's character. In fact, "Deep-Holes" could be read as something of a rewriting of *Lear* more generally. Alex and Sally have three children, one of whom demonstrates a very different form of love and loyalty to the father. In *Lear*, there is also a kind of fall from a cliff; recall that Gloucester wants to throw himself to his death and then is convinced by Edgar in disguise that he has survived a great fall. Kent also signifies as a place name; think also of the geographical and simple geological significance of Alex and Sally's two other children, Savanna and Peter. In this

sense, we see how each child is his or her father's message. And both Savanna and Peter apparently go on to be and do exactly what their parents expect of them. We have not even begun to unpack the significance of Lazarus and Jonah.

Works Cited

Freud, Sigmund. *Case Histories I: "Dora" and "Little Hans."* New York: Penguin, 1990.

_____. *The Interpretation of Dreams.* New York: Penguin, 1992.

Gay, Peter. *Freud: A Life for Our Time.* New York: Doubleday, 1989.

Hawthorne, Nathaniel. *The Scarlet Letter.* 1850. New York: Norton, 1988.

Laplanche, Jean. "An Interview with Jean Laplanche." Interview by Cathy Caruth. *Postmodern Culture* 11.2 (2001): n. pag. *Project Muse.* Web. 10 Feb. 2011.

_____. *New Foundations for Psychoanalysis.* Trans. David Macey. Oxford: Blackwell, 1989.

Laplanche, Jean, and J.-B. Pontalis. *The Language of Psycho-Analysis.* Trans. Donald Nicholson-Smith. New York: Norton, 1973.

Masson, Jeffrey Moussaieff, ed. and trans. *The Complete Letters of Sigmund Freud to Wilhelm Fliess, 1887–1904.* Cambridge, MA: Harvard UP, 1985.

Munro, Alice. *The Love of a Good Woman.* Toronto: McClelland, 1998.

_____. *Runaway.* Toronto: McClelland and Stewart, 2004.

_____. *Too Much Happiness.* Toronto: McClelland, 2009.

Margaret Atwood and Alice Munro: Writers, Women, Canadians _____

Carol L. Beran

The works of Canadian women writers Margaret Atwood and Alice Munro seem very different. For one, Atwood uses many genres, whereas Munro rarely writes outside the short-story form. Fans of Atwood can enjoy her thirteen novels, seventeen books of poetry, six children's books, nine volumes of nonfiction, and seven books of short fiction, not to mention numerous works published by small presses, a radio script, and three television scripts. Munro's publications include approximately thirty-three individual pieces described as "Essays, Memoirs, Letters, Poems, and Occasional Pieces" (Thacker 569–70), one book sometimes termed a novel, and fifteen collections of short stories. Nevertheless, comparing two of their short stories—Margaret Atwood's "Wilderness Tips," from the collection *Wilderness Tips*, and Alice Munro's "White Dump," from the collection *The Progress of Love*—with respect to the terms *writers, women,* and *Canadians* reveals significant similarities: both authors present their stories through similar narrative techniques, both stories depict women at various ages while exposing their victimization, and both portray Canada in ways that contribute to nationalistic projects in a postcolonial nation.

"Wilderness Tips" tells the story of a Canadian family—Prue, Portia, and Pamela, plus their brother Roland—that interacts with George, a Hungarian immigrant, for over three decades. In the present time of the story, George has had several affairs with Prue, has been married to Portia for many years, is interested in Pamela, and is disliked by Roland. "White Dump" uncovers the experiences of three generations of a dysfunctional family: Sophie, a single mother and teacher of Scandinavian languages; Laurence, her son; Isabel, Laurence's first wife; Denise, their daughter; and Magda, Laurence's second wife.

Writers: Narrative Technique

Atwood and Munro use third-person limited narration in "Wilderness Tips" and "White Dump"; in each story, three characters are used in succession to provide the viewpoint from which readers see the stories. Atwood filters the initial part of "Wilderness Tips" through George's mind, focalizes a short middle section through Roland, and opens up Portia's point of view in the final section. "White Dump" begins with Denise's perceptions, limits the viewpoint in the middle section to Sophie's experiences, and focalizes the final part of the story through Isabel's mind, with the possible exception of the last sentence. The translation of the quotation from *The Poetic Edda*, encased in parentheses at the end of the story, may be a comment from a third-person omniscient narrator, since Isabel would not be able to translate the line.[1] This causes a sense of fate to permeate the entire story, linking together the possibilities seen by the focalizers (the characters through whom readers view the story) with a pronouncement that seems to come from outside of their minds, and creates a feeling that possibilities may not be what the perceivers expect. For example, Denise's work helping battered women may be as futile as Laurence indicates (Munro 276), the frogs that Sophie moves to a better cove all return to their old habitat by the next day (294–95), and Isabel's affairs seem brightest "even before the beginning . . . when it flashes on you what's possible" (308). In both stories, the kaleidoscopic focalized narration has the advantage of giving readers privileged access to one person's perceptions at any given time while also, as the stories proceed, opening for readers the minds of other characters, thereby offering a more complete and complex look at each story than a single focalizer would provide.

Whereas "Wilderness Tips" uses one female and two male focalizers, "White Dump" uses only women as central intelligences. Munro's choice places a very strong spotlight on what the women think and feel, with only an outside view of how their actions affect the men. For example, by using Denise's childhood memories to recount the scene in which the pilot's wife tells Laurence that their spouses are having an affair, Munro thus conceals Laurence's emotions, which the child would not understand. In Atwood's story, the thoughts of the two male focalizers relate largely to the women, as, for example, George considers whether he wants to have another affair with Prue or why he might want to have an affair with Pamela, while Roland evaluates his sisters on the basis of childhood relationships. Therefore, although the focus on female perceptions is less strong than in Munro's story, the men's perceptions nevertheless illuminate the women's stories as well as their own. Seeing the situation at Wacousta Lodge through the powerful but amoral mind of George and the weak but idealistic mind of Roland prepares readers to sympathize with gentle Portia—and to be aware of more than she perceives—when she becomes the central intelligence. Characters such as Atwood's Pamela and Munro's Laurence, who never become central intelligences, seem mysterious in contrast to those whose perceptions readers know.

The kaleidoscopic narratives of "Wilderness Tips" and "White Dump" move flexibly among multiple locales and times. For example, George's segment of "Wilderness Tips" moves from the present time and place of the story (approximately 1990 on a lake in Ontario) back to George's childhood in Hungary, forward to the present, then back to the 1950s in Toronto, and finally forward to the present again. Similarly, Denise's segment in "White Dump" begins in a house on an Ontario lake in the present time of the story, moves to a conversation she had some time ago with her brother, then to her drive to the lake (which she thinks about as she has drinks with her father and his second wife in the present), next to typical quarrels Denise has had with her father regarding her career, then to her discussions of her father's opinions with her lover, next to the present again, and then to Laurence's birthday in 1969 for a quick summary of events that will be depicted in detail in the next segments. This extended time frame and supple movement among focalizers and times produces in "White Dump," according to Brina Caplan, "an illusion of real time that's rare in short fiction—an almost sculptural dimensionality" (499). Atwood and Munro use flexible and fragmented time lines in these and many other works to compress whole lifetimes into relatively brief short stories, while still providing depth in characterizations as readers access past experiences that impinge upon the present action.

Women: Women's Stories

Women's lives comprise the main subject matter of "Wilderness Tips" and "White Dump." Atwood and Munro tell the stories of women of many ages, exposing ways in which they are victimized.

Both writers show something of the childhood of the major characters. Like many stories by Atwood and Munro, these two stories consider the plight of older women, an age group often omitted from fiction in the past except when a villainess is needed. Atwood's Prue and Pamela can be seen as aging women eager to prove their continuing sexual viability by seducing George in the present time of the story, although they know that he has been victimizing them all for over three decades. In Munro's story, Sophie's fears in the plane and her subsequent absence from the lake—first for medical testing, then without explanation—highlight the aging process. Seeing Sophie's elderly body naked impels Isabel toward the lightning emanating from the pilot before time overtakes her body likewise. Isabel's tanned body and "the smooth stomach bared by Isabel's bikini" (285) contrast with Sophie's aged body: "all that white skin, slackly filled" (300). But growing old is the inescapable destiny even of young women, implicit in Sophie's presentation throughout the story as virgin, mother, and crone.

Both stories reveal women's victimization. In *Survival: A Thematic Guide to Canadian Literature*, Atwood posits that survival is the defining trope for Canada (32) and identifies four "victim positions." In "Wilderness Tips," Prue, the first of the sisters to connect with George, has had several affairs with him and seems, at the outset of the story, intent on embarking on yet another. Because Prue usually controls the timing of their affairs, she does not see herself as a victim, and yet George ignores her overtures in favor of Pamela's, which hurts her:

"Her tone is peevish, as if she's wondering the same thing"—that is, where George is (Atwood, *Wilderness* 201). Those who are victimized but deny it fit into Atwood's victim position one (*Survival* 36). Portia, George's wife, is endlessly accepting, endlessly eager to please. Hearing sounds of George and Pamela having sex, Portia acknowledges her victimization by using imagery of the *Titanic* sinking and a woman like the Greek prophetess Cassandra calling out danger but not being believed. This imagery suggests Atwood's victim position two, in which a person is aware of being victimized but sees her plight as inescapably fated (*Survival* 37). Portia's response is to sleep on the beach and then swim, perhaps drowning herself, perhaps accepting yet one more infidelity: "And nothing has happened, really, that hasn't happened before" (Atwood, *Wilderness* 204). For Portia, this is how things inevitably are.[2] Because the story never lets readers see into Pamela's consciousness, the degree of her victimization is unclear. Although her deliberate seduction of George resembles Prue's pursuit of him, Pamela's actions may be more intellectualized, less driven: "Pamela does what she wants, nothing more and nothing less" (199). Her feminist stance suggests that she is in victim position three, where the victim fights back (Atwood, *Survival* 37–38), or even in position four, the creative non-victim, aware of the victimization of women in general but able to transcend victimization by telling her story and the stories of others (38–39). Will she ultimately prove to be the clever sister of the folk tale who prevails over the sinister wizard and rescues her sisters?

Munro's "White Dump" similarly shows women—and men—in various stages of victimization. Sophie, victimized by Laurence's father, who failed to take any responsibility for her pregnancy, in turn victimizes her son, most noticeably when she embarrasses him by standing naked at the breakfast table after hippies have ripped her robe and tossed it into the lake. This passing on of victimization is a sign of victim position two (Atwood, *Survival* 38). Isabel, victimized by Laurence's "bullying" (Munro 307), rebels by having an affair with the pilot, who in turn victimizes her; she moves on to other liaisons, but her current relationship suggests that she repeats victim position three—taking action—with a series of different men. However, Isabel's belief that the best part of love affairs comes "before the beginning," "just when it flashes on you what's possible" (308), implies that her affairs will inevitably be this way, a stance of victim position two (Atwood, *Survival* 38). Denise, who works with victimized women, tries to elude her father's victimization. Yet their conversations suggest he never stops trying to denigrate her work and her mother's new life. Because her father's bullying prevents Denise from telling her own story, she appears to be in victim position two with respect to him, seeing victimization as inevitable, rather than moving on to position three or four, one or both of which undoubtedly characterize her work at the Women's Centre.

When Atwood and Munro show phases of women's lives that were omitted by many past storytellers and expose victimization in these stories and in many others, their stories connect with those of the many contemporary writers concerned about the social images of women.

Canadians: Reinventing Canada

In using kaleidoscopic focalized narration and revealing the victimization of women of many ages, Atwood and Munro share techniques and a vision with many writers. However, nowhere is the similarity within difference between Atwood and Munro more remarkable, and their difference from most contemporary women writers more evident, than in what each does with Canadian settings. Atwood publicly identifies as Canadian, frequently speaking out on topics ranging from those of national importance, such as free-trade agreements, to more local problems, such as funding for Toronto public libraries. In contrast, although Munro has spoken out about such things as censorship of books in schools, she seems less concerned with Canadian nationalism than with writing about individual women's lives. Nevertheless, a closer look at the way these two writers present setting, particularly Ontario lakes, in "Wilderness Tips" and "White Dump" indicates more commonalities than are usually noted.

The imaginary—that is, the set of constructs that impute meaning to a place—of the Ontario lakes values them for their location on the Canadian Shield. The lakes, indentations on the bedrock of Canada, offer not only recreational opportunities but closeness to nature in an authentic Canadian setting. When Margaret Atwood sets "Wilderness Tips" on one of these lakes and Alice Munro sets "White Dump" on another, part of the value of these settings comes ready made by way of a preexisting imaginary.[3] However, in using these locales, each author adds to the construct of Ontario lakes, thereby altering the attributed value of the place. Both stories challenge Ontario lakes as locations where people can have authentic experiences in natural surroundings, redefine the construct through spatial and temporal excursions outside the local setting, and invite readers, as tourists in the texts, to expand the popular imaginary as they interact with the people, in the place. The constructs of the lakes enlarge the local-color element in these stories to engage in building the national image of Canada.

On the Canadian Shield, six-hundred-million-year-old Precambrian rock is exposed in an area of over 4.6 million square kilometers that extends from the Arctic into the United States. "Repeated advances and retreats of ice sheets have scoured its surface and left it strewn with countless lakes, rivers, streams and ponds" (Marsh, "Shield" 1687). Algonquians developed the canoe to traverse these waters; later, voyageurs used canoes in their trapping and trading ventures on these waterways. "The Shield's stark and rugged beauty has attracted Canadian artists, writers, tourists and cottagers and has become almost synonymous with Canada itself" (1688). Because Ontario's lakes are in the Shield, writers who use this setting in their fiction invoke these connotations, particularly the idea that the location is a synecdoche for Canada.

Constructs of the lakes related to surviving pioneers and Canada as distinct from the Old World blend into a romantic imaginary. Tourism ads for Ontario lakes in the Muskoka district, where Atwood's story apparently takes place—the characters go north from Toronto (*Wilderness* 187)—promise an authentic wilderness setting, repeating words like *pristine*, *rugged*, and *paradise*. Tourist literature stresses that the area's national and provincial parks both preserve wilderness and make it accessible for various outdoor sports, from swimming and canoeing to bird watching and fishing.

Munro's story is set on the Canadian Shield in the Rideau Lakes region—the characters go flightseeing "all down the Rideau Lake system" (Munro 279)—where shores are rocky and islands stud lakes that were once an Indian canoe route (Helleiner 1584). Nowadays, dairy farms and maple-syrup production coexist with tourist pastimes such as boating and fishing. An aerodrome in Westport, presumably the model for Munro's Aubreyville, provides additional activities, including the sightseeing flight in "White Dump."

Challenging Authenticity

"Wilderness Tips" and "White Dump" make use of both contemporary tourist imaginaries and earlier, still-persisting pioneer imaginaries that attach to the Ontario lakes. According to the pioneer construct, Canadian lake country is wilderness, feared but available for taming. Northrop Frye emphasizes the fear:

> Small and isolated communities surrounded with a physical or psychological "frontier," separated from one another and from their American and British cultural sources: communities that provide all that their members have in the way of distinctively human values, and that are compelled to feel a great respect for the law and order that holds them together, yet confronted with a huge, unthinking, menacing and formidable physical setting—such communities are bound to develop what we may provisionally call a garrison mentality. (225)

Similarly, when Margaret Atwood names survival "the central symbol for Canada," she emphasizes fear and isolation in the wilderness: "For early explorers and settlers, it meant bare survival in the face of 'hostile' elements and/or natives: carving out a place and a way of keeping alive" (*Survival* 32). The tourist imaginary downplays the terror, displacing the fearfulness of the wilderness with ideas about confronting nature in its more benign aspects.

In "Wilderness Tips," Atwood's characters vacation at Wacousta Lodge, built by the family patriarch and given an apparently aboriginal name to reflect the earliest inhabitants of the land, lending the structure authenticity. However, because in John Richardson's novel *Wacousta; or, The Prophecy* (1832) the title character is actually a white man masquerading as a native, Atwood's choice of the name signals that this participation in the pioneer imaginary lacks authenticity. The bathroom has "only a sink and a ewer" (*Wilderness* 184), inflicting some pioneer privations on the modern vacationers. Like an early settler, Roland chops wood, although the family will probably not need to build a fire on a day warm enough for swimming. Roland is more like a Boy Scout than a mighty woodsman, as he regrets not having had a chance "to survive by [him]self in the woods" (196). Prue mimics pioneer women by making her own clothing. However, it seems unlikely that a pioneer woman would have fashioned a halter top by knotting bandanas together. At Wacousta Lodge, the canoe is not a means of transportation and commerce but a recreational craft useful for escaping the rest of the family, or else a decorative miniature on the mantelpiece (186). Hunting has been reduced to "a mangy bearskin rug complete with claws and head" and stuffed animals—"a duck, a loon, a grouse"— under glass (186). Nature has been subdued, but also rendered useless to humans except as ornament. Similes and metaphors link George with animals of the wilderness—"thin as a snake," "his foxy smile" (182), "a vulpine smile" (185), "eyes of a young goat" (192), "a lizard" (195)—and his self-identification with a dragon connects him with the hostility of nature: "He sees himself as a dragon, fumes and red flames pouring out of his ravenous maw" (193). Although the sisters try to tame George, unlike the bearskin and the animals under glass, he is not subdued. Taming the wilderness has reduced it to decoration and the danger of seduction; survival has to do with the continuance of a marriage, not the survival of humans battling natural forces and pre-European inhabitants for possession of the land.

In "White Dump," Munro's characters live in "the Log House," built "in the trees, like a hunting lodge" (296) by Sophie's father, Augustus Vogelsang, who "had left the comparative comfort of Bismarck's Germany to seek the freedom of the New World, in which all individuals might choose how they dressed, spoke, worshipped, and so on" (291). The "and so on" undercuts the authenticity of the explanation of Vogelsang's reasons for coming to Canada. An old-fashioned malfunctioning oven evokes the hardships of pioneer life as Sophie bakes "hard roast potatoes, cakes raw in the middle, chicken bloody at the bone" (279). However, Munro's story, like Atwood's, undercuts the pioneer imaginary of the lakes. The stove has been replaced in the present time of the story, providing modern convenience while subverting authenticity. It is not stereotypical hostile First Nations marauders but three hippies—"trespassers, nomads" (291)—who intrude on Sophie's early-morning swim, arousing her anger because they steal her cigarettes, tear her robe, and throw it along with her lighter into the lake, leaving her bereft of coverings. In 1969, the intrusion of inimical outsiders results in slight deprivation and embarrassment rather than scalping or captivity. In fact, rather than struggling to make the land support the family with bountiful harvests, the modern Log House family triumphs briefly over the land by surveying it from a sightseeing plane. Objects on the ground seem "toylike": "juniper bushes spread like pincushions in the fields, cedars charmingly displayed like toy Christmas trees." Sophie, however, has an *Alice in Wonderland* experience, "as if it was she, not the things on earth, that had shrunk" (296), which she counters by commanding her grandchildren in words that evoke the Creation story in Genesis: "Look here, look there, see the shapes on the earth, see the shadows and the light going down in the water" (297). But Sophie is neither Alice nor God, and the Log House is not a real pioneer cabin. Magda's "*calculated* jumble" of scarves (276; italics in orig.) implies the falseness of the ways the current inhabitants of the Log House exclude the chaos of wilderness while pretending to invite it indoors.

In both "Wilderness Tips" and "White Dump," then, the authenticity promised by the pioneer imaginary and its modern counterpart, the tourist imaginary, of Ontario lakes is shown to be simulated rather than real, which alters the value of the place. By referencing the pioneer and tourist imaginaries but then diluting and subverting them, both stories deny authenticity to the characters' experiences on the Ontario lakes.

Redefining and Enlarging Imaginaries

Atwood and Munro not only challenge the authenticity that is central to the imaginary of Ontario lakes but also enlarge the imaginary by redefining boundaries to include multiple times and a universe of locales.

For Atwood, the lake is the site of European fairy tales, which come true in perverted ways, linking the two continents. Writer and English professor Percival Everett sees "Wilderness Tips" as a reformulation of several folk tales: Prue, Pamela, and Portia play the three little pigs to George's wolf; like Goldilocks in the home of the three bears, George finds the sisters' beds too hard, too soft, and just right; and the reinvented woodchopper from "Little Red Riding Hood," Roland, rescues no one. George, with his wolflike qualities, may also come from "Little Red Riding Hood." One seductive but deceitful man connecting with three sisters suggests the fairy-tale character Bluebeard, perhaps from the Grimm brothers' "Fitcher's Bird" (Wilson 265, 378). Like Cinderella, Portia marries the prince, but the prince is a rogue, and two wicked stepsisters prevent her from living happily ever after.

The names of the characters make them alternative doubles of characters in European stories from the past, bringing cultures distant in time and space to Ontario. Prudence's name reminds readers of the

Puritan heritage, albeit ironically, since she is neither prudent nor puritanical. Her name adds England and France to the construct of the lakes. She may be an ironic descendant of one of the four virgins who invite John Bunyan's Christian in *The Pilgrim's Progress* (1678) to stay at their palace (37) on his journey to the Celestial City (38–46). In *Camille* (1848), by Alexandre Dumas *fils*, Mme. Prudence is the milliner who introduces the heroine and Armand (43), just as Atwood's Prue introduces Portia and George. Portia remains true to her literary ancestor in Shakespeare's *The Merchant of Venice*, which adds England and Italy to the imaginary along with "the quality of mercy" (*MV* 4.1.184). When the narrator points out the pun on Porsche (Atwood, *Wilderness* 170), contemporary Germany is added to the mixture of cultures. Pamela's name takes the story back to a story set in England; however, whereas Samuel Richardson's heroine in *Pamela; or, Virtue Rewarded* (1740) was the object of seduction by a predatory male, the new Pamela is the seducer of the predatory male. Is Roland a diminished version of the epic hero from the medieval French *Song of Roland*, who died protecting Charlemagne's retreat, or an ambiguous figure like Robert Browning's character in the poem "Childe Roland to the Dark Tower Came" (1855), the sole surviving knight alone in a wilderness? Either way, his name brings the chivalric Old World to an Ontario lake. As a Hungarian immigrant who has killed two men, George may come from the thriller genre, but his name ironically evokes St. George; these diverse aspects of his character add more European contexts to the imaginary of the lakes. Portia envisioning the *Titanic* sinking enlarges the lake into the Atlantic Ocean: "She thinks of a boat—a huge boat, a passenger liner—tilting, descending, with the lights still on, the music still playing, the people talking on and on, still not aware of the disaster that has already overcome them" (Atwood, *Wilderness* 204). As the image continues, it links Portia with the Greek prophetess Cassandra, "running naked through the ballroom" (204), warning of doom but not being believed, thus further widening the setting to include ancient Greece.

For Munro, as for Atwood, a Canadian lake can be the site of European fairy tales. In "White Dump," Isabel is a Cinderella, "a poor, bright girl from the factory side of town," working in a cafeteria in a "tight pink sweater" when she meets the prince, Laurence (Munro 282). When Munro parodies D. H. Lawrence as Laurence fails to engage Isabel in their lovemaking, much less make it the sensual and transcendent experience it generally is for Lawrence's characters, another part of the European past enters the place ironically. However, when the pilot lands the sightseeing plane and says that Isabel can go flightseeing tomorrow, their momentary eye contact contains "a promise" that "hit her like lightning, split her like lightning" (305), evoking gods in various ancient legends swooping down from the sky to ravish mortal women. Like Munro's pilot, who says he saw "flames . . . shooting out of [his] fingers" (287) during a thunderstorm, sky gods such as Zeus and Thor are often associated with lightning, bringing more ancient stories to enlarge the imaginary of the lake. Sophie's father emigrated from Germany; Sophie gave birth to Laurence on Bastille Day, teaches Scandinavian languages, and is the subject of family jokes about "Old Norse" (280–81), linking additional cultures distant in time and space to the lakes, attaching global qualities to seemingly local color writing. At the end of "White Dump," when Isabel reads a quote from *The Poetic Edda*, a thought about fate from an ancient culture interacts with modern Canadian culture.

A television rented to watch the 1969 moon shot brings the outside world into the Log House in "White Dump"; a TV special on the Galápagos Islands, another on America's national parks, and a serialized version of Dickens's *David Copperfield* connect the lake that Munro's characters inhabit with South America, the United States, and nineteenth-century England. The American moon shot and moon landing is mentioned twice in the story without being described in detail (Munro 278, 289), leaving readers to intuit the parallel between the dry craters of the lunar landscape and the water-filled craters in the Canadian Shield that are the Ontario lakes, expanding the imaginary of lakes in

Ontario by hinting at their likeness to the lunarscape. When the characters play charades, Peter acts out Orion, suggesting another link with places beyond an Ontario lake.

Both Atwood and Munro expand their settings to evoke the Eden myth,[4] making the Ontario lakes suggest the most nostalgic and ultimately unavailable place. George sees the lakeside lodge as "his refuge, his monastery, his sacred ground. Here he will perform no violations" (Atwood, *Wilderness* 183). The place represents something particularly attractive about Canada that distinguishes it from the Old World—innocence, possibility, authenticity—and he assimilates its qualities by marrying Portia (188–89). However, as Verena Bühler Roth points out, "Wacousta [Lodge] does not grant authentic, unalienated experience like a truly sacred place" (100). By the end of the story, the man as "thin as a snake" (Atwood, *Wilderness* 182) turns out to be the serpent in Eden as he begins an affair with Pamela at the lodge, not only denying the authenticity of the imaginary he formerly believed in but also mocking the Edenic attributes of this setting.

Munro does not endow the Log House with sacred-space status, yet Isabel is an Eve, tempted first as a child by the white dump of candy sweepings and then by the pilot/god who swoops down from the sky to strike her with lightning and ultimately foment storms in two families. As the elderly Sophie comes up from the lake naked and then wraps herself ineffectively with a tablecloth, she parodies Sandro Botticelli's *Birth of Venus* (1486), reducing the mythic to the mundane; yet, at the same time, she is ironically imputing value to the lake as birthplace of a goddess or a site dedicated to love. The setting of "White Dump" may extend the Rideau region into mythic territory, but the characters' actions devalue this Eden as a place of authenticity. The fact that Isabel has multiple lovers after her affair with the pilot, and that Denise works with battered women, subverts the ideal of authentic true love.

Enlarging the constructs of Ontario lakes, then, alters the imaginary but does not imbue it with authenticity. The boat in the lake at Wacousta Lodge is replaced by the *Titanic*, offering not recreation but death.[5] The Precambrian Shield is replaced by the moonscape, evoking an apocalyptic landscape to supplant constructs of Ontario's beautiful vacationland, while the quotation from *The Poetic Edda*—"It is too late to talk of this now: it has been decided" (Munro 309)—asserts that human actions are as fated now in Ontario as they were centuries ago in Norse legends.

Inviting Readers

Readers are tourists within texts. With the implied author and the narrative focalizers as tour guides, readers roam multiple imaginaries; they arrive at sentence one of the story with a single multifaceted imaginary and begin to let that imaginary interact within those that the author and the characters construct, forming a complex of linked images that imbue elements within the text with value and meaning. As tourists in these two stories, readers are asked to imagine quintessentially Canadian settings, but to do so in a deconstructed, globalized context through characters like George and Old Norse, and to contextualize recent times with the past through elements such as the wolf in fairy tales, characters from the British literary tradition, Venus, the moon landing, and the *Titanic*.

If the Precambrian Shield is "almost synonymous with Canada itself" (Marsh, "Shield" 1687), Tom Thomson and the painters in the early-twentieth-century Group of Seven,[6] in addition to finding artistic value in scenery that had formerly been considered unappealing, also made Ontario lakes symbolic of Canada's uniqueness and distinctness from England by emphasizing the isolated, windswept trees, the tangled underbrush, and the bare granite. The paintings acknowledge the dual reactions to Canadian lakes: fear of their wildness and awe at their beauty. The imaginary accompanying these paintings is constructed in terms that emphasize the uniqueness and power of the place. Stories set on the shores of Ontario lakes, then, partake of the qualities that differentiate Canada from England and help define its uniqueness; the environment is chaotic, mysterious, and inimical to humans, yet haunt-ingly beautiful.

Because Ontario lakes represent both Canada as a whole and Cana-da's uniqueness, by using Ontario lakes as settings, Atwood and Munro enter the conversation about Canada's national identity. Atwood has been a frequent commentator about Canada; in her essay "An End to Audience?," she asserts, "I've implied that the writer functions in his or her society as a kind of soothsayer, a truth teller; that writing is not mere self-expression but a view of society and the world at large, and that the novel is a moral instrument" (Atwood, *Second* 353). In con-trast, Munro's comment when Graeme Gibson asked her if she thinks in terms of being a Canadian writer indicates that she has not felt con-sciously engaged in constructing the imagined nation: "No . . . I'm be-ginning to feel guilty that I haven't, because it's being borne in on one that one should (laughter) but—no I haven't" (Gibson 247; ellipsis in orig.). Yet comparing "Wilderness Tips" and "White Dump" in terms of their challenges to and enlargements of the imaginary of Ontario lakes reveals Munro's participation in this nationalistic project.

Wacousta Lodge and the Log House are garrisons where families have an existence presumed safe from intrusions by the inimical as-pects of the wilderness or other outside threats to the Canadian ide-als of peace and order. Yet George, the Hungarian immigrant, invades Wacousta Lodge and ultimately profanes it, while the pilot lures Isa-bel away from the Log House and hippies invade the tranquility of Sophie's morning bath in the lake. Portia's survival is ultimately threat-ened; some critics argue that she drowns in the final scenes of the story as the surrounding landscape seems to tilt (for example, Roth 96–100). Similarly, Munro's characters acknowledge the fragility of the peace and order they have created for themselves. Having left the safety and security of marriage, Isabel, in the most recent time frame of the story, has a relationship described as "periodically 'unstable'" (Munro 278). Sophie's experience of shrinking as she sits in the plane presages her death: "She had a sure sense of changes in the offing, that were not her choice" (297). Thus Atwood and Munro engage with essential parts of the Canadian national ideals—peace and order—in their stories set on Ontario lakes. However, by challenging the authenticity and upsetting the boundaries, the stories also destabilize the nationalistic aspect of the imaginary.

Local-color writing presumes it can tap into authenticity through realism evoked via specific details. Laurie Ricou writes that regional literature is "tied to the conventions of realism because it attempts to distinguish accurately the features of a clearly definable region, either rural or closely linked to the land" (1562). "Wilderness Tips" and "White Dump" both fit within the regionalist tradition and go beyond it. Atwood and Munro embrace the popular imaginary of Ontario lakes, then challenge and enlarge it. The fact that the imaginary they use is iconic of Canada means they are also engaged in challenging and enlarging the imagined nation. Like Atwood, then, Munro is not only a writer expertly handling focalized kaleidoscopic narration, a woman writer recounting women's whole life spans and revealing their victimization, but also a Canadian woman writer engaged in imagining nation.

Notes

1. Alternatively, we might assume we are still in Isabel's mind, and that the book she reads presents the text in two languages. James Carscallen calls the narrator of "White Dump" third-person omniscient (35) but notes that the narrator is close to the women's minds, calling the women "experiencers" (21, 35) and speaking of "this succession of minds" (21). He refers readers to critics who find parts of the story outside the three experiencing minds (43).

2. Some critics see Portia's experience in the lake as a death and rebirth from which she may emerge as a creative non-victim (Atwood, *Survival* 38–39), able to rescue the family (Hengen 114–15).

3. An imaginary is a group of images that comprise the way a person or group of people imagine something. Imaginaries often contain components from the past, but also change as new components are added or existing ones deleted. Imaginaries of places have significant implications: "Places occupy core positions in human existence and everyday lives. People learn attitudes and behaviour patterns in places where they interact with others and to which they ascribe

meanings" (Johnston). The setting of a work of fiction functions similarly as a focal point for interaction and the making of meaning. Whether or not it seems to contain elements from the world outside the story, a fictional setting is a fiction, and it often includes elements from existing stereotypes—collective imaginaries—about a place as well as elements that the writer has altered or added. In *Imagined Communities*, Benedict Anderson asserts, "Communities are to be distinguished, not by their falsity/genuineness, but by the style in which they are imagined"; a nation, he says, is an imagined community (6–7). Similarly, the way writers imagine a locale creates or revises an imaginary of the place for readers; when the locale represents the nation, as it does in the case of the Canadian Shield and the lakes in it, the way the locale is imagined may contribute to and alter the way the nation imagines itself. For a more theoretical discussion of imaginaries, see Salazar 5–7, 184n5.

4. Verena Bühler Roth delineates how Atwood's setting in this story is Edenic: "The place is singled out as one where time is suspended, where the social differences of the city play no role, where special rules with respect to behaviour have to be observed, and where it is believed that the dead great-grandfather sees everything. All of these features, together with the wilderness location of the cabin, mark it as a pastoral" (91). As a holy place, the lodge has its holy books, "all related to the history and literature of Canada, a mythical past" (94).

5. When Atwood writes of E. J. Pratt's poem *The Titanic* (1935) in *Survival*, she says that the ship "—as its name implies—is a giant created by man as a challenge to Nature" and "a kind of Noah's Ark, carrying a microcosm of the society that has created it," but "instead of saving its passengers from the Flood it drowns them in it" (58–59). Portia's vision of land on the Canadian Shield tilting like the *Titanic*, then, refers to the whole nation, not just this particular lake.

6. Before World War I, Tom Thomson and other Canadian artists began painting the landscape of Ontario lakes. In 1920, Lauren Harris, A. Y. Jackson, A. J. Casson, F. H. Varley, J. E. H. MacDonald, Franklin Carmichael, and Arthur Lismer held their first exhibition in Toronto as the Group of Seven, asserting "a doctrine of aggressive nationalism and a style of painting derived directly from their experiences of the Canadian landscape," condemning many of the other artists of their time for holding "elitist, European-dominated ideals" (Shipton 7). During 1930s, the group became "an institution, wielding a national influence" (11). Many of their paintings can be seen at the Art Gallery of Ontario in Toronto and the McMichael Canadian Collection in Kleinburg, Ontario.

Works Cited

Anderson, Benedict. *Imagined Communities: Reflections on the Origin and Spread of Nationalism*. New York: Verso, 1991.

Atwood, Margaret. *Second Words: Selected Critical Prose*. Toronto: Anansi, 1982.

_____. *Survival: A Thematic Guide to Canadian Literature*. Toronto: Anansi, 1972.

_____. *Wilderness Tips*. New York: Doubleday, 1991.

Bunyan, John. *The Pilgrim's Progress*. 1678. New York: Oxford UP, 1984. Print.

Caplan, Brina. "Objects of Desire." *Nation* 243.15 (8 Nov. 1986): 497–99.

Carscallen, James. *The Other Country: Patterns in the Writing of Alice Munro*. Toronto: ECW, 1993.

Dumas, Alexandre, *fils*. *Camille*. 1848. *Project Gutenberg*. Project Gutenberg Lit. Archive Foundation, 26 Sept. 2008. Web. 11 Sept. 2011.

Frye, Northrop. *The Bush Garden: Essays on the Canadian Imagination*. Toronto: Anansi, 1971.

Gibson, Graeme. *Eleven Canadian Novelists*. Toronto: Anansi, 1973.

Helleiner, Frederick M. "Rideau Lakes." Marsh, *Canadian* 1584.

Hengen, Shannon. *Margaret Atwood's Power: Mirrors, Reflections and Images in Select Fiction and Poetry*. Toronto: Second Story, 1993.

Johnston, Ron. "Geography." *Encyclopaedia Britannica Online*. Encyclopaedia Britannica, 2011. Web. 1 Oct. 2011.

Marsh, James, ed. *The Canadian Encyclopedia*. 3 vols. Edmonton: Hurtig, 1985.

_____. "Shield." Marsh, *Canadian* 1687–88.

Munro, Alice. *The Progress of Love*. Toronto: McClelland, 1986.

Ricou, Laurie. "Regionalism in Literature." Marsh, *Canadian* 1562.

Roth, Verena Bühler. *Wilderness and the Natural Environment: Margaret Atwood's Recycling of a Canadian Theme*. Tübingen: Francke, 1998.

Salazar, Noel B. *Envisioning Eden: Mobilizing Imaginaries in Tourism and Beyond*. New York: Berghahn, 2010.

Shakespeare, William. *Shakespeare: The Complete Works*. Ed. G. B. Harrison. New York: Harcourt, 1952.

Shipton, Rosemary. Preface. *The McMichael Canadian Collection*. Kleinburg, ON: McMichael Canadian Collection, 1983. 5–11.

Thacker, Robert. *Alice Munro: Writing Her Lives; A Biography*. Toronto: McClelland, 2005.

Wilson, Sharon Rose. *Margaret Atwood's Fairy-Tale Sexual Politics*. Jackson: UP of Mississippi, 1993.

CRITICAL
READINGS

"My Mother's Laocoon Inkwell": *Lives of Girls and Women* and the Classical Past_____

Medrie Purdham

Alice Munro's interest in ancient Greece and Rome runs throughout her oeuvre. Three stories in *Runaway* (2004) feature Juliet, an academic whose field is classics. "Executioners" (*Something I've Been Meaning to Tell You*, 1974) retells the story of the fall of Troy.[1] *The Moons of Jupiter* (1982) makes a title reference to the Roman god Jupiter. And in "Wenlock Edge" (*Too Much Happiness*, 2009), a university student of Greek philosophy winds up in the odd position of reading, naked, to an older man who, referring to the bosom-baring attire of women in the Minoan civilization of ancient Crete, says resonantly, "It's odd the different things that are hidden in different eras. And the things that are displayed" (79). For Munro, the cultural values of the ancient world reveal our own, and a character's growth and change can be underlined by metaphorical changes of era, as in her 1971 novel,[2] *Lives of Girls and Women.* A coming-of-age story set in the years following World War II, this *Künstlerroman*[3] details the experiences of Del Jordan as she becomes a writer. The exuberant and maddening force driving Del's development is her mother, Addie, an encyclopedia saleswoman with a secular-humanist zeal. Addie drags Del through life lessons in personal excellence based on reason and achievement, projecting a world that is whole and systematic. Addie, in keeping with her generally classical outlook, has a "Laocoon inkwell," a kitschy miniature of a classical Greek sculpture that depicts the sufferings of the Trojan priest Laocoon as he tries to prevent Troy from being razed to the ground by the invading Greeks (Munro, *Lives* 102). Addie's pen is symbolically dipped in the forms of the classical past, and her association with this Greco-Roman tradition helps explain Del's rebellious artistic turn to Gothic forms and religious Christian themes. The novel is steeped in references to Greece, Rome, and early Christianity, as if to suggest a pagan-to-Christian arc. When Del refuses to be baptized in the Wawanash River, however, Munro leaves incomplete the conversion narrative that often subtly underlies the *Künstlerroman*.

Late in the novel, Addie announces that she has "always had a secret desire to learn Greek" (Munro, *Lives* 253). At this stage, Del is finishing high school, browsing university pamphlets, and preparing to leave her hometown of Jubilee, Ontario. Addie's attraction to Greek is perhaps not as secret as she thinks; the novel has always shown, in Addie, a classical sensibility tied to her hopes for Del's education and development. As *Lives of Girls and Women* opens, Del is in grade four, a bright girl renowned for her memory. Addie and Del move away from the family home on an unincorporated stretch of the Flats Road, where Del's father raises silver foxes in partnership with family friend Uncle Benny. Munro's novel has a literally "pagan" opening in that its setting is "of the country, rustic" ("Pagan"). The world of the Flats Road, which Del and Addie quickly leave behind, is a pastoral space. Del, as the adult narrator, may not look back at her childhood home in quite the same way that poets looked back on Greek Arcadia—as an ideal, agrarian world of nymphs and shepherds, of timelessness and simplicity—but the world of the Flats Road certainly strikes Del as innocent, and the people who seem to inhabit it most naturally are distinctly unworldly. When Uncle Benny goes to the city to pursue his mail-order bride, he is unable to use a road map to negotiate his way. And Del watches her "pure-hearted" (Munro, *Lives* 116) brother Owen, "without two dates or capitals or dead presidents to string together, as far as anybody knew, tenderly, privately, wrapping a long chewed-out piece of gum around his finger" (73). Addie, by contrast, is worldly and progressive, and she tries to nurture these qualities in her daughter.

Addie's decision to rent rooms in Jubilee with Del represents an embracing of the polis, a movement into the figuratively classical period of their lives together; Addie even goes so far as to refer to Jubilee as "the metropolis," however ironically (Munro, *Lives* 75). Though Addie will never be fully at home in Jubilee, her move into town is still a rejection of the outré world of the Flats Road, in which "anything could happen" (29). Uncle Benny's brief and hapless marriage to a "Tartar" (20) reveals the Flats Road to be a world governed by luck rather than law, an uncivilized world that Addie rejects on behalf of herself and her daughter. Jubilee is a modest civic space, but it gives Addie a form of experience that is grounded in rational order and civic participation. When Del finds that she approves of the "order, the wholeness, the intricate arrangement of town life" (76), her praise of wholeness, regularity, and order are as yet in line with her mother's classical values.

The term *classical*, used to describe the Greeks and Romans of antiquity, implies a humane and immediate responsiveness to the world itself and to mortal life, rather than to a heavenly or transcendental realm. Addie, for her part, has an almost aggressive vitality, as though her "sharpness, smartness, determination, selectiveness" were, as Del observes, "qualities . . . developed for her assault on life" (Munro, *Lives* 156). The ancient Greeks expressed their appreciation of life in a love of beauty, of forms that are strong and simple in their line and without excess or mannerism. (Del differs from her mother in that she maintains a taste for the lurid and the ornate.) They valued wholeness and strove to let their actions, thoughts, and morals reflect what they perceived as the world's own potential for wholeness and perfection (Schaper 92). Addie is a resolute agnostic, with a utopian belief in the ability of humans to perfect their own existence in a self-created future. She is confident, for example, in the "change coming . . . in the lives of girls and women," by which they will no longer depend on their connection to men (Munro, *Lives* 193). She insists on personal excellence to such an extent that Del fears the possibility of her own mediocrity in her mother's eyes. The ancient Greek idea of virtue is closer to our idea of excellence than to that of moral rectitude (Kitto 172), and Addie appears to adopt Aristotle's ethic that we will find our happiness by dedicating ourselves to the shaping of the superior parts of ourselves: our intellect and moral intelligence (Kenny 95).

Addie begins selling encyclopedias and recruits Del as her young prodigy. She requires Del to learn and recite a dazzling array of facts:

"Del, name the presidents of the United States from George Washington down to the present day, can you do that?" (Munro, *Lives* 73). Addie's mentorship of Del seems classically Greek in the sense that Greek philosophy predates the specialization of discourses. Addie, like a classical pedagogue, has a drive to know and communicate absolutely everything: "the social system of ants, the methods of sacrificial butchery used by the Aztecs, the plumbing in Knossos" (72). Marjorie Garson detects a different note of ancient Greece in these memorized encyclopedia demonstrations, suggesting that their scope is epic, almost like Homeric poetry: "This is a performance, like those of the ancient bards who recited epic catalogues" (56). Whether in poetry or in philosophy, the Greek impulse was to know and to describe the world in its wholeness, which is implicitly also Addie's aim.

In her passion for the encyclopedia and its grand systematization of natural and human history, Addie might remind us of Aristotle, who "set out to produce, in a series of lectures, and by written records, a kind of encyclopedia of all human knowledge" ("Peripatetic" 370). In classical Athens, two competing institutions of study arose. One was Plato's Academy; the other, the Lyceum, was where Plato's former student Aristotle assembled vast collections of worldly specimens in order to systematize material knowledge, partly as an alternative to the idealist teachings of his former master. His Lyceum was formerly a sanctuary to Apollo Lykeios, or Apollo in the persona of the Wolf-God or Wolf-Slayer (Lynch 9). From the Lyceum, Aristotle established the peripatetic school, so named because lectures took place while mentor and student wandered the colonnaded gardens.[4] Addie's encyclopedia pitches are peripatetic, wandering; Del's maiden great-aunts like to say that Addie is always "going on the road" (Munro, *Lives* 70). (Of course, from the perspective of Aunt Elspeth and Auntie Grace's more domestic femininity, Addie is not just peripatetic but wayward.) The town of Jubilee happens to have a Lyceum Theatre at its center, and Addie happens to be associated not with a wolf slayer but with a breeder and slayer of foxes, her husband. It would also appear that Addie's intellectual rival in town is a reader of the works of Plato. Irritated by Mrs. Comber's attitude of superiority at the book club, Addie makes a nasty little slight that seems to suggest Aristotle's materialism in contrast with Plato's idealism: "What good is it if you read Plato and never clean your toilet?" (81). Munro's classical references seem to crystallize around Addie's hopes of living in a civilized space and showing Del that the "function of man . . . is activity of soul in accordance with reason, or not apart from reason" (Aristotle 91).

Addie is unlike the classical Greeks, however, in being reserved about the body. The Greeks, in their humanism, delighted in and celebrated the body—even the pained body, as the Laocoon sculpture will show. In later stories, Alice Munro illustrates that the stereotype of Greek rationality gives us only a partial picture of their culture and fails to reveal the sensuous Greeks; in *Runaway*, her heroine Juliet happens to be reading a book about the irrational element of Greek culture.[5] But Addie, reacting to her dogmatically religious upbringing and to the unspecified sexual torture she endured at the hands of her younger brother in the family barn, will only acknowledge bodily experience in a limited way. Consequently, she rejects the Greek celebratory "bacchantic note" as well (Hatfield 81).[6] She is startled when Del brings up birth control, though she herself has advocated for it in principle. Barbara Godard observes that in growing to maturity and becoming a writer, thus "begetting both self and body" (49), Del must do so independently, because her mother cannot help her. Though Addie takes an Aristotelian materialist view of the world, she offers Del no hint that the body itself can be expressive and significant. Later, in turning to religion, Del will come to ponder the ways in which the body lends itself to communion and sacrifice, the ways in which the body can generate meaning.

The death of Del's great-uncle Craig in the chapter entitled "Heirs of the Living Body" gives Addie the perfect platform for teaching Del a secular-humanist view of existence. Uncle Craig is writing a painstakingly detailed history of Wawanash County when he unexpectedly dies.

Addie makes the disastrous decision to bring Del to the funeral, which involves giving Del, who is still just a child, an explanation of death and the vulnerability of the body. Addie explains life and death in a way that minimizes the suggestion of the body's susceptibility to harm and also avoids any mention of the soul. Her description of physical life is in line with the view espoused by some philosophers of the peripatetic school, who "denied the existence of the soul and said that life depended on the arrangement of elements in the body" ("Peripatetic" 371). Aristotle, the son of a physician, wrote detailed accounts in his *Organon* of the functioning of animal systems; Addie, too, is interested in the systematic function of the body, but not in the body's personal and symbolic value. Inspired by an article she has read about the emergence of organ-transplant technology, Addie produces a memorable speech about the "elemental" body, a speech that might appeal even to an ancient Greek who took *elements* to mean earth, water, air, and fire:

> Well, first off, what is a person? A large percent water. Just plain water. Nothing in a person is that remarkable. Carbon. The simplest elements. What is it they say? Ninety-eight cents' worth? That's all. It's the way it's put together that's remarkable. The way it's put together, we have the heart and the lungs. We have the liver. Pancreas. Stomach. Brain. All these things, what are they? Combinations of elements! Combine them—combine the combinations—and you've got a person! We call it Uncle Craig, or your father, or me. (52)

Addie exuberantly explains that these parts may break down and re-combine in new and different forms, so that "Uncle Craig doesn't have to be Uncle Craig! Uncle Craig is flowers!" (53). When the body can be endlessly reconstructed in this way, it ceases to be in any way personal or tragic. Addie tries to comfort Del with the suggestion that nothing of significance is done to the person when the body is broken, has ceased to function, or is stigmatized or degraded, because there is always a way in which it can be recomposed. Addie's view of the body promotes the interchangeability of its parts in a way that does not account for the vulnerability of the whole—in death, in pain, in degradation or humiliation.

Addie cannot respond to the intuition of violence that nonetheless haunts Del. Munro masterfully places her account of Uncle Craig's death alongside a somewhat buried story (buried because it is euphemistically relayed to nine-year-old Del) of a sexual attack on Mary Agnes Oliphant, Del's mentally handicapped cousin. Mary Agnes goes off with a group of boys, only to be abandoned, naked, in a puddle on a fairground. Between Craig's death and Mary Agnes's victimization, between a dead cow that Del and Mary Agnes find in a ditch and the story of the birth trauma that is assumed to have produced Mary Agnes's handicap, Del is struck all at once by the grotesqueness and terror of physical life. She is suddenly, forcibly impressed by the violence that can be visited on the body. This is a violence that Del associates with every act that breaks down something that is whole, including her mother's analytical (and thus inadvertently segmenting) explanation of the human being and her Uncle Craig's unfinishable manuscript, weighed down by detail.

Because civilized analysis breaks things down, Del rejects civilization completely and responds to her intuition of mortality with a primal savagery. She does the unthinkable and bites Mary Agnes on the arm: "When I bit Mary Agnes I thought I was biting myself off from everything. I thought I was putting myself outside" (Munro, *Lives* 61). The civilization that has been represented to this point by Addie's classicism and her Greek view of the elemental body has failed. Addie condemns herself as "barbaric" for bringing a child to a funeral, and Mary Agnes's mother, Aunt Moira, paints Del as virtually a cannibal: "Aunt Moira . . . would always say she had to pull me off Mary Agnes's arm with blood on my mouth" (61). Though the young Del who bites her cousin would not understand it this way, the incident marks the beginning of Del's search for a way of responding artistically and morally to the fact of physical suffering, to the unbeautiful and irrational parts of existence.

At the heart of the collection is "Age of Faith," in which Del senses that her questions about sex and death are possibly questions that religion can address. Secretly (given her mother's hostility to religion), Del looks for a place to worship in Jubilee. The title, "Age of Faith," could almost be an entry in one of Addie's encyclopedias, describing the passage of a whole culture from a pagan to a Christian orientation. The question that drives Del is whether the ordeals of the body, like Christ's on the cross, mean anything—whether the body has any real power to signify. The appeal of religion to Del is primarily artistic. She is drawn to the Gothic imagery of the Catholic Church, at least as it is represented in local superstition, with "babies' skeletons, and strangled nuns under the convent floors, yes, fat priests and fancy women and the black old popes" (Munro, *Lives* 103). She is also drawn to the ritual practices of the Anglicans, as ritual suggests formality, and formality suggests art. Her appearance in church is mainly theatrical; she designs to appear before others in the tableau of a lone, devout child. Del's "faith" is an artistic posture before it is a personal commitment: in worshipping, she creates an image of herself that she likes. Religion is also a kind of art to her in the sense that she uses it to test the limits of her own creative and determinative power. After the strength of her prayer unexpectedly saves her from the hated task of threading the sewing machine in her home-economics class, she must quickly confront the fact that she cannot, through prayer, help save Owen's dog, Major, from being put down. To an extent, Del's religious questing is sincere. On a significant level, though, her search for religion is metaphorical, describing her growth as an artist. What Del's search for religion really shows the reader, in other words, is her urge to fit her life to some kind of form.

Art ideally does for the artist what religion does for some others: it assigns a spiritual unity to a disorganized host of experiences. The *Künstlerroman*, like all forms of autobiographical writing, real or fictional, has its roots in a genre of spiritual narrative: the literary confession (Spengemann xiii). A confession, in the tradition of St. Augustine, is a narrative that aims to absolve the speaker, putting her objectively outside her experiences so that she may see the whole. Similarly, the *Künstlerroman* is interested in the search for a "creative awareness of things" (Henry James, qtd. in Beebe 227). Cynda Gault suggests that Del rejects "secular knowledge" in favor of "religious mystery" (450), and in fact the genre of the *Künstlerroman* invites this contrast. Following the model of St. Augustine's *Confessions* (and coincidentally, there is a town called St. Augustine near Jubilee), the *Künstlerroman* is often spoken from the point of view of a "converted" narrator who looks back on the progress of an "unconverted" protagonist (Spengemann 7). The young protagonist who has these various life experiences is tentative, while the older narrator who looks back on events is surer of the moral shape of things. The older narrator is converted mostly in the sense that he or she has a sense of the whole to which the parts belong, a model for meaning.

One mark of the conversion of the mature Del who narrates *Lives of Girls and Women*, as opposed to the young Del who is its protagonist, is that the narrator has a more "whole" vision of the events of that time. Del's churchgoing is a rebellion against Addie's agnosticism, but it would seem that, as the adult narrator, Del finds continuity between her faith and Addie's skepticism. Though Del remembers Addie's skeptical questions as the "heresies" that "riddled" her upbringing (Munro, *Lives* 41), she also hints at commonalities between classical and Christian imagery. Del remembers liking a Holman Hunt painting of Christ in which "he looked . . . more pagan, somehow, or at least [more] Mediterranean" than in other depictions (107). Along the same lines as her approval of this "pagan" Christ, the mature Del seems to recognize the convergence of pagan and Christian iconography in another object that she found perplexing at the time of her girlhood: her mother's Laocoon inkwell.[7] The statue *Laocoon and His Sons*, sculpted on the Greek island of Rhodes by Agesander, Athenodoros, and Polydoros in the year 25 BCE, depicts the Trojan priest Laocoon and his two sons wrestling with an attacking serpent. The sea serpent was sent by Athena, protector of Greece, to punish Laocoon for broadcasting his (correct) suspicion that the Trojan horse carried the attacking Greek army concealed within itself. As a young girl, Del has absolutely no idea what to make of the inkwell, a prize her mother won at school. She imagines that it is of value to robbers, and she gingerly peeks under the coils of the serpent entwined around Laocoon and his sons for evidence of male genitalia. But the adult Del's conscious inclusion of this inkpot in the opening passages of "Age of Faith" suggests that she now thinks of the Laocoon sculpture as being related, in some way, to her own religious search. The image of Laocoon pierced under the ribcage by a serpent's fang and turning his eyes upward as if for explanation mirrors the image of Christ on the cross, pierced by a centurion's spear, looking heavenward for the reason for his suffering. Though Del certainly does not realize it yet, the Laocoon image is also a humanist example of the way beauty and suffering can come together in art.

If Del herself suffers at this point in the novel, it is because things are not clear to her: the nature of feminine experience, the intricacies of sex—the very things that drive her to inspect Laocoon's anguished body in the childish way that she does. If Laocoon is an alternative Christ figure, or, as has been suggested, "a saint of *Humanität*, a pagan St. Sebastian" (Hatfield 127), then it should also be apparent that the human condition has long been depicted in terms of the assaults borne by the male body. Del's interest in Christ's suffering body, and similarly in Laocoon's, calls attention, by contrast, to the obscurity of female suffering in the novel. The physical ordeals of girls and women seem too secret, too inexplicit, to communicate anything to Del about the nature of feminine experience. What happened to Mary Agnes Oliphant on the fairground? What happened to young Addie Morrison in the barn? Did Fern Dogherty, Addie's boarder, have a baby, and what happened to it? Why did Miss Farris, Del's teacher, throw herself into the Wawanash River? Why did Marion Sherriff do the same thing? The martyrdom of the male is meaning-producing in culture, both before and after the Common Era, but the martyrdom of the female is more obscure. The female body is "without authority" (Kamboureli 35). Perhaps Munro was attempting to speak back to this inequality when she gave her work the hagiographic title (that is, a title modeled on the literature of saints' lives) *Lives of Girls and Women.*

Laocoon and His Sons is one of the most discussed masterworks of Western art, and one debate that surrounds it—the question of whether art is most responsible to beauty or to morality—is a question that is also important to Munro's novel. Although the bodies of Laocoon and his sons are twisted in effort and agony, Laocoon's mouth is open in a rather sedate *O*. The German art historian Johann Joachim Winckel-mann (1717–68) found this unexpectedly composed expression to be the sign of Laocoon's heroic forbearance of pain. He suggested that because Laocoon suffers gracefully, the statue shows us that art can be moral as well as beautiful (Lessing 2). Winckelmann's contemporary Gotthold Lessing counters that the ancient Greeks did not consider it virtuous to be reserved about bodily experience and so would not have deemed it "moral" of Laocoon to have contained his agony. Lessing demonstrates how often heroes and demigods in Homer's epics scream, wail, and moan (4). He claims that if the sculptors of the Laocoon declined to make Laocoon's face express pain, it was only because pain is unbeautiful.

The religiously inflected idea that the endurance of suffering is moral is openly repulsive to Addie's classical sympathies. She finds the religious impulse to find meaning in suffering and crucifixion excessive, gross, even barbaric:

> "Christ died for our sins," said my mother, jumping up. In the hall mirror she peered aggressively at her own dim face. "Well, well, *well*. Redeemed by the blood. That is a lovely notion. You might as well take the Aztecs cutting out live hearts because they thought the sun wouldn't rise and set if they didn't. Christianity is no better. What do you think of a God that asks for blood? Blood, blood, blood. . . . What about a God who isn't satisfied until he has got somebody hanging on a cross for six hours, nine hours, whatever it was?" (Munro, *Lives* 117)

But to Del, who enjoys all forms of excess and yearns to know what the body can reveal, blood remains the ultimate signifier; in fact, Del defines faith as "surrender . . . to the body" (239). For her, blood cannot help but mark the importance, the quasi-religiosity, of an experience. When later she loses her virginity to Garnet French against the side of her house, Del remarks, "When I saw the blood, the glory of the whole episode became clear to me" (249). Munro links female rites of passage to blood rites, and she also places those blood rites right on the line between pagan and Christian beliefs, the precise line where the novel dwells.

In the chapters following "Age of Faith," Addie's influence over her daughter fades, and Munro suggests a change of era. In the chapter called "Lives of Girls and Women," Del's innocent schoolgirl crushes from "Changes and Ceremonies" have become more serious sexual investigations, in pursuit of which she rebels against her mother's authority. To underline Del's insurgency, the chapter's imagery and references are now Roman, decadent and even martial. Rome has succeeded Greece and in turn looks forward to the rise of the medieval Christian Gothicism that will mark Del's own style, as predicted by "Age of Faith." As Addie loses her dominance over her daughter, Munro repeatedly mentions Del's study of Latin, contrasting, of course, Addie's "secret desire to learn Greek" (Munro, *Lives* 253). Del is also reading Erich Maria Remarque's 1945 novel *Arch of Triumph* (191), the title of which refers to the triumphal arch of Roman conquest.

Munro develops the Roman motif through the introduction of Art Chamberlain, whose military service in Italy during World War II allows her to introduce a range of Italianate and martial references. Although Mr. Chamberlain is dating Fern Dogherty, Addie's boarder, he makes crude, confident passes at Del and her school friend Naomi. Del, wanting to discover something about the "magical, bestial act" of sex (Munro, *Lives* 167), does not rebuff him. Chamberlain uses Del to invade Fern's privacy. He asks Del to go into Fern's room and steal back his letters, presumably so that Fern cannot compel him to marry her by citing breach of promise, and pays Del back for this favor with sexual attentions. Through Chamberlain, Del indulges a fantasy of sexual danger and self-abandonment, and her goal is ultimately artistic: she wants to narrate her affair to Naomi. She finds herself decadent and revels in it. Del comes to her voluptuous notions of love and sex, and love as conquest, through opera, but the blunt reality of the situation is that Mr. Chamberlain is an adult who is exploiting Del, a high-school student. Chamberlain masturbates in front of Del and suggests that, because he is doing only this, she has had a lucky escape (186). He expects her to find the spectacle of his exposed penis "quite a sight" (187), but she finds it "raw and blunt, ugly-coloured as a wound" (185) and refuses to feed his self-congratulation. Before Chamberlain's "valedictory" show, the word itself a Latin descriptor for a parting triumph, Del remembers the Latin passage she has just translated: *"Having pitched camp and slaughtered the horses of the enemy by means of stealth, Vercingetorix prepared to give battle on the following day"* (180). Del figures herself as the Gallic captain Vercingetorix, who futilely but resolutely stood up to Julius Caesar in the course of Caesar's Gallic campaign. Del knows she is being used by Chamberlain but she persists anyway, to show that she is not "damageable" (193), even in a situation in which she is being dominated.

In this chapter, Del sullenly confronts the fact of male privilege in art and in life. Art Chamberlain presides over the Jubilee radio, mostly because he has a rich voice and can be counted on not to pronounce Bach *"Batch"* (Munro, *Lives* 189). Meanwhile, a conversation about his tour of Italy, prompted by Addie, reveals his total lack of interest in art and culture. Though he acts in bad faith toward Fern Dogherty, she still pines for him as though he were a legitimate beau. And though he may have been guilty of killing his comrades-in-arms in a friendly-fire episode, he still enjoys being addressed as "soldier," grasping at all forms of unearned status. (He narrates the fatal, tragic incident as though it were just an amusing anecdote, a military comedy of errors.) A self-gratifying figure, Art maintains an attitude of *render unto Caesar that which is Caesar's* that incites Del, as she did in "Heirs of the Living Body," to throw off the yoke of civilization and identify instead with the "barbarian," here the tribal Vercingetorix.

In "Baptizing," Del reclaims an independent and metaphorically heathen self. She refuses to be baptized in the Wawanash River by her lover, Garnet French, who wants to marry her in his evangelical church and make her respectable. Del's resistance to this baptism is a resistance to the social ideology of love and marriage, along with its tie to Garnet's faith. Del's residually "pagan" self, cultivated by her mother, is, in a sense, still her true self. Garnet tests Del's personal commitments on all fronts; she comes with him to revival meetings, but will she join the church? She loses her virginity to him, but will she marry him and bear his children? Garnet dunks Del in the river in a playful imitation of baptism, only to have Del arrive at a moment of personal clarity. The game, through "layers of incredulity" (Munro, *Lives* 262), becomes serious, even violent. In fighting back, Del draws a clear line of demarcation around herself: she will not be his. Garnet feels snubbed, punished, even excluded along class lines: "You think you're too good for it . . . for anything. Any of us" (260). But Del's refusal of baptism seems to be a final acknowledgment that her flirtation with the revival meetings was only an experiment, a posture, from which she is liberating herself. The romantic relationship itself was a self-mythologizing game, one of many in the novel, in which Del enjoyed thinking of herself as someone's lover. As Del walks home from the Wawanash River, she "repossesse[s] the world" in its fullness, its detail, its reality (265). She comes back to the world in its wholeness and its appearance of rational organization—her mother's world, almost—but she comes back to it independently, untied now to anyone's ideological interpretation of it. If the world suddenly seems more whole, it is because Del more fully possesses herself.

Thomas Tausky reveals how difficult it was for Munro to conclude her novel in a way that satisfied her, how often she reworked the material of the novel's epilogue. In a sense, the novel ends with "Baptizing," in Del's simultaneous refusal of both conversion and marriage. With this double refusal, Del fulfills her mother's prophecy that the day will come "in the lives of girls and women" in which women will need not attach themselves to the lives of men, or, as we have seen, to the movements governed by the ideas, the enterprises, and even the sufferings of men. The epilogue shows how, having achieved a kind of independence of thought and action, Del is able finally to start to reunite her aesthetics with her ethics.

The residue of Del's religious impulse is still with her in the form of her Gothic tastes (in architecture, Gothicism is associated with medieval Christianity in the sense that it describes the ornate carvings of demons on medieval churches, meant to ward off the evils of the world), but in the epilogue, she starts to evolve a new personal style. She is writing a juvenile work, a "black fable," that uses the lives of the Sherriff family as raw material for a sensationalistic tale. Del's lurid story is indifferent to the lives of the real Sherriff family, the lives she must unexpectedly address when Bobby Sherriff makes contact with her. In a way that is reminiscent of Munro's stories "Family Furnishings" (*Hateship, Friendship, Courtship, Loveship, Marriage*, 2001) and "Material" (*Something I've Been Meaning to Tell You*), Del is called upon to reconcile her ethics and her aesthetics by deciding how to represent the lives of others in art. Bobby Sherriff calls to her from his garden gate to offer her a slice of cake, a good wish for luck in her life, and an odd, unreadable gesture: "He rose on his toes like a dancer, like a plump ballerina" (Munro, *Lives* 273). Del looks at Bobby Sherriff in all his ordinariness and all his mystery. She appreciates, in an instant, how the world exceeds her grasp of it. Though she admits that "no list could hold what I wanted," she still wants to write things down in such a way that "every last thing, every layer of speech and thought, stroke of light on bark or walls, every smell, pothole, pain, crack, delusion" is "held still and held together—radiant, everlasting" (277). In this moment of fledgling maturity, Del is caught between the limits of the known world and the limitless and unknowable dimensions of everyday mystery.

It has been suggested that the difference between a classical world-view and a Christian one is the difference between an outlook that is "whole" and one that is "infinite" (Hatfield 183). Perhaps this binary also expresses an orientation toward beauty as opposed to morality. When Del refuses baptism, she finds herself poised richly between a knowable world something like her mother's and an infinite world for which she also longs. The *Künstlerroman* tends to trace the progress of an artist figure, not to the point of producing a significant work, but rather to the point where the artist *could* produce one. And so it seems that, even in her state of confusion and betweenness, Del has reached an ideal phase in the evolution of her self-consciousness and her world consciousness. The state of mind in which Del tries to reconcile these opposites seems to be the state of mind from which art is made. Munro also implies in Del's desire to make lists that she has reconciled herself somewhat with her upbringing, with Addie's own style of thought, though she also realizes that "no list could hold what I wanted." Addie appears less and less frequently in the last chapters of *Lives of Girls and Women* and not at all in the epilogue. Some critics, following Godard, suggest that Del liberates herself from her mother in order to move forward as a writer. It seems, rather, that the novel stages an important return to origins. Like many other contemporary female authors of the *Künstlerroman*, Munro "inscribe[s] the maternal subplot more emphatically" than any of the romantic plots (Abel 163), subtly suggesting Addie's continuing and ultimately productive influence on Del's thought. Del's observation about the "solid, intricate structure of lives supporting us from the past" (34) applies just as well to her mother, Addie, as to the various cultural traditions that the novel explores.

In *Lives of Girls and Women*, Del passes metaphorically through different phases of history: Greece, Rome, and the "Age of Faith." This passage helps underline the way experience itself is episodic, the way different selves, clearly marked as separate in time, are reunited in the course of a *Künstlerroman*. The particular arc of *Lives of Girls and Women*, from the pagan to the Christian, seems also to acknowledge the roots of the *Künstlerroman* in the confession. It has a modern twist, however, in that there is no conversion, except in the metaphorical sense that the epilogue shows Del to be at a first, important moment of maturity or even personal enlightenment. The novel seems to suggest that Jubilee may be finally "radiant" with meaning when, from the standpoint of the adult narrator, it is finally illuminated from within by gratitude. Del does not thank Bobby Sherriff for the cake or the odd gesture, but the narrator retrospectively believes that she should have. Del's "selves," as represented by the different chapters of this "episodic novel" (Besner 39), are almost historically separate entities. They are reunited in the acknowledgment of the thanks due to others, for all their offerings and for making the crucible in which the self is formed.

Notes

1. The status of "Executioners" as a retelling of the Trojan War is discussed by Ralph Stewart, who is cued by the names of the misfit Helena and the "country boy, Howard Troy" (Stewart 159), whose house is set on fire. Other critics who have written articles on classical allusion in the works of Alice Munro include Ian Rae and Klaus P. Stich. Rae sees the Juliet stories from *Runaway* as fictionally resonant with the life of poet and classicist Anne Carson and as evidence that Munro is not strictly the local, autobiographical writer that she is made out to be; Stich finds allusions to Dionysus and Medusa running through Munro's story "Meneseteung" (*Friend of My Youth*, 1990).

2. I am calling *Lives of Girls and Women* a novel, but some would describe it as a collection of interconnected stories. Janet Beer argues that the male bildungsroman is typically a novel but believes that the story of Del's development is suited to the episodic form of the interconnected short-story cycle. This structure shows not only how Del emerges from episodic interactions with men but also how she contains the influence of each man within a discrete period of her life (Beer 126–28). Neil K. Besner most helpfully addresses the question of whether *Lives* is a novel or a collection of short stories by proposing the term "episodic novel" (39).

3. The *Künstlerroman* (novel of artistic development) is a subgenre of the bildungsroman (novel of development). *Lives of Girls and Women*'s relationship to the archetypal modernist *Künstlerroman*, James Joyce's *Portrait of the Artist as a Young Man* (1916), has been extensively discussed.

4. There is some debate as to whether the name of the peripatetic school is actually derived from the noun *peripatos*, meaning the colonnaded walks in which philosophers rehearsed their learning, or whether it comes from the verb *peripateien*, which describes the physical act of traveling or wandering (Lynch 74). Though Lynch, following Busse and Brink, argues that the school is named for the noun, there is evidence that the ancient Greeks themselves were confused on this point (Lynch 73–74), so I will consider both meanings to be available.

5. Ian Rae believes that Munro's Juliet is a figure for the Canadian poet and academic Anne Carson, whose doctoral thesis, out of which she published the monograph *Eros the Bittersweet* (1986), explores the irrational, erotic, lyric, and elegiac aspects of classical Greece.

6. Klaus P. Stich, like Rae, demonstrates that Munro herself is more of a "bacchantic" classicist, one who is interested in the affiliation of the god Bacchus/Dionysus with the arts. Bacchus was associated with inspiration, wine, and revelry, and Stich is interested in the motif of grapes and alcohol in Munro's "Meneseteung."

7. I am adopting Munro's spelling of Laocoon. It is often given as Laocoön elsewhere.

Works Cited

Abel, Elizabeth. "Narrative Structure(s) and Female Development: The Case of *Mrs. Dalloway*." *The Voyage In: Fictions of Female Development*. Ed. Elizabeth Abel, Marianne Hirsch, and Elizabeth Langland. Hanover, NH: UP of New England, 1983. 161–185.

Aristotle. *On Man in the Universe*. Ed. Louise Ropes Loomis. Roslyn, NY: Black, 1943.

Becker, Susanne. *Gothic Forms of Feminine Fictions*. Manchester: Manchester UP, 1999.

Beebe, Maurice. *Ivory Towers and Sacred Founts: The Artist as Hero in Fiction from Goethe to Joyce*. New York: New York UP, 1964.

Beer, Janet. "Short Fiction with Attitude: The Lives of Boys and Men in the *Lives of Girls and Women*." *Yearbook of English Studies* 31 (2001): 125–32.

Besner, Neil K. *Introducing Alice Munro's* Lives of Girls and Women: *A Reader's Guide*. Toronto: ECW, 1990.

Garson, Marjorie. "I Would Try to Make Lists: The Catalogue in *Lives of Girls and Women*." *Canadian Literature* 150 (1996): 45–63.

Gault, Cynda. "The Two Addies: Maternity and Language in William Faulkner's *As I Lay Dying* and Alice Munro's *Lives of Girls and Women*." *American Review of Canadian Studies* 36.3 (2006): 440–54.

Godard, Barbara. "'Heirs of the Living Body': Alice Munro and the Question of a Female Aesthetic." *The Art of Alice Munro: Saying the Unsayable; Papers from the Waterloo Conference*. Ed. Judith Miller. Waterloo, ON: U of Waterloo P, 1984. 43–71.

Hatfield, Henry. *Aesthetic Paganism in German Literature: From Winckelmann to the Death of Goethe*. Cambridge, MA: Harvard UP, 1964.

Kamboureli, Smaro. "The Body as Audience and Performance in the Writing of Alice Munro." *A Mazing Space: Writing Canadian, Women Writing*. Ed. Kamboureli and Shirley Newman. Edmonton, AB: Longspoon/NeWest, 1986. 31–39.

Kenny, Anthony. *Aristotle on the Perfect Life*. Oxford: Clarendon, 1992.

Kitto, H. D. F. *The Greeks*. Baltimore: Penguin, 1951.

Lessing, Gotthold Ephraim. *Laocoon: An Essay upon the Limits of Painting and Poetry*. 1766. Trans. Ellen Frothingham. Boston: Roberts, 1894.

Lynch, John Patrick. *Aristotle's School: A Study of a Greek Educational Institution*. Berkeley: U of California P, 1972.

Munro, Alice. *Lives of Girls and Women*. Toronto: Penguin, 1971.

_____. *Too Much Happiness*. Toronto: McClelland, 2009.

"Pagan." *The Oxford English Dictionary*. 2nd ed. 1989. *OED Online*. Web. 15 July 2011.

"Peripatetic School." *Encyclopedia of Classical Philosophy*. Ed. Donald J. Zehl. Westport, CT: Greenwood, 1997. 369–76.

Rae, Ian. "Runaway Classicists: Anne Carson and Alice Munro's 'Juliet' Stories." *Journal of the Short Story in English* 55 (2010): 141–56.

Schaper, Eva. *Prelude to Aesthetics*. London: Allen, 1968.

Spengemann, William C. *The Forms of Autobiography: Episodes in the History of a Literary Genre*. New Haven, CT: Yale UP, 1980.

Stewart, Ralph. "A Note on Munro's 'Executioners' and the Fall of Troy." *Journal of the Short Story in English* 42 (2004): 159–65.

Stich, Klaus P. "Letting Go With the Mind: Dionysus and Medusa in Alice Munro's 'Meneseteung.'" *Canadian Literature* 169 (2001): 106–25.

Tausky, Thomas. "'What Happened to Marion?' Art and Reality in *Lives of Girls and Women*." *Studies in Canadian Literature* 11.1 (1986): 52–76.

Who Does Rose Think She Is? Acting and Being in *The Beggar Maid: Stories of Flo and Rose*

David Peck

The Beggar Maid may be the best known of Alice Munro's short-story collections, if only because half its contents have been reprinted in other collections; four of the stories from this 1978 volume are included in Munro's 1996 *Selected Stories* alone. Two of its ten stories, "Royal Beatings" and "Wild Swans," are probably her most reprinted, and "Royal Beatings" and "The Beggar Maid" were the first of fifty stories over the next thirty-five years to be sold to the *New Yorker*. The volume won the Governor General's Award, Canada's highest literary prize, and was short-listed for the Booker Prize in England. It is, as biographer Robert Thacker writes, "*the* critical book of Munro's career" (294; italics in orig.).

The history of the construction of this collection—Thacker calls it "the most complex, and fraught, publication history of any of Munro's books" (341) —is revealing. Based on the success of two previous collections, *Lives of Girls and Women* (1971) and *Something I've Been Meaning to Tell You* (1974), Munro and her editors prepared a new volume, in which about half the stories centered on the Rose character and the others were about a new character, Janet, who would turn out at the end of the volume to be the author of the Rose stories. After further reshuffling of these contents, galleys were prepared, and review copies had already been sent out (which is why some early reviews may be confusing to readers today) when Munro, unhappy with the volume's arrangement, paid the publisher to make the alterations necessary to produce a new collection. Six Rose stories were retained; three Janet stories were dropped, later to appear in Munro's 1983 collection, *The Moons of Jupiter*; three other Janet stories—"Mischief," "Providence," and "Who Do You Think You Are?" —were rewritten to become Rose stories; and Munro added one story she had just reworked from a much longer version, "Simon's Luck." The original Canadian volume was titled after the last story in the collection, but the American publisher, Knopf, did not think that the US audience would understand the social class reproach behind the question "Who do you think you are?" and replaced it with the more colorful title of a middle story, "The Beggar Maid." The tighter coherence of the collection may be at least partly attributable to this frantic reassembly of the stories just before publication and Munro's active oversight of the new collection. Instead of being a volume of stories written at different times, published in various venues, and assembled with the editorial direction of the publisher, as many short-story collections are, *The Beggar Maid* is a volume of interconnected or "linked" stories (Munro's term), a fragmentary novel centering on the narrator-protagonist Rose and assembled under the white heat of direct authorial intervention.

As shown in W. R. Martin's most useful analysis of the structure of *The Beggar Maid*, the collection focuses on the three main stages of Rose's life. The first four stories in the collection deal with Rose growing up in the 1940s in Hanratty, Ontario, with her dying father, her stepmother, Flo, and her younger half brother, Brian. The middle four stories follow Rose through college, courtship, marriage, motherhood, and divorce, and the final two return to Hanratty, as Rose comes back in order to care for an aging Flo in the 1970s. The first and last sections, featuring Rose and Flo in Hanratty, are clearly the strongest of the three, but all the stories in the collection are tied together by character and theme, metaphor and motif, and by a central character who progresses through life by learning to play different roles. This opposition between acting and real life, or seeming and being, lies beneath the collection's sporadic portrait of Rose's search for identity, culminating in the final two stories when Rose, a professional actress, returns to Hanratty and confirms her identity as a performance made up of various parts.

The first four stories in *The Beggar Maid* include Munro's two most reprinted stories and set out the themes in the collection most vividly. The first of the four stories focusing on Rose's childhood and adolescence, "Royal Beatings," dramatically displays Rose's impoverished and dysfunctional beginnings. Rose's mother died while Rose was still a baby, and her father has married the woman who came to help him out and then bore Rose's half brother, Brian. Rose's father repairs furniture in a shed behind the house, while Flo tends a small store they have opened in a front room of the house to make ends meet. Hanratty, Huron County, Ontario, is poor and will decline further in the course of the collection, and West Hanratty, where Rose and her family actually live, across the river, is even poorer. This is just one of a series of oppositions in the story, such as between past and present, that underpin the central split between the childhood Rose is trying to leave behind and the adolescence she is entering. In "Royal Beatings," Rose marks this passage through her conflict with Flo. Her stepmother is resentful of the rebellious Rose, often threatening the girl with "a Royal Beating" for her language and her tone, both of which show her disrespect. To the young Rose, everyone around her seems to have a dual personality: the person making noises in the kitchen bathroom "was not connected with the person who walked out"; the father who works in his shop murmuring lines about Spinoza and Botticelli and quoting Shakespeare's *The Tempest* "and the person who spoke to her as her father were not the same, though they seemed to occupy the same space" (Munro 6).

This split culminates in the beating Rose does get when her antagonistic language ("Two Vancouvers fried in snot! / Two pickled arseholes tied in a knot!") finally drives Flo to summon the father from his workshop, and a scene the three actors have performed before is played out, as the father hits and kicks his daughter in a brutal pantomime. Rose thinks, "He is like a bad actor. . . . That is not to say he is pretending, that he is acting, and does not mean it. He is acting, and he means it" (Munro 18). Still, "Rose must play her part in this with the same grossness, the same exaggeration, that her father displays, playing his" (19). The drama ends with Rose, finally unhurt, crying in her room, and the remorseful Flo bringing her a tray of her favorite foods.

The theatricality of the scene is underscored by contrast to the story Flo told earlier of the savage beating of Becky Tyde's father by Hat Nettleton and two others, which led to his death. In the coda to "Royal Beatings," an adult Rose in Toronto hears a radio broadcast that she at first imagines must be "a scene from some play," but turns out to be the 102-year-old Hat Nettleton being interviewed from the same nursing home where Rose has placed the senile Flo. Rose concludes from the broadcast that everything can change over time, as the "horsewhipper" Hat Nettleton has turned into a lovable "living link with our past" (24). More importantly, though, Rose yearns to tell someone the story of Hat on the radio and thinks immediately of Flo, the key figure in her childhood, who first filled her head with dramatic stories—like the story of the beating of Becky Tyde's father, another "performance," with Becky Tyde as sole spectator. The coda anticipates the final two stories in *The Beggar Maid*, in which Rose will return to Hanratty to take care of Flo. In that return, she will prove that everything does, in fact, change and that the unhappy child has managed to become the adult Rose, but only through her ability to act in the roles she has created, in performances she first learned from Flo in her childhood.

In psychological terms, Rose is a case of arrested or poor ego development. Lacking a mother or any other useful female role model, she must forge her older selves by her own imagination, and she does so by mimicking others, her journey through life marked by a series of performances as she takes on and then discards various roles. The remaining three stories in this first section of *The Beggar Maid* show early roles Rose plays. "Privilege" displays her learning to survive the poverty and squalor of elementary-school life, in part by falling in love with an older girl and "trying to *be* her" (Munro 34; italics in orig.). In her high school in "Half a Grapefruit," Rose pretends to be a "town" girl (instead of a "country" girl, or someone from the even more impoverished West Hanratty, as she really is) and is caught in the pretense. She is also learning performance, as she now "change[s] herself into chronicler" (42) and returns from school each afternoon to relate stories of her day for Flo, as Flo earlier shared tales and gossip with her. Rose has no models for her impending womanhood; her father's only advice is, "Look out you don't get too smart for your own good." His ideal woman? "Flo was his idea of what a woman ought to be . . . energetic, practical, clever at making and saving" (47). Rose has none of the skills necessary to step into such a role, so instead she imagines herself as others; when she reads Shakespeare, "she imagine[s] herself *being* her, being Lady Macbeth" (50; italics in orig.). Unwittingly, Rose is training to become an actress.

In "Wild Swans," Rose's father has died, and she is making her first train trip alone into Toronto. Flo warns her about sexual predators, especially "people dressed up as ministers," and of course that turns out to be exactly the person she encounters: an older man who sits down next to her, claims to be a minister, and pretends sleep while he fondles Rose under the cover of his newspaper. Rose is unable to act in her own defense against this sexual attack, and much of the criticism of this story argues about whether the incident truly happens or she just imagines it, but it hardly matters. The point is that part of Rose longs for adult sexual contact: "She had a considerable longing to be somebody's object. Pounded, pleasured, reduced, exhausted" (Munro 63). But she is finally not able to deal with the attack. "Her imagination seems to have created this reality, a reality she was not prepared for at all. She found it alarming" (63). In the coda to this story, Rose remembers another story of Flo's, about a fellow worker in the Toronto train station gift shop years before, who went to a resort for the weekend and called herself "Florence Farmer" to give people the idea she was the 1940s movie actress Frances Farmer. Rose is learning about life by learning about transformations—even from a dirty old man pretending to be a minister—and she admires people who can transform themselves into other characters and "get away with it, . . . enter on preposterous adventures in your own, but newly named, skin" (67).

The middle four stories, which carry Rose through university, marriage, motherhood, divorce, and final independence, are generally weaker than the four stories in the first section and the two in the last. In part, it is because the tension Munro creates between past and present in Hanratty, seen in the codas to both "Royal Beatings" and "Half a Grapefruit," is missing in this middle section, so the stories appear flatter and less resonant. "The Beggar Maid" is one of the better stories in this section, along with the last one, "Simon's Luck." In "The Beggar Maid," Rose has left Hanratty to attend university as a scholarship student. Living cheaply in the home of Dr. Henshawe, a retired classics professor, Rose is courted by Patrick Blatchford, a graduate student in history who falls in love with her in the university library where she works, and where a man grabs her bare leg in the book stacks one Saturday afternoon.

Patrick is incredibly romantic and full of "chivalric notions," and for him, Rose "turn[s] herself into a damsel in distress" in a library that actually resembles a castle, with "casement windows, which might have been designed for shooting arrows through" (Munro 75). Patrick insists on calling her "*The White Goddess*" or the "Beggar Maid," from the Pre-Raphaelite painting *King Cophetua and the Beggar Maid* (1884) by Edward Burne-Jones, a romantic rendering of the medieval story of a king marrying a beggar woman. Patrick comes from a wealthy Vancouver family, and Rose knows they represent two different worlds. Their visits to each other's homes are disastrous; his home is luxurious but full of "true malevolence" (89), while she only feels shame when he is in Hanratty. She resists the roles that some people, like Dr. Henshawe, assign her, yet claims she wants to be an actress: "She wanted to perform in public" (72). She does not think that Patrick really knows her, but of course she really does not know herself, made up as she is of bits and pieces of others, and she reluctantly takes on the romantic role he assigns her. She tries to break up with him, but then visualizes a scene in the library in which they are reconciled—and finally acts it out.

The coda to the story takes place in the Toronto airport nineteen years later. They were married for ten years and have been divorced for nine, and she is now a successful television interviewer. She sees him again, in a tableau remarkably like the reconciliation scene in the library, and again imagines she could "surprise him with his happiness" (Munro 99); then he turns, sees her, and makes a "truly hateful, savagely warning, face . . . a timed explosion of disgust and loathing" (100). It has taken her nineteen years, but she has finally learned that she cannot create a role for herself with another, cannot imagine their scenes together and then act them out happily.

"Mischief," the next story in the middle sequence, takes place in Vancouver, where Rose and Patrick have moved so that he can work in his family's department store, having given up his academic plans for her. Rose still wants to be an actress, "though she was too much of a coward ever to walk on a stage" (Munro 106). She makes a new friend, Jocelyn, in the maternity ward where she gives birth to her daughter, and then falls in love with Jocelyn's husband, Clifford, at a party the new friends throw. Clifford is a professional violinist who tells her that she looks "delicious"; Rose thinks "he ha[s] taken on a role. . . . He might be adept at disguises"—just as, she believes, "she herself [i]s getting to be" (109). When he kisses her, Rose is "transformed, invulnerable" (112). They launch an affair that is never consummated, but Rose learns that "deceitfulness, concealment," seems "to come marvelously easy to her; that might almost be a pleasure in itself" (114). When they finally arrange a long-planned rendezvous, Clifford changes his mind and backs out at the last moment. What Rose sees is that "his life in that house, Jocelyn's house, [i]s all pretense, and waiting, like her own life in Patrick's house" (127). The pretense will soon end, at least for Rose and Patrick; meanwhile, in the coda to this story, Clifford and Jocelyn are living in Toronto, near where Rose teaches drama at a community college. After a party, they have a three-way sexual encounter. Rose rises angry the next morning and resolves never to see them again, but after writing a letter to that effect, she decides "to go on being friends with Clifford and Jocelyn, because she needed such friends occasionally, at that stage of her life" (136). In "Providence,"

Rose has left Patrick and her daughter, Anna, and has taken "a job at a radio station in a town in the Kootenay mountains" (137) in British Columbia to be close to Tom, a married teacher at the University of Calgary. Like the near-affair with Clifford, the affair in "Providence" is mostly a series of failed assignations.

"Simon's Luck," the fourth and final story in the middle section of *The Beggar Maid*, is a better story of a more successful affair. Rose has been teaching theater for two years at a community college outside Kingston, Ontario. At a party in the city, she meets and takes home Simon, a classics teacher, and they spend an idyllic weekend together. Simon has survived World War II in Europe as a displaced Jewish orphan, and, like Rose, he plays various roles, usually for comic effect. "She already knew a few of his characters. This was The Humble Workman. Some others were The Old Philosopher . . . and . . . The Mad Satyr" (Munro 165–66). Like Rose, Simon has escaped an earlier life, with much luck, and the two find fleeting happiness together (in another romantic fantasy, like the one she bought into with Patrick in "The Beggar Maid"). However, when Simon does not show up again the next weekend, Rose becomes desperate and packs her car and drives west from house and job; after driving all night, she stops at a café and undergoes an epiphany. "She realized then that she had come into this café without the least farfetched idea of Simon, so it seemed the world had stopped being a stage where she might meet him, and gone back to being itself" (175). The failed affair has pushed Rose out of a place where she was stuck, for in Vancouver she gets a role in a new television series. In the coda to the story, on a ferry in British Columbia during the shooting of one of the episodes of the popular series, she meets a woman from the Kingston party who tells her that Simon is dead, that he had pancreatic cancer when Rose met him; readers can only assume he ended the affair before she would learn the truth and have to suffer with him. Simon's luck ran out, but not before he passed some of that luck on to Rose.

In the final two stories of the collection, Rose is back in Hanratty, taking care of her failing stepmother. Flo and Hanratty have disappeared from the reader's view since "The Beggar Maid," when Rose brought Patrick back for the brief but disastrous visit before they were married, and something was lost in the following stories in their absence. This is partly because Flo's character is probably the strongest in the book. She is a singular creation: uneducated but intelligent, opinionated and superstitious, imaginative and dramatic, telling her stories in unique solo performances. Rose has missed her, and readers have as well; after all, as the subtitle to the collection declares, these are supposedly "stories of Flo and Rose." Hanratty itself provides the contrast that creates some of the tension in the story, for it is here that past and present clash and the old and new Rose struggle for recognition. It is only in Hanratty, and with her old nemesis Flo, that Rose can validate the adult woman she has become and bring closure to her own development, her own history.

In "Spelling," not all the changes are bad. West Hanratty looks better, having "got itself spruced up with paint and aluminum siding; Flo's place [is] about the only eyesore left" (Munro 180), and the lone inhabitant of the dilapidated house has dementia, lives amidst dirt and debris, and only occasionally recognizes Rose. Rose is now close to fifty herself and has not been back for two years. Earlier, she went to visit her half brother, Brian, an engineer living in Toronto with his wife, Phoebe, and their children, in order to discuss what to do with Flo. Rose assumed that Brian, being Flo's son, would have done more, but he has not, leaving it up to his wife to maintain contact with Flo. Visits with Brian have never been successful, as "they could never stop the old, old competition; who is the better person, who has chosen the better work?" Phoebe looks on in amazement as her husband and sister-in-law disclose "their contest, their vulnerability, their hurt" (184). The poverty and deprivation that Rose suffered growing up in Hanratty, as revealed in the first section of *The Beggar Maid*, apparently also afflicted her half brother. Both have been making up for the pain of childhood, and Brian has moved away to become successful but rigidly self-satisfied, not unlike Rose's ex-husband, Patrick, while Rose has become a successful actress.

The plan the three come up with is for Rose to return to Hanratty to make arrangements to get Flo into the Wawanash County Home, but Rose secretly opposes their plan. She imagines "going to Hanratty and looking after Flo, living with her, taking care of her for as long as . . . necessary" (Munro 185), but this idea does not last the first days of being home. Rose spends some time with Flo, visits the depressing County Home, and tries to convince the only occasionally rational Flo that it is a good idea to move there. One morning, she wakes up to find Flo dressed and ready to go to "The Poorhouse," as she calls it. After she is admitted, Rose finds a thick gray-blue wig in the house that Flo wore from Hanratty to a drama awards ceremony in Toronto to which Rose had invited her years before. The ceremony had ended disastrously when Flo, being Flo, pointed out loudly that there was a black man in the cast. Rose takes the wig out to the home and models it for Flo for comic effect, as Flo slips back into believing it is forty years earlier, when Rose and Brian were children. The stories in *The Beggar Maid* are coming full circle; now Rose is performing for Flo, instead of the reverse, as Flo reverts into Rose's childhood.

The final story—and remember, Munro and her Canadian editors thought the title of "Who Do You Think You Are?" appropriate for the whole collection—concludes the volume by bringing its first themes and motifs to some kind of conclusion. Rose has taken Flo to the County Home but is staying in West Hanratty to clean up the house and get it ready to sell. Her neighbors, thinking that Rose might be lonely on a Saturday night, invite her to the Legion Hall. There, she meets Ralph Gillespie, a classmate from high school in Hanratty who dropped out, joined the navy, was wounded, and is living out his life back in Hanratty on a disability pension. Rose talks to him, and later remembers the "wave of kindness, of sympathy and forgiveness" she felt in this conversation:

That peculiar shame which she carried around with her seemed to have been eased. The thing she was ashamed of, in acting, was that she might have been paying attention to the wrong things, reporting antics, when there was always something further, a tone, a depth, a light, that she couldn't get and wouldn't get. And it wasn't just about acting she suspected this. Everything she had done could sometimes be seen as a mistake. She had never felt this more strongly than when she was talking to Ralph Gillespie, but when she thought about him afterward her mistakes appeared unimportant. (Munro 209)

Earlier, a woman sits down next to her in the Legion Hall, introduces herself, and says she recognizes Rose from television. Whenever someone does this, Rose has "an absurd impulse to apologize. Here in Hanratty the impulse [i]s stronger than usual. She [i]s aware of having done things that must seem high-handed." In Hanratty, Rose thinks, her "beguiling confidence and charm" must seem "a sham" (207). At the end of the story, living back in Toronto, Rose reads in the Hanratty paper that Ralph has died, and—like with the story of Hat Nettleton on the radio at the end of "Royal Beatings"—there is no one she can share his story with. "What could she say about herself and Ralph Gillespie, except that she felt his life, close, closer than the lives of the men she'd loved, one slot over from her own?" (210).

The story of Rose's encounter with Ralph in the Legion Hall takes up only the last quarter of "Who Do You Think You Are?" The story opens with the tale of Milton Homer, a developmentally stunted man who lives in Hanratty with his two old-maid aunts. One, Miss Hattie Milton, taught English at the high school, and it was Miss Hattie who, when Rose learned a poem by heart in class instead of copying it down, as she had been assigned, told her, "You can't go thinking you are better than other people just because you can learn poems. Who do you think you are?" (Munro 200). The class consciousness of the rebuke, the warning not to try to rise above one's station in life, is, as Rose says, one she has heard before—from Flo, in the very first story in the collection, "Royal Beatings," and from her father in the third, "Half a Grapefruit." But Rose has in fact moved out of her social class, as she has left Hanratty for university and marriage and a professional career. Yet when she returns to Hanratty, her accomplishments seem somehow diminished; only in talking to Ralph does she feel free of her shame.

Milton Homer is the last in a long line of misfits, like Becky Tyde in the first story, who crowd Munro's pages here, just as in the fiction of her American peer Carson McCullers. "The village idiot," as Brian's wife Phoebe calls Milton, wanders around Hanratty talking to himself and visits homes where babies have been born to give his blessing. Hanratty's mock–Jesus Christ, he is also "a mimic of ferocious gifts and terrible energy" (Munro 196) who marches in parades and imitates, and thus parodies, the movements of the other marchers and dancers. He is, in short, an actor, performing publicly for Hanratty in almost a caricature of what Rose does professionally. A similar connection to Ralph Gillespie is first made in the story when, in Miss Hattie's English class, Ralph changes the title of the John Keats poem they are studying, "On First Looking into Chapman's Homer," and shows Rose what he has written in his book: "*On First Looking into Milton Homer*" (198). Ralph soon becomes another "ferocious" mimic, known mainly for his imitations of Milton Homer. In fact, it is while watching Ralph perform his Milton Homer imitation in school that Rose's desire for acting is first crystallized: "She wanted to fill up in that magical, releasing way, transform herself; she wanted the courage and the power" (204). She has achieved this childhood goal in some small measure through her acting, her television work, her teaching, and her creation of her own adult identity. When she returns to Hanratty, she is reminded of just how far away she has moved. At the same time, she feels guilty for having abandoned her roots, Flo, and her Hanratty self, and she falls back into those childhood roles that Flo and the town assigned her. Meeting Ralph at the end of the book, however, she is somehow reconciled, imagining him "one slot over" from her life and feeling closer to him than to other men. Ralph somehow validates her own trajectory, through acting, out of Hanratty and into adulthood. As Coral Ann Howells has written, all three characters are outsiders "with the same transgressive delight in performance" (64). Milton Homer became a mimic, but could not develop as a person any further; Ralph Gillespie became a mimic, left Hanratty, but had to return, wounded. Rose was wounded in childhood but learned to survive by playing roles she created for herself or had thrust upon her—often unhappily—that took her far from Hanratty. If Milton Homer is the parodic Christ baptizing babies (including Rose) and thus freeing them from original sin, then Ralph is the imitation priest absolving Rose of transgressions and granting her some kind of peace; she feels a sense of recognition, feels the "sympathy and forgiveness" that emanate from Ralph. To the question "Who do you think you are?" Rose would earlier have had to answer, "I don't know," but in the closure of her story, she returns to Hanratty and is validated in the composite identity she has created.

Arguments over whether to call *The Beggar Maid: Stories of Flo and Rose* a short-story collection or a novel seem ultimately pointless. All of the stories can stand on their own and have done so in separate magazine and anthology publications; "Spelling," to cite just one example, was selected for *The Best American Short Stories, 1979* by the volume's editor, Joyce Carol Oates. Together, as the portrait of a central character's journey through life, they are also united by theme and metaphor as a fragmentary novel. Perhaps *The Beggar Maid* can best be described as a story cycle, like Sherwood Anderson's *Winesburg, Ohio* (1919) or Eudora Welty's *The Golden Apples* (1949). Regardless of the label, *The Beggar Maid* stands on its own as one of Alice Munro's unique achievements, and remains, as Robert Thacker concludes, "the single most important book in her *oeuvre*—at least as regards her development as a writer" (533). In later stories and collections of stories, Alice Munro will explore other regions (as far away as Scotland and Russia), as well as other subjects, and her style will deepen and coalesce. But her mature voice and themes are here first, in this collection of ten distinctive linked stories that carry Rose from childhood to adulthood and show her working out her identity, in a series of roles she takes on and those she has thrust upon her, through scenes of poverty and sickness, violence and death, love and loss.

Works Cited

Howells, Coral Ann. *Alice Munro*. New York: Manchester UP, 1998.
Martin, W. R. *Alice Munro: Paradox and Parallel*. Edmonton: U of Alberta P, 1987.
Munro, Alice. *The Beggar Maid: Stories of Flo and Rose*. New York: Knopf, 1979.
Thacker, Robert. *Alice Munro: Writing Her Lives; A Biography*. 2011. Toronto: McClelland, 2005.

Alice Munro's *The Progress of Love:* Free (and) Radical _____

Mark Levene

As a writer, above all a writer exclusively of short stories, albeit often very long ones, Alice Munro seems to have had a blessed life. (Whether she would call it her "real life" is a permanent mystery.) She has not suffered neglect or misapprehension from readers and critics. She has not even suffered much from the cultural question or puzzlement about the ways in which her works are recognizably Canadian—or not. The problems she has encountered, as she describes in an early interview with Graeme Gibson, were inevitable ones: overcoming even temporarily her community's aversion to the shameful fecklessness of a life with books, "getting enough time" (Gibson 250) to write when facing the natural imperiousness of young children, and managing the jolts to the psyche that are always hovering when one places words on a page. From early on, it was clear to anyone who read her stories that there was something unique unfolding in the books under her name. That she was determined to hold to both the rural world of southwestern Ontario and the short-story form, and that she seemed indifferent to the possibilities for her career in aligning herself with literary society, appeared to be markers of independence, strength, and at the same time an essential modesty. Initially, praise focused on her often-startling ability "to get at the exact tone or texture of how things are," "the sights and sounds and smells" of "the external world" (Gibson 241, 243–44).

Early in my involvement with Munro's work, I gave a lecture that was attended by a former teacher of hers from Wingham, Ontario. During the intermission, the sharp-eyed, elegant, elderly woman said to me in a near-whisper, sounding like Munro's prose, "That's how it was, that's how it felt" (Levene 844). This hushed quality, a note reserved for the most luminous of the world's writers, extends to the responses of colleagues and friends when one mentions writing about Munro's work. Her identification as a deft, inventive chronicler of girls' and women's lives, inclined to any perception except the psychologically simplified or morally categorized, goes some way toward illuminating the range of admiration for her now-abundant but still muscular body of writing. In his introduction to *The Progress of Love* (1986), Richard Ford, himself a deeply talented writer of short fiction, adds something crucial to the celebration and understanding of Munro's dense yet accessible creativity: "Myself, I always marvel at what I think of as Munro's *freedom* (my word) . . . from the hammerlock of any story's chosen formal features," whereas "most *other* stories operate solidly, obediently, unfreely *within* their formal decisions" (xi). These decisions are "any story's scaffolding" (xii)—its narrative voice, "its internal transitions, its diction, its unities" (xi):

> But Munro the writer has use only for those boundaries that serve, with no obedience to tell us anything but (apparently) the right thing, using the best word in whatever lingo, in whatever time frame, to whatever surprising extent (long or short), in whomever's "point of view," in whatever verb tense, no matter what's gone before or seems ordained to come next. Hers is freedom to stray beyond the story's apparent unities and amenities and hard sides and never to come back unless she wants to. To us readers it all feels unstrained, effortless and right. (xii–xiii)

Every story in *The Progress of Love* confirms the rich subtlety in Ford's perception of Munro's creative freedom: in the title story, the separate, almost separable, internal story of the narrator's grandmother's apparent attempt to hang herself; in "Miles City, Montana," the deferral of a resolution to the framing story until its internal story is played out; the severe, even ugly, controlled language of "Lichen" leading to the beautiful ending note of "a pause, a lost heartbeat, a harsh little break in the flow of the days and nights as she keeps them going" (Munro, *Progress* 52); in "A Queer Streak," the sudden leap forward in time, which here and often in Munro's stories means the stark, abrupt abridgement in the life of someone who had seemed significant to the preceding narrative;

and the tightly coded relation of afternoon, morning, and evening set against the open time sequences of the future in "Circle of Prayer." All these instances of Munro's freedom are her "lovely tricks, honest tricks," shapes within "the marvelous clear jelly" of her unsparing yet generous creativity (Munro, *Something* 43).

With the right temperament and analytical gear, one can go pretty well anywhere in exploring Munro's fiction and come out ahead, which reflects her startling comment about writing and reading in her ironically very brief essay "What Is Real?": "I don't take up a story and follow it as if it were a road, taking me somewhere, with views and neat diversions along the way. I go into it, and move back and forth and settle here and there, stay in it for a while" (825). Where I want to go in this essay are some of the rooms in her house of fiction, the places in *The Progress of Love* that extend Ford's perspective, especially Munro's radically complex genius at conclusions—or, as is often the case, the compound, layered endings in a single story.

Endings have rightly occupied the attention of many theorists of the short-story form. As Munro is a writer deeply affected by James Joyce, the early master of elliptical conclusions, her singular and often singularly enigmatic conclusions are a necessary subject. But her radical freedom from conventionality also shows forth in her transformation of parentheses, endowing them with a subversive centrality, even a cool whimsy, about what we really know of the characters. The conclusion of "White Dump," which is also the end of the collection and comments on the earlier endings, is an extended parenthesis followed by a short one, a translation by an unknown translator of a cryptic passage from an Old Norse saga. Munro's one-page essay about fictional reality, "What Is Real?," is also dominated by parentheses, so much so that the answer to the question "what is real?" is for Munro likely a parenthesis, or an idea once thought of, if at all, as parenthetical. So, as strange as it may sound, the parenthesis-shaped room in Munro's fictional structure is where I will go—and end.

144   Critical Insights

First, however, there are metaphors, or more exactly characters who make metaphors as an expression of their deep, private freedom, primarily in the first two stories, "The Progress of Love" and "Lichen." A writer's freedom is not necessarily matched by a character's freedom; indeed, they may be inversely proportional. Declared, badge-wearing satires are particularly given to this imbalance. In *The Secret Agent* (1907), for instance, Joseph Conrad's almost wild freedom to erode every distinction he can think of—between policeman and thief, organic and inorganic, first- and third-person narration—exists because of the servitude of the characters to the novel's controlling ideas. But for the time at which he wrote, Conrad was, as always, an unusual case, and in much of the high modernist fiction of Joyce, D. H. Lawrence, and Virginia Woolf, freedom seems to flow from creator to character to reader. But those were the 1920s. In *Nineteen Eighty-Four* (1949), one of the grimmest examples of reciprocity between character and author occurs: Winston Smith's illusion about the private integrity of his consciousness is entwined with George Orwell's awareness that in a world of relentless destruction, psychological intricacy is an extinct species, and metaphors are not expansive but limited, repetitive, and horribly fragile. Writer, character, and their bond in language operate "unfreely," not because of artistic constraints, but because of the curtailment, the erosion, of personal life itself.

However, in "The Progress of Love" and "Lichen," this literary troika of author, character, and language is political only in the special sense of organizing the need—sometimes desperate, sometimes Zen-like—of an apparently helpless person to exert the power to penetrate or alter stultifying and love-denying external, received stories. In the title piece, allusions to freedom are initially more like notations, their significance not quite at the center of the unfolding narration. The narrator's father's phrase for her mother's death, "I think your mother's gone," prompts an ambiguous association: "The word 'gone' seemed full of nothing but a deep relief and even an excitement—the excitement you feel when a door closes and your house sinks back to normal and you let yourself loose into all the free space around you" (Munro, *Progress* 3). Concluding the primary version of the story about her grandmother in the barn with a rope around her neck, Fame (that is, Euphemia, named after the grandmother) looks beyond the claustrophobic tie between mothers and daughters—"like a cloud you couldn't see through, or get to the end of"—to her brothers and again sees freedom: "My brothers weren't bothered by any of this. I don't think so. They seemed to me like cheerful savages, running around free, not having to learn much. And when I just had the two boys myself, no daughters, I felt as if something could stop now—the stories, and griefs, the old puzzles you can't resist or solve" (13).

But the connection Fame makes between freedom and biology, a link expanded on and darkened immeasurably in the collection's fourth story, "Miles City, Montana," occurs after something more directly purposeful, courageous, and verbally inventive on her part. When she begins to retell her mother's story, her instinct, since she already knows how calcified and cruel the story is, is to add details to what her mother would almost certainly never have said:

> "Mama?" called Marietta. She walked through the house to the back yard. It was late spring, the day was cloudy and mild. In the sprouting vegetable gardens, the earth was damp, and the leaves on the trees seemed suddenly full-sized, letting down drops of water left over from the rain of the night before.
> "Mama?" calls Marietta under the trees, under the clothesline. (9–10)

Here, recalling Richard Ford's admiration for Munro's choice of "whatever verb tense" she and a character need, we realize, somewhat startled, how author's and character's freedoms inform and shade one another: Munro's burden is how best to articulate a character's emotional whirl; Fame's burden is to breathe rather than suffocate within the inherited story by modifying and altering its deterministic nature.

So "it was late spring, the day was cloudy and mild," although perhaps it really was not.

Fame is a metaphorist in training. As dramatic as a possible suicide is, the essential and even more exciting drama in "The Progress of Love" is the conflict of competing and irreconcilable stories: her mother's version, which takes the noosed rope with absolute seriousness, and later on her aunt Beryl's version, as told by the culpable father. The mother "wanted to give Daddy a scare" (Munro, *Progress* 20), Beryl is sure, and she saw that the rope was "just flung there—it wasn't tied at all!" (21). Skeptical as we are about the accuracy of a very young child's perception, the two stories combine to make an all-encompassing, impenetrable toxic cloud that keeps Fame exiled from her mother in a shameful separateness. In "Jesse and Meribeth," later in the collection, Jesse, "seeing the power of [her] own lies, [her] own fantasy," says, "I am a person capable of wizardry but helpless" (175). The relation of wizardry—that is, the creation of metaphor and stories—to both power and helplessness is at the core of Munro's unparalleled art. Helpless before the "tall, firm front" of her mother (13), Fame intuitively becomes a wizard. Instead of deciding between the two separate stories, she eventually creates another one. She tells Bob Marks, a "good-hearted" man not entirely devoid of imagination, "My mother once burned up three thousand dollars . . . She burned three thousand dollars in that stove" (24). Despite the family's poverty, Fame's mother is so driven by hatred for her father, the presence behind the noosed rope, that she burns her portion of his legacy, bill by bill. Contextual details, which are rare in Munro's work—"in the summer of 1947, when I was twelve" (7) —confirm the factuality of the mother at the stove. But the rest is metaphor, the expression of Fame's newfound freedom. "She put it in just a few bills at a time, so it wouldn't make too big a blaze," she tells Bob. "My father stood and watched her" (25). Despite strict empirical evidence to the contrary, that her father had not been in the kitchen, had not known about the money, "it seems so much the truth it is the truth; it's what I believe about them" (29):

I see my father standing by the table in the middle of the room . . . and there is the box of money on the table. My mother is carefully dropping the bills into the fire. She holds the stove lid by the blackened lifter in one hand. And my father, standing by, seems not just to be permitting her to do this but to be protecting her. A solemn scene, but not crazy. People doing something that seems to them natural and necessary. At least, one of them is doing what seems natural and necessary, and the other believes that the important thing is for that person to be free, to go ahead. They understand that other people might not think so. They do not care. (28)

Fame's choice of freedom, of wizardry, in creating this story not only endows her otherwise constrained parents with freedom as well but also elicits a sense of forgiveness, once unavailable, for them and for herself.

The following story, "Lichen," is a sort of companion piece in its differences from "The Progress of Love," differences that amplify the sense of doubleness increasingly prominent in the volume. "Lichen" is a cruel study in physical revulsion built on two opposing transformations. The first and apparently dominant one is the male pathos in David's horror at aging, which becomes a blackly comic misogyny: "You know, there's a smell women get. . . . It's when they know you don't want them anymore. Stale" (Munro, *Progress* 37). Munro even allows the story to recoil from the general identification of her work as a celebration of women's lives, because outside David's perspective, she has Catherine, his now-"stale" girlfriend, announce, "I feel a change coming in my life. I love David, but I've been submerged in this love for so long. Too long" (42). This thin self-lavishing on a thin self draws into the narrative the famous and exuberant, if naive, announcement by Del's mother in Munro's second book: "There is a change coming I think in the lives of girls and women. Yes. But it is up to us to make it come" (*Lives* 192). The irony of this doubling of story on story is disquieting; it hints at a subversion of the earlier optimism by what seems a submersion in a new language of power, of assault, where metaphor is the inventiveness of loathing, a weapon in wars everyone loses. Forgiveness has gone missing, and what is left is relentless clarity; if there is still freedom, it is in Munro's choice to turn herself momentarily into a corrosive writer like V. S. Naipaul. Again outside David's scabrous insight, the story describes an utterly incidental character: "Mary is not in the least fat, but something had happened to her chin that usually happens to the chins of fat women. It has collapsed into a series of terraces flowing into her neck" (*Progress* 36). Munro is not playing a game. She seems to know that to enter fully into an alien perspective is a dangerous thing, a potential contaminant, but she does enter, if only to shift again at the end to a grace note of transcendence, a metaphor of great beauty, made even more precious and welcome by how it doubles a slightly earlier metaphor that remains in the language of revulsion.

During the visit to the nursing home to see his father-in-law (held over or deferred, like many central passages in *The Progress of Love*, through characters' fears and anxieties, which override the logic of ordinary sequence), David tries "to think of him as a post-human development, something new in the species. Survival hadn't just preserved, it had transformed him." When he speaks, the "sound seem[s] to come from a wet cave deep inside him, to be unshaped by lips or jaws or tongue. These could not be seen to move" (Munro, *Progress* 48). David's picturing is brutal, but not as brutal as he wants to be to Stella, his "pensioned-off" wife (34), by showing her a genital-focused photograph of his "new girl." "'It looks like lichen,' says Stella, her paring knife halting. 'Except it's rather dark. It looks to me like moss on a rock'" (39). After David and his current girl have left, Stella finds the picture half-hidden, a last effort through metaphor to disquiet her, to confirm her irrelevance and passivity:

> Lying in the sun had faded it, of course. . . . She sees that the black pelt in the picture has changed to gray. It's a bluish or greenish gray now. She remembers what she said when she first saw it. She said it was lichen. No,

she said it looked like lichen. But she knew what it was at once. It seems to her now that she knew what it was even when David put his hand to his pocket. She felt the old cavity opening up in her. But she held on. She said, "Lichen." And now, look, her words have come true. The outline of the breast has disappeared. You would never know that the legs were legs. The black has turned to gray, to the soft, dry color of a plant mysteriously nourished on the rocks. (52)

Both verb and noun, *liken* and *lichen*, are parts not so much of speech but of Stella's inner grammar, which allows her to elude David's gender-driven coercions and what may be a fear of mortality also rooted in gender. Like Fame in the previous story, she turns *seems* into *is*, but where Fame's creativity, her assumption of freedom, is a form of conscious and paradoxical belief, Stella's arises from a privacy without need, a mysterious intactness entirely separate from other people. "Stella's words have come true. This thought will keep coming back to her—a pause, a lost heartbeat, a harsh little break in the flow of the days and nights as she keeps them going" (52).

In the *Poetics*, Aristotle announces that "the greatest thing by far is to be a master of metaphor. It is the one thing that cannot be learnt from others; and it is also a sign of genius" (Aristotle 22). His view that man's "creation of likenesses" and the "innate desire for knowledge" (Heath xiii) are inextricable gathers tremendous force through the centuries and informs our thinking of metaphor "as the concept at the crux of all thought, and maybe all human understanding" (Romano). For Friedrich Nietzsche, there is *"no real knowing apart from metaphor"* (qtd. in Kofman and Large 57; italics in orig.), the formation of which is "the fundamental human drive" (155n5). Since Munro has emphatically said, "I'm not a writer who is very concerned with ideas. I'm not an intellectual writer. I'm very, very excited by what you might call the surface of life" (Gibson 241), the invocation of these philosophical titans as footnotes to her fiction might seem to her anything from amusing to interesting. But whatever she would think of the company, what is inescapable and crucial about her writing is that surface and depth are not fixed, and what relates them is metaphor. Munro is brilliant at using metaphors, at their placement in a sentence and in the perception of a character. More oblique and intellectually daunting is that this use is part of her dramatizing how, and sometimes even why, metaphors come into being, and her locating them at the core of selfhood.

But with Munro's writing, our straying from specifics for too long is a mistake. What led to Stella's luminous moment (let us call it, tentatively, an epiphany on the order of the snow at the end of Joyce's story "The Dead") are two metaphors that are not as easily elaborated upon as the union of lichen and liken. David thinks of "a wet cave deep inside" Stella's father, and then, alone with the photograph and not having heard David's words, Stella "felt the old cavity opening up in her." Lichen and liken are one thing, cave and cavity quite another. Aside from being spaces linked by resemblances in sound but disharmony in visual associations—inorganic, nonhuman rock versus organic and utterly human genitalia—there is no available abstract reconciliation between the metaphors. In the story "The Moon in the Orange Street Skating Rink," the possibility that Callie is exercising almost "miraculous" powers leads to a parenthesis that is almost miraculous in its own way, in the freedom Munro extends from herself to her narrator and her characters. She backs off from elaboration and rests on a gentle hypothesis: "Maybe Edgar, in particular, felt this" (*Progress* 148). But with cave and cavity, as with Peg's character in "Fits," narrative reticence has no note of transcendence or generosity. Her declining to explain leaves her language and our reading just on the edge of bleak, dreadful implications.

That Munro neither reveres nor laments the unknowable, those always-distinct but elusive silhouettes of human mystery, leads us back to her claim that she is not an intellectual writer. Intellectual or beyond intellectuality, Munro is free too, perhaps, of the constraints the word and the activity may conjure up for her. She is a writer whose subtlety and toughness are in the tradition of the modernists, the poet-explorers of doubleness and multiplicity who had no difficulty with being "intellectual." Joyce and Woolf and Henry James and William Faulkner, and now Munro, are, in Irving Howe's brilliant terms, "committed to the view that the human lot is inescapably problematic" (9). They are "disdainful" not only of "certainties" but of the assumption, both personal and cultural, that certainties are desirable and possible (Howe 10). The dualities of Leopold Bloom in Joyce's *Ulysses* (1922), Clarissa in Woolf's *Mrs. Dalloway* (1925), and Quentin Compson in Faulkner's *Absalom, Absalom!* (1936) are open to everything but strict synthesis and resolution. Their authors knew that the "commitment to the problematic" nature of perception and knowledge "is terribly hard to maintain, it requires nerves of iron" (Howe 21). Munro's cave and cavity, metaphor and prayer, exist in their fine tension because of her "firm grip on the idea of the problematic" (21). But the two stories most in this grip on the problematic—that is, on a complex irresolution—are "Miles City, Montana" and "Fits," the first rooted in one of the densest metaphors Munro has yet created, the second in an impenetrable white space and an undermined conclusion.

In "Miles City, Montana," as in "The Progress of Love," the narrator's perceptions and questions emerge through a layering of stories; the difference is that the framing story seems "separate" (one of the prime words in Munro's writing life), the transition from the past to the ostensible present sharp but ambiguous. As a girl, the narrator both witnessed and reconstructed the picture of a "boy who had been drowned" (Munro, *Progress* 80), which is not quite the same as a boy who had drowned. This relocation of responsibility from the boy, Steve Gauley, to someone or something else is quickly associated with the picture of Steve's one parent, whose "fatherhood seemed accidental, and the fact that the child had been left with him when the mother went away, and that they continued living together, seemed accidental" (81). The full meaning of *accidental* arises only at the end of the entire story, after the narrator's proximity to "accidental" in her own life and her daughter's brush with "accidental" drowning. Here, the word suggests something not deliberate or chosen, unlike the purposefulness the narrator's own parents flaunt, which prompts in her "a furious and sickening disgust" (82).

Munro has a stunning way of approaching beginnings, middles, and endings, which often is to write a double opening and a multiple ending, making middles protean parts of a thoroughly fluid structure. In the second opening of "Miles City, Montana," the narrator thinks of her family's trip across the continent as her "shedding" of domestic responsibilities and neighborhood "sociability" (*Progress* 84). In the house, "I wanted to hide so that I could get busy at my real work, which was a sort of wooing of distant parts of myself. . . . But on trips . . . those bits and pieces would be flying together inside me. The essential composition would be achieved" (84). Despite how striking the word *wooing* is, the entire metaphor is unemphatic and yet is central to the increasingly complex perception of freedom in Munro's stories, including her own as a creator. Wooing suggests conventional romance or the courting of something external, but here concerns no one other than the "I" (female and male, both wooer and wooee). Her pursuing "distant parts of herself" draws us into the realm of ancient mythologies, of fertility rituals and the process of destroying and then recreating the figure and potency of a divinity. Munro's allusiveness is much quieter and more oblique than is T. S. Eliot's in *The Waste Land* (1922). We follow Munro in this unusually decorated hallway in her house of stories—or we do not. It is her choice not to increase the interpretive odds, not to alter the "accidental" nature of reading. She lets it be. What it is possible to see is that, unlike other mothers, with their defining and imperious "need to be burdened" (Munro, *Progress* 86), the narrator senses the separateness of her "essential composition," which is that of a "watcher, not a keeper" (84)—a distinction that places her, we are startled to realize, closer to Steve Gauley's "accidental" father than to her own parents, with their delusions of benign care and family purpose. Although the word *free* is not used directly in this brief, beautiful meditation on the perilous romance of the private self, it is a modest inference that the coming together of the distant yet inner "bits and pieces" of herself is a condition of freedom, although not necessarily the only one.

However, it is the nature of accident to unsettle even so subtle a process as the narrator's solitary wooing. Reprising the transformations in "The Progress of Love" and "Lichen," the narrator's older daughter, Cynthia, invokes a pool, and in Miles City there is one, though not quite as lyrical an incarnation as Cynthia has imagined. But in this story, the metamorphosis of *maybe* or *seems* into *is* changes again, now into the terrible danger of the lifeguard's inattention. The mother suddenly asks herself on the other side of the pool fence, "*Where are the children?*" (Munro, *Progress* 95). The answer she and her (then-)husband, Andrew, discover is that both girls are swimming, not floating or submerged: "'I didn't know it was deep,' Meg said. 'I didn't drown'" (97). Andrew invokes "some kind of extra sense that mothers have" (100) to explain the question. But having seen herself as a "watcher, not a keeper," the narrator is not so sure. "Partly I wanted . . . to bask in my extra sense. Partly I wanted to warn him—to warn everybody—never to count on it" (100). Her bits and pieces may include an instinct to preserve and safeguard her children, which puts her alongside her own parents as well as Steve Gauley's accidental father, a doubleness that allows her to grasp her revulsion and disgust during the boy's funeral. "I was understanding that they were implicated. . . . They gave consent to the death of children and to my death not by anything they said or thought but by the very fact that they had made children—they had made me." Children "should have sprung up free, to live a new, superior kind of life, not to be caught in the snares of vanquished grown-ups, with their sex and funerals" (99). Steve Gauley, however, "was neglected, he was free, so he drowned," and his father "was the only one I didn't see giving consent" to either the boy's life or his death. The proportion of accident and purpose in the narrator's attachment to her children is, once more, something unknowable in Munro's writing. But we know two things: the narrator has given consent, yet does not ooze "religion and dishonor" (99); and, despite her remarkable question, she does not rescue Meg. This deeply private person is happily, gratefully present at a dramatic expression of Meg's independence within the space of what is here a benign accident.

There is also the suggestion of another consent that brushes the reader, butterfly-like: the mother's consent to Meg's freedom to be what she is, separate from the people and the world of which she is a tenuous part. She has a "forthright independence," a "ferocious bashfulness" (Munro, *Progress* 95), and her body still possesses a "sweet indifference" (94). Her mother's lament for the mortality of children has an element of celebration. Steve Gauley "was free, so he drowned"; Meg was free, so she lived, even perhaps into "a new, superior kind of life." The narrator slides from watcher to keeper to watcher again, lives through Miles City, and, in the company of parts of herself—if there are surrounding figures, they are accidental—moves on, somewhere and possibly someone else.

Independent girls and women are hardly unfamiliar to Munro's readers. But *The Progress of Love* is unusual not only in the number of these characters but also in the often disquieting and paradoxical ways they silhouette one another. Peg Kuiper in "Fits" is a "keeper" only in the sense of keeping secrets. Her primary secret is what she watched: the aftermath of the murder-suicide of their neighbors, the wonderfully named Weebles. Robert, her (second and more passive) husband, "once told her he had never met anyone so self-contained as she was" (Munro, *Progress* 103). Peg, centering in herself the question of what "fits," says, edgily, "I know what the words mean . . . I just don't understand how you mean it about me" (104). The most independent, vexing, and, for many readers, terrifying of all the figures in the collection, Peg possesses a literalness at odds with a repeated insistence on what cannot be known; one hinges on belief in causality, the other on its irrelevance. The fit between parts of herself is far from perfect. When Robert asks her why she did not contact him after her discovery of the bodies, her answers are flat and eerie: "You were up on the roof. . . . What good would that have done?" (111). She explains to her sons why she did not scream: "I didn't. I guess because there wasn't anybody to hear me. So I didn't" (118). At the same time, however, she circles back to what she knew, which is mainly cast in the negative: "I knew there wasn't anybody but me alive in the house"; then, later, "I hardly knew them. We hardly knew the Weebles" (119). Peg is one of Munro's few anti-poets, almost tragically bereft of the instinct to create metaphor. Through the conclusion to the inner story of Peg's ascent of the staircase, the most dramatic of the framed narratives in *The Progress of Love*, Munro takes the rare, drastic step of shutting down her readers' freedom of understanding and interpretation. It is here that her radical genius at endings, her transformation of the epiphany's luminous intensity, most fully shows itself.

In response to a comment about the unusualness of her endings, Munro became impassioned: "The moment evaporates, or the insight leads to something else. That's what I meant when I said flippantly that [the apparent epiphanies are] wrong" (Munro, "Interview" 292). The essential rhythm of "Fits" is an unarticulated epiphany followed by a negated one and then back again. What Peg actually sees at the top of the stairs becomes a crucial element of inference (the constable's report, Robert's juggling of details and possibilities), but the moment of perception itself, the meeting of the Weebles' bodies with Peg's eyes, and its route through her are buried, sealed off in a typographical white space, the largest blank in Munro's writing. At the technical end of the story, when Robert walks away from the house, a double of the neighboring, empty house, he becomes aware of a "congestion of shapes" that, neither simile nor metaphor, "did not look like anything he knew" until, repeating Peg's earlier motion, "he got very close" (Munro, *Progress* 124). The old wrecks of cars and trucks abandoned in the snow prompt a "moment of insight": "He thought of himself telling Peg about this—how close he had to get. . . . They needed some new thing to talk about. Now he felt more like going home" (125). But his realization is a delusion; if what he perceives is an epiphany, it is immediately negated, in a sense buried by the earlier encapsulation of what Peg sees in a white space. "Some new thing to talk about" is, like Peg's inner and probably fractured self, unavailable. Robert will give her a passionate, innocent description; Peg will give him a fact or a lie, either one through her "quick transactional smile" (103).

Not all the stories in *The Progress of Love* have such radical and upending conclusions, where stasis meets negation. "Lichen," "Miles City, Montana," "The Moon in the Orange Street Skating Rink," and "Circle of Prayer" end with luminous, even transcendent moments that are shapes for Munro's generous sense of how people can break through the encroachments of mortality on the self and the power others attempt to exert in their evasions of that mortality. The sentences in "Moon"—"They were just laughing. They were happy. They were free" (*Progress* 153)—reflect the core of this kind of ending: open, often lyrical, and densely nuanced. But like her chronologies, there is a restlessness about the rhythms of Munro's years of work. She moves on, very often in deeply surprising directions. In his celebration of her freedom from formal constraints, Richard Ford says nothing directly about punctuation, but in Munro's world, where categories never hold—happiness and unhappiness, accident and purpose, fact and fiction—parentheses may be anything but conventionally parenthetical, something explanatory, an afterthought. Often Munro makes parentheses work in their ordinary, subordinate way; even more often she does not. An analogy for this particular kind of literary subversiveness may be the rampant, maddening proliferation of parentheses in William Faulkner's *Absalom, Absalom!*, which is also a book about the elusiveness of what we know and the deep presence of what we do not know.

However, Munro is drawn to mystery, not to mystification. Brief as it is, the parenthesis in "The Moon in the Orange Street Skating Rink"— "(Maybe Edgar, in particular, felt this)" (*Progress* 148)—is at once an embracing of human possibility and an unobtrusive upending of convention. In its layered parentheses, the conclusion of "White Dump," the final story, has a more diffuse power, extending forward into that "somewhere" Munro likes to think her stories continue, and backward to the more intact endings of "The Progress of Love," "Lichen," and "Miles City, Montana." The first parenthesis, a page long, is the memory of the start of the affair that, we learned earlier, split the family apart. But what we see here is the essential privacy of Isabel's response to the pilot. It seems to have nothing to do with her husband or her children, but rather is an extension of her own childhood: "She felt rescued, lifted, beheld, and safe" (298), a sentence where the last word, an adjective, is virtually created by the preceding verbs. Isabel is free; yet her "ending" is a prologue or a companion to another parenthesis, a terse sentence full of voices that resonates with the power of fate and determinism. Unread and unreadable to her husband and children, she reads—that is, watches—the indecipherable Old Norse words in a book left by her medievalist mother-in-law. The narrator, utterly separate and sealed off from Isabel, merges with a previously absent translator of the passage: "(It is too late to talk of this now: it has been decided)" (299).

Every element of this quiet, bleak ending—the generation of voices, the paradoxical doubling, the weaving of perception and blankness—is a mark of that incomparable imaginative freedom this essay has followed. It is presumptuous and crude to seek an explanation of that freedom. But I will put forward a striking repetition, not as anything clinical, but because, using an element of Munro's unaggressive aesthetic, it is "interesting." In an interview after she had published her second book, Munro said that writing "has something to do with the fight against death, the feeling that we lose everything every day, and writing is a way of convincing yourself perhaps that you're doing something about this. You're not really, because the writing itself does not last much longer than you do" (Gibson 243). Thirty-six years later, in "Too Much Happiness," Munro gives Sophia many of the same words about her mentor, as she too wonders whether "his life" of achievement is "so much more satisfactory to contemplate than his sisters'" (*Too Much* 281). "The writing itself does not last much longer than you do," Alice Munro said—but now, look, just this once, her words have not come true.

Works Cited

Aristotle. *On the Art of Poetry*. Trans. Ingram Bywater. *Project Gutenberg*. Project Gutenberg Lit. Archive Foundation, 1 Oct. 2004. Web. 27 Jan. 2012.

Ford, Richard. Introduction. Munro, *Progress* ix–xvi.

Gibson, Graeme. *Eleven Canadian Novelists*. Toronto: Anansi, 1973.

Heath, Malcolm. Introduction. *Poetics*. By Aristotle. Trans. Heath. London: Penguin, 1996. vii–lxvi.

Howe, Irving. *Decline of the New*. New York: Horizon, 1970.

Howells, Coral Ann. *Alice Munro*. Manchester: Manchester UP, 1998.

Kofman, Sarah, and Duncan Large. *Nietzsche and Metaphor*. Palo Alto, CA: Stanford UP, 1994.

Levene, Mark. "'It Was about Vanishing': A Glimpse of Alice Munro's Stories." *University of Toronto Quarterly* 68.4 (1999): 841–60.

Munro, Alice. "An Interview with Alice Munro." By Eleanor Wachtel. *The Brick Reader*. Ed. Linda Spalding and Michael Ondaatje. Toronto: Coach House, 1991. 288–94.

_____. *Lives of Girls and Women*. Toronto: Penguin, 2009.

_____. *The Progress of Love*. Toronto: Penguin, 2006.

_____. *Something I've Been Meaning to Tell You*. Harmondsworth, Eng.: Penguin, 1990.

_____. *Too Much Happiness*. Toronto: McClelland, 2009.

_____. "What Is Real?" *The Art of Short Fiction: An International Anthology*. Ed. Gary Geddes. Toronto: HarperCollins, 1993. 824–26.

Romano, Carlin. "What's a Metaphor For?" *Chronicle Review*. Chronicle of Higher Education, 3 July 2011. Web. 20 Jan. 2012.

Friend of My Youth: Alice Munro and the Power of Narrativity _____

Philip Coleman

The relationship between short-story theory and the practice of writing short stories has always been strong. Since Edgar Allan Poe first posited his theories in relation to both his own work and the stories of Nathaniel Hawthorne in the 1830s, many short-story writers—from Poe to Henry James, Ernest Hemingway, Frank O'Connor, Raymond Carver, and David Foster Wallace—have also been at the vanguard of short-story theory and criticism, offering important insights into the aesthetic and epistemological decisions and strategies that combine to make this particular form of narrative art one of the most popular and compelling, at least to authors.

In a rare comment on the art of writing short stories, Alice Munro has said, "Writing or talking about writing makes me superstitiously uncomfortable. My explanations have a way of turning treacherous, half-untrue" ("Colonel's" 191). Unlike some of her closest contemporaries, Munro has been curiously reticent about the explicit mechanics of short-story writing. Apart from comments in interviews and occasional pieces of nonfiction, she has not published collections of essays of the kind that Wallace and Jonathan Franzen have undertaken, for example. It is fair to say that in terms of her pure dedication to the art of the short story, she is almost unparalleled in modern literature; of her published works to date, only one, *Lives of Girls and Women* (1971), was published as a novel, and even that may be read as a collection of interconnected stories. Nonetheless, Munro's works of short fiction often contain important reflections on the nature of narrative and the process of what Susan Lohafer has called "storying" (300). The self-reflexive activity of using short stories to think about the existential and emotional importance of narrative in human life allows Munro to be read as a writer whose work embodies an impulse toward critical and theoretical agency; her work, for all of its primary motivation toward storytelling, also tends toward reflection on the nature of the art itself at its deepest level. This is not to say that she engages in the same kind of metafictional play that characterizes the work of writers such as John Barth, Robert Coover, or Donald Barthelme, but rather that her stories frequently remind readers of the profound place that stories have in the formation of different kinds of personal and public identity. As Lohafer puts it, "Storying is a way of processing experience in the interests of human well-being" (310).

In Munro's seventh book, *Friend of My Youth* (1990), the activity or process of storying is manifest in both the manner of her artistry—that is, the way in which she handles the short-story form—and the ways that the characters in the book's strongest stories, most notably the title story, make sense of themselves and the lives of those around them. Some of the earliest essays and reviews on the book focused on its explorations of feminist themes and issues, prompting Barbara J. Eckstein to comment, "Whether or not Munro's reader thinks of the stories here or any of her short fiction as feminist depends upon the friends of that reader's youth" (639). The stories of *Friend of My Youth* have been usefully interpreted in relation to the discourses of theoretical feminism articulated by theorists such as Hélène Cixous, Luce Irigaray, and Julia Kristeva, and critics such as Ailsa Cox, Gayle Elliott, and Pam Houston have drawn attention to the ways in which Munro's work participates in the construction and interrogation of female identity. For example, in an essay that Elliott has aligned with the work of Cixous and Irigaray (Elliott 76), Houston argues that the stories in this collection display radically different understandings of male and female narrativity, while Cox offers a compelling reading of Munro's work from a Kristevan perspective, focusing on its depictions of what "Kristeva identifies [as] the subversive potential of the abject in literature" (Cox 92).

Despite the persuasiveness of these readings, however, Cox's claim that "there has never been a writer who relished the diversity of language as much as Alice Munro" (97) does not need to be read solely in relation to feminist critical theory. Indeed, because storying is always a function of language, Munro's relishing of language may also be related to her belief in the importance of stories in themselves, which transcends or subsumes her interest in sexual or any other kind of politics. While the experience of being Canadian is central to her work, for example, Munro could hardly be described as a writer for whom the question of Canadian identity is a subject of major ideological concern. While many of the stories in *Friend of My Youth* are narrated by women and appear to be concerned with themes that touch on issues related to female sexual experience in very important ways, an interest in the general human significance of stories and storytelling—for men as much as for women, irrespective of social class or background—is also present throughout the collection and, indeed, across the entire range of Munro's oeuvre. Jonathan Franzen has suggested that her work "strives for and achieves, in each of her stories, a gestaltlike completeness in the representation of a life" (xi). He has also argued, "Her subject is people. People people people" (vi). One could press this a bit further and say that Munro's subject is people, both women and men, and how they relate to each other, how they become themselves and are disclosed to each other through stories. As the novelist Michael Cunningham has written, "Alice Munro tells the large stories of people whose lives are outwardly small. . . . I don't know a writer better able to chart the intricacies of human beings, the incredible complexity and ambiguity of emotions" (91–92).

The stories of *Friend of My Youth* may then be said to demonstrate a pervasive and general concern for the nature of narrative and its profound importance to understanding human subjectivity. Indeed, they call to mind the philosopher Richard Kearney's claim that, "whether as story or history or a mixture of both (for example testimony), the power of narrativity makes a crucial difference to our lives." Moreover, Kearney's contention that "the unnarrated life is not worth living" (14) may be seen to pertain to the narrators and characters of many of Munro's short fictions, figures for whom the prospect of life being known at all is rarely if ever possible beyond the structures and forms of narrative formulation and projection. Despite what some critics have seen as an ostensible focus on the experience of gender, what Kearney terms the "power of narrativity" encloses many kinds of stories for Munro—male and female, individual and communal, erotic and political, local and international—and since the start of her career, her work has been marked by an ability to move smoothly between different real and imagined historical and social contexts. Her work may be focused to a large extent on a clearly discernible Canadian backdrop; as Coral Ann Howells puts it, "Munro's fictions are set mainly in her home territory, the rural communities and small towns of southwestern Ontario, in that quietly rolling countryside, 'back where nothing seems to be happening, beyond the change of seasons'" (200). At the same time, though, her stories aspire to a condition of universality in their recognition of the fact that people everywhere are driven by the same fundamental desire to understand the ways in which their lives are formed and reformed through narrative, as her story "Goodness and Mercy" demonstrates.

"Goodness and Mercy" is one of three stories in *Friend of My Youth* set outside of southern Ontario; its central drama is staged upon a ship in the Atlantic Ocean, while "Hold Me Fast, Don't Let Me Pass" is set in Scotland and "Differently" takes place in the Canadian city of Victoria, the capital of British Columbia. In the opening paragraph of "Goodness and Mercy," the ship is described as "passing through the Strait of Belle Isle, on its third day out from Montreal" (Munro, *Friend* 156). This setting provides a large-scale backdrop for the human dramas staged in the story between the young woman Averill and her mother, June "Bugs" Rogers, and also between Averill and the ship's captain. Averill has agreed to take her terminally ill mother on a transatlantic voyage, but during the voyage, Averill strikes up a relationship with a number of other people on board, including the captain. At one point, the narrator says, in parentheses, that she "often told herself stories—the activity seemed to her as unavoidable as dreaming" (169); the thought is bracketed off to reinforce the idea that it refers to some deep and secret part of Averill's being. Equally, it is through the telling and retelling of stories that Averill's life and the lives of those around her acquire meaning, and that meaning is constantly subject to narrative renegotiation:

> The captain had told [the story of a woman buried at sea] as if the mother and daughter [in the story] were sisters and he had transported the boat to the South Atlantic and he had left off the finale—as well as supplying various details of his own—but Averill believed that it was her story he had told. It was the story that she had been telling herself night after night on the deck, her perfectly secret story, delivered back to her. She had made it, and he had taken it and told it, safely.
>
> Believing that such a thing could happen made her feel weightless and distinct and glowing, like a fish lit up in the water. (178)

The poetry of Munro's prose here—the brilliant and suggestive clarity of the fish simile following the adjectives *weightless, distinct,* and *glowing*—augments the sense of mystery that always accompanies the idea of the story in her fiction. Her stories, or the stories told within her stories, are rarely if ever purely factual, even if they appear to contain many details that afford them a degree of contextual specificity, such as place names, dates, or references to historic events or personalities. Rather, as in this passage from "Goodness and Mercy," Munro is ultimately concerned with exploring and exposing the ways in which one person's story can become another's through acts of imaginative engagement in the process of storying. The "power of narrativity" allows strangers to connect, even in the most unfamiliar of circumstances, and it brings people such as Averill into a new and heightened state of self-understanding. The story Averill has assumed is the story of her life becomes most profoundly her own when it is told back to her by a stranger.

Friend of My Youth, a collection of ten stories, takes its title from the opening story. The phrase "Friend of My Youth" resonates with broad cultural significance in its allusions to Jeremiah 3.4 ("Wilt thou not from this time cry unto me, My father, thou art the guide of my youth" in the King James version), Charles W. Chesnutt's haunting and important short story "The Wife of His Youth" (1899), and section 7 ("The Friends of His Youth") of W. B. Yeats's poem "A Man Young and Old" (1928). The titular story, perfectly placed as the opening story of the collection, is important, not just because it gives the collection its title, but also because it introduces some of the key themes explored in more detail throughout the other nine stories—especially the theme of the power of stories and storying in human relationships and the pursuit of self-knowledge through memory and recollection. On one level a story about a woman's relationship with her mother, "Friend of My Youth" is also about the relationship between an individual and the various communities through which her identity is formed. The story is concerned in a very explicit way with Canadian history; its final section (it is divided, like many of Munro's stories, into several unnumbered sections) takes the form of an extended note on the Presbyterian sect called the Cameronians, a "freak religion from Scotland" (Munro, *Friend* 5), but the supposedly factual details revealed about the sect contrast with the narrator's earlier admission that her view of her mother, and her mother's view of her, is based on stories that might ultimately be made of the same stuff as dreams, mere notions and ideas. Note in the following passage the movement from statements of apparent historical fact, as suggested by the use of proper nouns, toward the more open-ended kind of fictive narration with which the story concludes:

The Cameronians, I have discovered, are or were an uncompromising remnant of the Covenanters—those Scots who in the seventeenth century bound themselves, with God, to resist prayer books, bishops, any taint of popery or interference by the King. Their name comes from Richard Cameron, an outlawed, or "field," preacher, soon cut down. The Cameronians—for a long time they have preferred to be called the Reformed Presbyterians—went into battle singing the seventy-fourth and the seventy-eighth Psalms. They hacked the haughty Bishop of St. Andrews to death on the highway and rode their horses over his body. One of the ministers, in a mood of firm rejoicing at his own hanging, excommunicated all the other preachers in the world. (26)

The passage begins in the voice of a researcher who has made an important scholarly discovery, but within a few sentences objective historical detail gives way to legend and the marvelously Hawthornian closing image of the minister who excommunicates "all the other preachers in the world" at the moment of his own execution. Indeed, if Hawthorne is alluded to in this passage—and Arthur Dimmesdale and John Endicott usually lurk somewhere in the background whenever religious separatism or extremism is discussed in North American culture—it also relates to Munro's play on the relationship between romance and realism throughout her fiction, the modes between which her nineteenth-century American precursor's work is at times very delicately poised. As Henry James put it, "The fine thing in Hawthorne is that he cared for the deeper psychology, and that, in his way, he tried to become familiar with it" (63).

Munro's interest in "the deeper psychology" has been read by Ailsa Cox in relation to Julia Kristeva's theories of intertextuality, specifically in terms of what Kristeva calls the interplay between the "symbolic" world of texts and signs and the underlying "semiotic chora" of subjective experience (Cox 89–90). The dialectical relationship between dreams and reality, and the author's movement between the poles of narrative possibility represented by romance and realism, is also suggested at several points in "Friend of My Youth" through the voice of the narrator, who is also a writer. The story is framed through dreams, a gesture that perhaps reveals Munro's indebtedness not just to Hawthorne but also to the poetry of Yeats, for whom dreams and other forms of visionary experience were of profound and lasting importance. But "Friend of My Youth" also contains a description of a writer arranging and rearranging the different elements of her story and the stories of those around her. Centrally, her mother's experience with a woman named Flora, whose story is in fact at the heart of "Friend of

My Youth," is retold so that the writer-narrator can tell her own, imagined version of events:

> I had my own ideas about Flora's story. I didn't think that I could have written a novel but that I would write one. I would take a different tack. I saw through my mother's story and put in what she left out. My Flora would be as black as hers was white. Rejoicing in the bad turns done to her and in her own forgiveness, spying on the shambles of her sister's life. A Presbyterian witch, reading out of her poisonous book. It takes a rival ruthlessness, the comparatively innocent brutality of the thick-skinned nurse, to drive her back, to flourish in her shade. But she is driven back; the power of sex and ordinary greed drive her back and shut her up in her own part of the house with the coal-oil lamps. She shrinks, she caves in, her bones harden and her joints thicken, and—oh, this is it, this is it, I see the bare beauty of the ending I will contrive!—she becomes crippled herself, with arthritis, hardly able to move. (Munro, *Friend* 20–21)

This remarkable passage is not only central to the development of the story's core meaning, which has to do with the ultimate impossibility of representing one's own life due to the distortions of memory, but also revealing in the way that it describes the action of writing in relation to experience, how literature makes and indeed remakes the self. As Yeats put it:

> Myself I must remake
> Till I am Timon and Lear
> Or that William Blake
> Who beat upon the wall
> Till Truth obeyed his call; (347)

Tellingly, at an earlier stage in "Friend of My Youth," the narrator describes how "the truth" of her story "somehow" eventually "came out" (Munro, *Friend* 10).

If "Truth" may ultimately be said to obey the narrator's call in "Friend of My Youth," then, it comes out in a radically reconstructed and therefore highly subjective form. In the passage quoted, the narrator's "own ideas" and "different tack" lead to the creation of a "Presbyterian witch" with a "poisonous book," but that book sustains the growth of the imagination and allows characters from another time—indeed, from her mother's childhood—to persist in memory. Without the narrator's retelling of the stories of Flora, her sister Ellie, and Robert, they might well have been forgotten, but she keeps them alive in works of fiction. While "the power of sex and ordinary greed" are essential elements to her narrative re-conjuring of their lives, as they are in most of Munro's stories, it is the power of narrativity itself that makes them larger than life and sustains them within the realm of art, where closure is presented in terms of the "bare beauty" of a novel's contrived formal ending. In this story and throughout *Friend of My Youth*, however, the power of narrativity exceeds the formal or structural limits of the printed text on the page: Flora "becomes crippled" as a character in a story, but the new life she is given in fiction haunts the narrator as "a phantom—something useless and uncalled for, like a phantom pregnancy" (Munro, *Friend* 26). This image is used in the story in relation to the narrator's mother—how she helped her, in dreams, to come to terms with her past and her background and to show her "options and powers [she] never dreamed she had" (26)—but it also describes the way that the narrator uses stories to arrange and understand her experience, to comprehend her life as separate from, but deeply involved in, the lives of those who have gone before her, right back to her Scottish ancestors.

It is tempting to read such instances of spectral imagery in Munro's fiction in relation to what Andy Belyea has presented as her "Gothic Realism." As he argues in his detailed study, the narrator's difficult relationship with her mother in "Friend of My Youth" may be read in relation to a long line of gothic works such as those explored by Juliann Fleenor and others in their studies of the gothic in Canadian fiction

(24). It is important, however, to stress the worldly aspects of Munro's fiction, and to realize that her imaginative projections into the realm of the gothic are still very much rooted in her observations of the real world. Her characters use stories to understand the worlds they live in, which is one of the reasons why Lohafer's idea of storying "as a way of processing experience in the interests of human well-being" (310) is so useful in relation to Munro. The image of Flora's "poisonous book" in "Friend of My Youth" is but one of several book images through-out this collection, and this is central to Munro's interest in the ways that individuals look for traces of truth in the worlds of fiction and art. Again and again—in "Goodness and Mercy," for example, as well as in "Oranges and Apples," where a character's reading of "heavy books" appears to make her "gr[o]w heavier herself" (*Friend* 112)—Munro's characters turn to books and texts to make sense of themselves and the worlds in which they live. Indeed, Munro makes another clear allu-sion to Hawthorne, this time to his tale "The Minister's Black Veil," in her description of the same character in "Oranges and Apples," whose hair has turned white "as if a piece of veiling had been thrown over it" (112). The point here, however, is that Munro herself writes stories that are often clearly written, if not over earlier narratives, then along the margins of narratives by Hawthorne and others.

Moreover, at a deeper level, her characters are also often presented as figures who strive to find some truth about their own lives in the things they have read, from the stories of their youth to snippets of poems and songs recollected from childhood. As Munro writes of a character in "Oh, What Avails," the title of which is taken from English Romantic writer Walter Savage Landor's poem "Rose Aylmer" (1806), "She knows a lot of poetry, from school or somewhere. She will fix a couple of lines on somebody, summing them up in an absurd and unforgettable way. She looks out the window and says a bit of poetry and they know who has gone by" (*Friend* 183). Munro's characters, consequently, use existing stories—often found in poetry and song, of-ten misremembered and recast in new forms—to tell their own stories.

Indeed, they frequently wonder whether their stories matter—whether, as the narrator asks of Murray in "Oranges and Apples," one's story "deserve[s] to be called a classic" (109). Beyond the mere telling and retelling of stories, in other words, Munro's fiction also challenges readers to think about what makes stories last, what elements make them worth revisiting and retelling by future generations.

The process of reading the world through textual evidence is very much a part of "Meneseteung" also, the third story in *Friend of My Youth*. Each of its six sections begins with a verse epigraph taken from the work of a fictional nineteenth-century poet named Almeda Joynt Roth, referred to in the narrator's local newspaper as "our poetess" (Munro, *Friend* 51). It is worth pointing out that the story's title refers to the First Nations name for the Maitland River, near which Munro grew up in Huron County, southwestern Ontario. Everything, then, from the author's sense of place to the imaginative creation of a fictional character, involves processes of reading and rereading, storying the world and the self into the new realities forged by Munro's short fiction. "Meneseteung" is particularly interesting in this regard because it imagines both a fictional writer and her work, therefore transporting the reader into a world beyond the most immediate Ontario locale of Munro's story, the world of Almeda Joynt Roth's imagination. This kind of narrative layering and imaginative framing is a common strategy in Munro's fiction, one she shares with her modernist progenitors James Joyce and Virginia Woolf. However, in her hands, it serves to reinforce the idea of life as a narrated phenomenon, to paraphrase Richard Kearney. Both Munro and her characters participate in active and continuous processes of narrative framing and reframing that allow them to resist the stultifying strictures by which life, and art, might be frozen into states of absolute paralysis. In "Meneseteung," a clear contrast is established between the world as it is created in imaginative writing (in Almeda's poems, crucially) and the claims to truth and factuality made in the reports of "the local paper, the *Vidette*" that are scattered throughout the text (50). Lacking the structural authority or mystery of the poetic epigraphs, these italicized sections, which are said to "[run] on, copious and assured," make a claim to understanding the life of the poetess; in the context of Munro's short story, however, the assured tone of the journalistic report is undercut by the more precise crafting of, and questing after, meaning that lies at the heart of poetic creation. The complexity of this process, of trying to represent the world in writing as an act of cognitive, cultural, and social awareness, is laid bare in a description of the composition of a poem called "The Meneseteung":

> [Almeda] has to think of so many things at once—Champlain and the naked Indians and the salt deep in the earth, but as well as the salt the money, the money-making intent brewing forever in heads like Jarvis Poulter's. Also the brutal storms of winter and the clumsy and benighted deeds on Pearl Street. The changes of climate are often violent, and if you think about it there is no peace even in the stars. All this can be borne only if it is channelled into a poem, and the word "channelled" is appropriate, because the name of the poem will be—it *is*—"The Meneseteung." The name of the poem is the name of the river. No, in fact it is the river, the Meneseteung, that is the poem—with its deep holes and rapids and blissful pools under the summer trees and its grinding blocks of ice thrown up at the end of winter and its desolating spring floods. Almeda looks deep, deep into the river of her mind and into the tablecloth, and she sees the crocheted roses floating. They look bunchy and foolish, her mother's crocheted roses—they don't look much like real flowers. But their effort, their floating independence, their pleasure in their silly selves do seem to her so admirable. A hopeful sign. *Meneseteung.* (70)

This is a brilliant description of the difficulty of artistic creation and poetic composition—the "fascination of what's difficult," as Yeats described it in a poem of the same title (104). It describes the numerous sources that feed into the work of art to suggest that art's origins are manifold, ranging from observations of one's immediate physical and social-geographical environment to the sense one might have of what is going on inside the head of another person ("the money-making intent brewing forever in heads like Jarvis Poulter's"). The passage presents the writing of literature as a form of (self-)knowledge that aims at a deeper understanding, not just of the self who creates (the author), but also of her subjects; it is directed toward an unearthing of truths that journalistic writing cannot even begin to approach in its "copious and assured" cataloguing of mere facts.

Through writing, then, Almeda keeps a firm hold on reality, even at its most tumultuous moments, and throughout *Friend of My Youth*, Munro celebrates the power of narrativity—that is, stories in themselves and the processes of storying—in the creation and representation of self and world. In the story "Differently," the character Georgia is a short-story writer: "Georgia once took a creative-writing course, and what the instructor told her was: Too many things. Too many things going on at the same time; also too many people. Think, he told her. What is the important thing? What do you want us to pay attention to? Think" (Munro, *Friend* 216). Later in the story, Georgia's husband, Ben, reads to her from James Joyce's *Dubliners* (1914), one of the most significant collections of short stories published in the twentieth century and the work in which Joyce famously explores the theme of paralysis. Later in "Differently," it is no surprise, given the reference to *Dubliners* earlier in the text, that Georgia describes her intense heartbreak after the end of an affair as "*a paralysis of grief*" (237; italics in orig.), but the Joycean reference is more than just an echo of Munro's master's voice. The allusion to Joyce, together with the allusions to figures ranging from Landor to Yeats in other stories throughout *Friend of My Youth*, confirms Munro's sense of the way that people use literature, and stories in particular, to make sense of their lives. Moreover, it reveals the dynamic process by which lives *mean*, no matter how paralyzed or contained individual characters might appear to be. In the same way that the characters in Joyce's stories from "The Sisters" to "The Dead" all participate in the life of the city, and by extension the nation, so do Munro's characters, for all of their apparent isolation and containment within the provincial backwater towns and villages of southwest Ontario, represent a broad cross section of human life that is described in the stories of *Friend of My Youth* in profoundly moving detail. Whatever critical lens might be applied to them, from the feminist readings of critics such as Cox and Houston to the postcolonial and eco-critical appropriations of Rowland Smith and Faye Hammill, Alice Munro's stories resist critical and theoretical reduction precisely because they affirm, above all else, the primacy of stories and the place of the storyteller in human existence.

For Jonathan Franzen, Munro is a writer who, like Joyce, has "always had a genius for developing and unpacking moments of epiphany" (xi). Seen by Belyea as a volume that marked an important change of direction in Munro's career as a writer—he describes it as "the first of Munro's collections to concentrate on such issues as marriage, infidelity, divorce, lost friendships, broken families, grave illnesses, and death" (99)—*Friend of My Youth* also affirms Munro's career-long belief in "the power of narrativity." Writing in 1936, Walter Benjamin suggested, "Familiar though his name may be to us, the storyteller in his living immediacy is by no means a present force. He has already become something remote from us and something that is getting even more distant" (83). Alice Munro was born in the same decade in which Benjamin made this claim. Her short fiction does not just affirm the profoundly important place of the storyteller in the contemporary world, however; it also reveals the pervasiveness of stories and the processes of storying in all areas of subjective and intersubjective experience. A reading of *Friend of My Youth* is necessary for a full understanding of the shape of Munro's career, as its stories show her to be one of the most important writers of recent decades to explore the nature and meaning of narrative agency and its power in all aspects of human life.

Works Cited

Belyea, Andy. "Redefining the Real: Gothic Realism in Alice Munro's *Friend of My Youth*." Diss. Queen's U, 1998. Web. 27 Jan. 2012.

Benjamin, Walter. *Illuminations*. Ed. Hannah Arendt. Trans. Harry Zorn. London: Pimlico, 1999.

Cox, Ailsa. *Alice Munro*. Tavistock, Eng.: Northcote, 2004.

Cunningham, Michael, et al. "Appreciations of Alice Munro." Ed. Lisa Dickler Awano. *Virginia Quarterly Review* 82.3 (2006): 91–107.

Eckstein, Barbara J. Rev. of *Friend of My Youth*, by Alice Munro. *World Literature Today* 64.4 (1990): 639.

Elliott, Gayle. "'A Different Tack': Feminist Meta-Narrative in Alice Munro's 'Friend of My Youth.'" *Journal of Modern Literature* 20.1 (1996): 75–84.

Franzen, Jonathan. "What Makes You So Sure You're Not the Evil One Yourself?" Introduction. *Runaway*. By Alice Munro. London: Vintage, 2006. i–xvi.

Hammill, Faye. *Canadian Literature*. Edinburgh: Edinburgh UP, 2007.

The Holy Bible. Cambridge: Parker, 1844.

Houston, Pam. "A Hopeful Sign: The Making of Metonymic Meaning in Munro's 'Meneseteung.'" *Kenyon Review* 14.4 (1992): 79–92.

Howells, Coral Ann. "Writing by Women." *The Cambridge Companion to Canadian Literature*. Ed. Eva-Marie Kröller. Cambridge: Cambridge UP, 2004. 194–215.

James, Henry. *Hawthorne*. New York: Harper, 1879.

Kearney, Richard. *On Stories*. London: Routledge, 2002.

Lohafer, Susan. "A Cognitive Approach to Storyness." *The New Short Story Theories*. Ed. Charles E. May. Athens: Ohio UP, 1994. 301–11.

Munro, Alice. "The Colonel's Hash Resettled." *How Stories Mean*. Ed. John Metcalf and J. R. (Tim) Struthers. Erin, ON: Porcupine's Quill, 1993. 189–91.

_____. *Friend of My Youth*. London: Vintage, 1996.

Smith, Rowland. "Rewriting the Frontier: Wilderness and Social Code in the Fiction of Alice Munro." *Telling Stories: Postcolonial Short Fiction in English*. Ed. André Viola and Jean-Pierre Durix. Amsterdam: Rodopi, 2001. 77–90.

Yeats, W. B. *Collected Poems*. London: Picador, 1990.

In Search of the Perfect Metaphor:
The Language of the Short Story and
Alice Munro's "Meneseteung"

J. R. (Tim) Struthers

> And this kaleidoscope uniting all,
> this tube, this conduit optical,
> this lens
> is magic. Through it—see
> (who dares?)
> the perfect, all-inclusive metaphor.
> (P. K. Page, "Kaleidoscope")

Words and phrases in Ojibway, according to renowned ethnologist and mythographer Basil H. Johnston, have three levels of meaning: first, "the surface meaning," which is denotative or literal; second, a more intricate, more fundamental level created by adding prefixes to other terms; and third, "the philosophical meaning," which is deeper still ("Is That All" 349). Consider Johnston's example of the term *Anishinaubae*, the original, aboriginal name for the nation now known in English as Chippewa in the United States and Ojibway in Canada. The word means, first, a member or members of that nation. More generally, the term combines the adjective and noun *Onishishi* and *naubae*, meaning "good, fine, beautiful, excellent" and "being, male, human species," respectively; that is, *Anishinaubae* stands as an answer to the question "What are you?": "I am a person of good intent, a person of worth" (349). Taken a little further, Johnston adds, the word suggests how his people view both themselves and all of human nature as good.

Finally, there is the philosophical level to which a nation's stories, both ancient and modern, so significantly contribute—stories including those by Basil H. Johnston, beginning with what I would term his "myth cycle," *Ojibway Heritage* (1976), and those by Alice Munro, beginning with her story collection *Dance of the Happy Shades* (1968).

On this third level, Johnston explains, the word *Anishinaubae* calls to mind Ojibway stories about Nanabush, "the tribe's central and principal mythical figure who represents all men and all women" and who "was always full of good intentions" ("Is That All" 349). Further, Johnston comments, the word *Anishinaubae* expresses "a strong sense of pride as well as a firm sense of place in the community" (349), a feeling that, he stresses, derives in no small part from his people's stories.

In sum, then, as Johnston passionately and convincingly argues elsewhere, language, literature, and culture must be taught or understood or appreciated together ("How Do We Learn"). And just as this is the case for Ojibway, so too is it for literary language in English—and, most emphatically, so it is for the language of the short story. It is a language that, by drawing on the ideas presented by Canadian literary theorist Northrop Frye in works like *The Great Code* (1981) and its companion *Words with Power* (1990), by American short-story theorist Charles E. May in essays like "Metaphoric Motivation in Short Fiction: 'In the Beginning Was the Story,'" and by Canadian critic James Carscallen in *The Other Country: Patterns in the Writing of Alice Munro* (1993), I would describe as the language of metaphor. Or, to state this in a way that comes closer to identifying the diverse riches of Munro, the language of metaphor, of allusion, of puns and portmanteau words, of allegory, of myth.

I believe that as readers, we can discover in Johnston's observations about understanding Ojibway language, literature, and culture a highly useful analogy for comprehending the magnificent verbal textures in Alice Munro's writing. Foremost amongst the possible examples with which to begin (or end) such an analysis is Munro's very deservedly acclaimed story "Meneseteung" from her book *Friend of My Youth* (1990), a story that focuses on a fictional nineteenth-century southwestern Ontario poetess named Almeda Joynt Roth. Not surprisingly, however, many aspects of Munro's mature deployment of language, narrativity, and form are strikingly evident even in the work that launched her career, *Dance of the Happy Shades*—like James Joyce's

Dubliners (1914), a collection of fifteen stories. Possibly the most impressive amongst these first collected stories are the works she placed first and third in this introductory volume: "Walker Brothers Cowboy," her mesmerizing North American creation myth—or, as I have termed it, genesis story (Struthers, "Alice Munro" 296)—and the powerfully haunting "Images."

We experience these sophisticated qualities of language, narrativity, and form a little later, and to a degree previously unfelt in Munro's oeuvre, in "Royal Beatings," a self-described "*big* breakthrough story" artistically for the author, "a kind of story that I didn't intend to write at all" (Munro, "Real Material" 21; italics in orig.). For good reason, therefore, it was the first of now a very long list of stories that Munro has published in the *New Yorker*. Subsequently published as the opening piece in the story cycle issued in Canada under the title *Who Do You Think You Are?* (1978) and in the United States and Great Britain as *The Beggar Maid: Stories of Flo and Rose* (1979), "Royal Beatings" interweaves two seemingly different but actually eerily parallel, not to mention decidedly violent, narratives. The first involves the historically based[1] but gothic-like tale of the town butcher, Old Man Tyde, a widower who reputedly beats his entire family and molests his dwarfish and polio-stricken daughter, Becky Tyde, resulting in his being dragged from his house one night and beaten virtually to death by local youths. The second involves the more subtle, everyday-like, and contemporary—and therefore much more disturbing—tale of the sexually charged, evidently recurring, apparently mutually gratifying strapping of the story's preadolescent protagonist, Rose, by her own generally admirable father.

We experience still further advances on these bold, layered, beautiful textures in any story you might choose from *The Progress of Love* (1986), the volume that I believe stands as Munro's big breakthrough story collection. To cite just one example, though an astonishing one, consider the shocking but illuminating ending to "A Queer Streak." Here, in the concluding exchange between the dementia-diminished and therefore "queer" (in the idiomatic sense of "not right in the head") main character, Violet Thoms, and her "queer" (in the sense of gay) nephew, Dane, we hear Violet utter the wholly incomprehensible, thoroughly terrifying noise "*Annhh.*" Then we hear her make a declaration that eventually registers for us with great clarity and significance, but which initially seems like complete madness, thereby proving to be even more horrifying later than at first: "There is a wild pig running through the corn" (Munro, *Progress* 253)—a remark that, once we realize it is pure metaphor, functions as a poetic revelation allowing us to look back on the story and interpret anew the very complex, dark, and sexually fraught web of family relationships portrayed therein.

We continue to experience Munro's astonishing textures of language and narrativity and form, I would argue, in every story she has published over the now quarter-century since the release of her masterly collection *The Progress of Love*. This is most formidably and therefore most satisfyingly the case, I believe, and will presently illustrate, in "Meneseteung," the only Canadian work honored by being selected for (as a Canadian, I cannot resist saying) the not-quite-accurately titled *The Best American Short Stories of the Century* (1999), edited by John Updike and Katrina Kenison.

I

Literary language is far more complex than we might assume at first, even with considerable formal education. In his essay "The Four Master Tropes," collected in his book *A Grammar of Motives* (1945), American literary theorist Kenneth Burke identifies the following four figures of speech as keys to understanding the operation of language in literature: *metaphor*, in which a person, place, or thing stands for another; *metonymy*, in which the subject or object identified is some kind of replacement for, or displacement of, something else; *synecdoche*, typically used to suggest times when a part is substituted for the whole, as we do in discussing one story as illustrative of a writer's entire oeuvre; and lastly, *irony*. Later, American theorist of history

Hayden White, in his book *Metahistory: The Historical Imagination in Nineteenth-Century Europe* (1973), adapted these four terms to suggest four types and phases of the writing of history. Very interestingly, White notes that when the last of these, irony, so prevalent in the postmodern era, is itself subjected to irony, we find ourselves coming around again to metaphor.

Subsequent to these seminal works by Burke and White, Canadian literary theorist Northrop Frye set forth in the opening chapter of *The Great Code* his own set of four kinds of language and four corresponding ways of thinking: *description*, the literal level; *metonymy*, the allegorical level; *metaphor*, the poetic level; and *proclamation*, the visionary or mythic level. Each kind of language we use, Frye persuasively argues, is an embodiment of, indeed a metaphor for, a kind of thinking we do. The first kind of language, description, permits descriptive thinking, what we might call literal-mindedness or plot summary. The second kind of language, metonymy, permits metonymic thinking, what Frye identifies as a restricted sort of allegorical reading or, to use a different word he employs, "commentary"—to my way of thinking, an attitude that sees the function, the very essence, of both literature and criticism as involving acts of what many critics today consider to be representation rather than acts of what I regard as transfiguration.

But it is the final two kinds of language and thinking that merit Frye's sustained attention and, as a result, our own. The third kind of language, the poetic language of metaphor, permits metaphoric thinking, which Frye rightly regards as more expansive in nature; this observation squares exactly with the view, expressed by short-story writer and essayist Clark Blaise in his essay "The Craft of the Short Story," that the short story, which we know depends heavily on metaphor, is "an expansive form" rather than a "contractive" one (Blaise 183). The fourth kind of language, which Frye calls the visionary language of proclamation, a term that he explains is derived from the Greek word *kerygma*, permits a still more all-encompassing mythic thinking that ultimately prepares us to experience what Frye, like Flannery

O'Connor in the title of a deservedly famous short story (O'Connor 191–218), calls *revelation*.

Without particular examples, such terms and concepts may seem a matter for theoretical discussion alone—something of no direct benefit to either our tasks or our pleasures as readers of literature, here specifically as readers of the stories of Alice Munro. But consider Munro's many-leveled image, in her story "Meneseteung," of the cheesecloth bag of grape pulp and juice hanging between two chairbacks in the kitchen of the darkened house of poetess Almeda Joynt Roth and dripping into a basin beneath. On a literal level, the image denotes the making of grape jelly, but it can also be seen as functioning, in both art and life, on many more levels than the literal—that is to say, metaphorically.

On one level beyond the literal, the image in "Meneseteung" of the dripping bag is a metaphor for a process in nature: the way a river builds up silt to form islands. *Meneseteung* is the original name in Ojibway for the river later called in English the Maitland, which flows into Lake Huron at Goderich, Ontario, the basis for this story's unnamed fictional town. And the word *meneseteung* in Ojibway, according to my understanding, means "place of little islands," with the additional suggestion, intended or not, of the form of the short story as a metaphoric island. Indeed, islands, such as the "women-ruled" Isle of Women in Mexico that figures in Munro's "A Queer Streak" (*Progress* 246), are a frequent metaphor, not only in Munro's depiction of the psychological situations of her different characters, but also for her metafictive depiction of her stories themselves.

On a different level, the image of the dripping bag is a metaphor for another sort of build-up, for a process not in men's but in women's bodies, for Almeda's menstrual "flow" (Munro, *Friend* 70) or menses—a physical phenomenon and, very importantly, also a metaphor, as William Butt discusses in his essay "Southwestern Ontario, the Narrator, and 'Words with Power' in Alice Munro's 'Meneseteung.'" Indeed, as Munro refigures the Ojibway word and name *Meneseteung* into her own multileveled literary language, we can hear in her chosen title "Meneseteung" resonant echoes of numerous English words. In the first half of the title, in addition to the word *menses*, we can hear, at the outset, the word *men*; then, intriguingly, especially in juxtaposition with men (and perhaps in some ways with menses), the word *menace*, as Magdalene Redekop observes (227).

In the second half of the title "Meneseteung," it is possible to hear not only the theatrical term of a stage *set* but also the literary term of a fictional *setting*. The concept of a stage set is definitely pertinent, given the strongly theatrical nature of Munro's stories. And the concept of a fictional setting is especially significant, being a crucial term, like *place* and *region*, for considering fiction in general and for appreciating Munro's stories in particular. At the very end of the title, as Louis K. MacKendrick discusses in his essay "Giving Tongue: Scorings of Voice, Verse, and Flesh in 'Meneseteung'" and as Redekop also notes (227), we can hear the word *tongue*, a metaphor that clearly functions usefully in, as well as for, a story involving various efforts at creative articulation.

Finally, and very importantly, the image in "Meneseteung" of the bag dripping with grape pulp and juice is a metaphor for yet another kind of buildup, not from grapes or of silt or menstrual blood, but of an imaginative process or flow. This creative rivering, the Ojibway word or name *Meneseteung*, the title "Meneseteung," Munro's complete story, and our own precise and intense reading of it not only identify but also perform. Again we encounter four different levels to this "flow of words" (Munro, *Friend* 69): that of Almeda, who has published one book of poems called *Offerings* (50) and is now composing in her head (so she fantasizes) "one very great poem that will contain everything," a long poem she intends to entitle "The Meneseteung" (70); that of the narrator, who should not be considered identical to Munro, as we must realize even when reading Munro's book of what I propose calling story-memoirs and memoir-stories, *The View from Castle Rock* (2006); that of Munro as artist, using form, technique, style, and especially language to her utmost capacity; and last, but by no means least, our own now greatly amplified imaginative process as readers of "Meneseteung."

II

Certainly one of the most diverse and powerful instances of Alice Munro's use of what Northrop Frye calls the poetic language of metaphor and the visionary language of proclamation is the name she gives to her nineteenth-century southwestern Ontario poetess in "Meneseteung," Almeda Joynt Roth. The extraordinary network of associations generated by this name is a brilliant example of Munro's demand, as W. H. New explains, that we "listen closely" (*Dreams* 210) to the full range of what I am calling the language of metaphor, of allusion, of puns and portmanteau words, of allegory, of myth.

On one level, the surname Roth, as Magdalene Redekop also has noticed, is a pun on the word *wrath* (225), a word sometimes pronounced like Roth and one that evokes the Old Testament God of wrath. This figure, both in divine form as the heartache-inflicting God of the book of Job and all its literary descendants—including, in some important respects, a great many of the stories by Thomas Hardy and Alice Munro[2]—and in human form as Almeda's literally and metaphorically harness-making father (Munro, *Friend* 50), presides over "Meneseteung" with a masculinist or patriarchal sternness, even ferocity. Metaphysically, socially, psychologically, and artistically, the powerfully entrenched, always expansive, strongly invasive, and fundamentally harmful nature of this set of attitudes compels an equally forceful feminist or matriarchal counter-expression, by Almeda as well as by the story's narrator, its author, and its readers.

The name Roth also suggests a genealogy and lineage for "Meneseteung" in terms of women's writing in English, stretching forward from such early groundbreaking work as that of seventeenth-century English poet and fiction writer Mary Sidney, Lady Wroth.[3] Furthermore, on a somewhat joking but still serious note, Munro's use of the name Roth in this strongly but subtly feminist story may well be a satiric reference to the masculinist structures (and strictures) that in some ways typify the work of American writer Philip Roth.

Allusions to literature or theater, further verbal play, and instances of Munro's very considerable knowledge of the local history of her home county and region are all involved in Munro's choice of Almeda Joynt Roth's middle name. On a historical level, Joynt, presumably her mother's surname, is an actual family surname of long standing in Munro's native Huron County. In a literary or theatrical context, devotees of Shakespeare—and based on a considerable number of sophisticated allusions to the bard's work in her stories, Munro must be counted as one—might also connect, first verbally and then thematically, the name Joynt with the darkly prophetic remark by the title character of Shakespeare's *Hamlet*, "The time is out of joint" (*Ham.* 1.5.188). To suggest also that the name Joynt might be related to that of Snug the Joiner in Shakespeare's *A Midsummer Night's Dream*, with the verbal connection inviting comparison between Snug's work and some metaphorically equivalent female activity in "Meneseteung," is undeniably playful, some might say frivolous, and perhaps completely fanciful. Very likely this occurs to me alone on account of Snug the Joiner being the sole Shakespearean character I have ever played on stage. But then again, can we be sure that this notion is not right? At the very least, a second, comic reference provides a meaningful counterbalance, in terms of our sense of the nature and the breadth of Munro's vision, to the first, tragic reference.

Still more interesting are the associations of Almeda Joynt Roth's middle name on a verbal level. Joynt, Redekop notes, suggests both *joint*, in the sense of a body part, and *joined* (226). The former, I would say, contains a satiric reference to the masculinist or patriarchal diminishment of women's bodies, and of women as "mere" bodies; the latter contains an ironic echo of the spousal injunction, drawn from Matthew 19.6, that "what therefore God hath joined together, let not man put asunder," especially given Almeda's ultimate rejection of her neighbor Jarvis Poulter's overtures of marriage. The middle name Joynt also operates, I suspect, as a contraction of "joy not," a verbally playful but thematically somber characterization of many aspects of Almeda's life of more than sixty years, from her birth in 1840 (like Thomas Hardy) to her death in 1903.

Proceeding to the richly suggestive associations of the protagonist's first name, Almeda, we can see a further illustration of Munro's capacity to simultaneously joke and be serious, in this case as she satirizes as well as applies the famous psychological formulation of the Oedipus complex that Sigmund Freud developed from the story of the tormented hero Oedipus in ancient Greek tragedy. "Al-me-da," as syllables said or heard just a little differently—as "all my dad"—wittily hints at the protagonist's possible Freudian fixation on her father, *da* being a common Irish version of *dad*. The middle syllable of Almeda, *me*, is of course a reminder of the very important autobiographical impulse toward creative acts of identity formation and personal expression, which is felt in different ways, but nevertheless still shared, by Almeda, the narrator, Munro, and ourselves as readers.

Furthermore, as Redekop points out, the name Almeda evokes the tormented heroine Medea (220), also from ancient Greek tragedy. And speaking of representations of women in epic literature—not inappropriately, since I believe Munro's "Meneseteung" to be a world-class example of a "brief epic"—surely it is no accident that Almeda is extremely close in sound to the name of the Spanish village Alameda, which, we are told by James Joyce's epic heroine Molly Bloom a few lines from the end of *Ulysses* (1922), is the place where she had an early romantic adventure with the man who became her husband, Leopold Bloom. "O that awful deepdown torrent O and the sea the sea crimson sometimes like fire and the glorious sunsets and the figtrees in the Alameda gardens yes" (Joyce 643), Molly exults, employing a style and imagery with which, I would argue, certain passages in "Meneseteung" definitely bear comparison.

In addition, as Redekop notes, the name Almeda suggests the concept of *media* (220), exemplified in a primitive way by the story's fictional and fiction-making (that is, gossipy) local paper, the *Vidette*, as well as in a far more sophisticated way by "Meneseteung" itself. As well, once its opening syllable, *Al*, is translated from the Arabic *al* to the English *the*, Almeda's first name suggests "the medium," the sort of person who possesses the capacity for what Frye calls proclamation—that is, someone with visionary and creative and transformative powers. That this is a subject of great importance to Munro is suggested by her choice of title for the story "Powers" in *Runaway* (2004) and by her placement of this story last in that volume. "Powers" is just one of many stories by Munro that include instances of female or male "fool-saints" with extraordinary modes of perception and messages that have the potential to be life-transforming for other characters and readers alike.

To these numerous resonant associations with the first name of the protagonist of Munro's "Meneseteung," I would add only one more, but a very important one: that Almeda's name is the hitherto unidentified key to uncovering what I am convinced is by far the most important historical model for Munro's fictional poetess. Not the late-nineteenth-to-early-twentieth-century Goderich, Ontario, author of *Golden Leaves* (1890), Eloise A. Skimings,[4] though various Munro critics such as Coral Ann Howells have made a good case for her (Howells 107–8, 166), but rather Munro's oldest, and very possibly her favorite, literary precursor: Emily Brontë, the late-Romantic, early-Victorian English author of the magnificent lyric novel *Wuthering Heights* (1847). Among a few different pseudonyms that Emily selected for herself in the richly developed childhood fantasy about an imaginary place called Gondal that she cocreated with her sisters, Charlotte and Anne, and her brother, Branwell, was the name Almeda.[5]

III

For us to investigate the subject of the language of Alice Munro—her use of the full range of allusion, puns, portmanteau words, allegory, myth, and in particular the language of metaphor—it is crucial that we consider Charles E. May's discussion in "Metaphoric Motivation in

Short Fiction." Here, May speaks of two conceptions of how knowledge can be framed in literature, two definitions of motivation, two views of metaphor, emphasizing that "it is helpful to keep both the relationships and the distinctions between these terms in mind" (64). May outlines a first literary (and by extension, I would add, critical) method that uses a framework that views knowledge according to "the natural, the social, or the psychological" (72)—in other words, that privileges verisimilitude or so-called realism. In so doing, this first method attempts, it would seem far less successfully, to present and to honor what May refers to as "the mystery" (72), or what, borrowing Basil H. Johnston's translation of the Ojibway word for supreme being, *Kitchi-manitou*, I would call "The Great Mystery" ("Is That All" 350). May contrasts this literary (and critical) method with a second, which uses a framework that views knowledge as being "inchoate, metaphysical, and aesthetic" (72) —that is, which realizes the ascendancy of the artistic over the realistic. In so doing, this second method attempts, it would seem far more successfully, to present and to honor the Great Mystery.

It is, of course, the second conception of how knowledge can be framed in literature—not mimetically but diegetically, we might say, employing the more sophisticated opposition described by Gerald Prince in *A Dictionary of Narratology* (1987); or, alternatively, not realistically but artistically—that the eminent short-story theorists, critics, historians, and editors Mary Rohrberger, Charles E. May, and W. H. New favor (as I do myself).[6] Just as importantly, it is the second way in which language can be used in literature, not ideologically but aesthetically, that these three pioneers favor. The astuteness and importance of their tastes and judgments are confirmed by the inimitable and enduring nature of the subjects they have chosen for detailed attention: Nathaniel Hawthorne, Edgar Allan Poe, Anton Chekhov, Katherine Mansfield, Flannery O'Connor, Alice Munro. And recognizing that metaphor is central to the thought and sense of form and expression of the story writers we most admire, Rohrberger, May, and New (and

I) also have chosen to make metaphor central to our own thought and sense of form and expression.[7]

Great works of art, by which I mean great musical, visual, and verbal performances, do not only indirectly represent the Great Mystery beyond, around, and within us; they also directly give it life, making it real, vivid, and palpable in themselves as art, so that with sufficient openness and preparation we can experience this mystery fully for ourselves. To employ the metaphor that Munro herself uses in her essay "What Is Real?" to describe the workings of her stories in general and "Royal Beatings" in particular, the site of transfiguration and transformation in her stories is "the black room" (334). Whether in its primary form or in some elaborate variant, such as the geological formation that Munro selects as the governing metaphor for her story "Deep-Holes" in *Too Much Happiness* (2009)—a formation that she describes evocatively as "deep chambers, really, some as big as a coffin, some much bigger than that, like rooms cut out of the rocks" (94)—this is the metaphor that I regard as absolutely central to both the writing of Munro's stories and the reading of them.[8] The black room. It is the place where everything we hold dear can be demolished. It is also the place where we can begin again.

In "What Is Real?," after Munro likens how a story functions for her as both a reader and a writer to how a house "encloses space and makes connections between one enclosed space and another and presents what is outside in a new way" (332), she uses the metaphor of the black room to convey what is most essential to her story "Royal Beatings." "It is the black room at the center of the house with all other rooms leading to and away from it," she explains, adding that it is there because she needs it there and because "it belongs there" (334). As readers preparing to engage with Munro's metaphorical structures, her black rooms and their variants, it is our challenge and our responsibility to ready ourselves both psychologically and aesthetically so that we will not hesitate before them. When we enter them—as we must, overwhelmingly but transformatively, in "Images" from *Dance of the*

Happy Shades, "Royal Beatings" from *Who Do You Think You Are?*, the murder-suicide story "Fits" from *The Progress of Love*, "Mene-seteung" from *Friend of My Youth*, and "Save the Reaper" from *The Love of a Good Woman* (1998), to name but a few examples—we experience, in the words of Edgar Allan Poe in his landmark review of Nathaniel Hawthorne's *Twice-Told Tales* (1842), "the immense force derivable from *totality*" ("Poe on Short Fiction" 61; italics in orig.). We experience the initially devastating, yet paradoxically finally replenishing, intensity that Munro brings to her writing and demands we bring to our reading.

Charles E. May, commenting on certain section divisions in his anthology *The New Short Story Theories* (1994), says, "The 'Early Formalist Theory' section could also be called 'The Poe Tradition,' just as 'The Modern Short Story' section might be called 'The Chekhov Tradition'; for the two most significant 'beginnings' of the form are marked by the contributions of those two masters" (Preface xii). Could it be any more appropriate, then, that the two significant antecedents of Munro's use of the black-room metaphor that I have found so far are classic stories by these two authors—namely, Poe's "The Masque of the Red Death" (1842) and Chekhov's "The Kiss" (1887)? Anything more than brief comparison of Munro's work to these individual stories by Poe and Chekhov lies beyond the scope of the present essay. However, the importance of the sort of phenomenon that greatly interested Northrop Frye—the considerable meaningfulness of the effect that literature has on us as a result of the often remarkably close resemblances, and therefore very strong connections, existing between elements in different works, and indeed the special power with which they interact to reinforce one another when viewed on and from a metaphoric plane as being essentially identical—is well worth emphasizing.

Such are the masterfully detailed situations or mise-en-scènes, the intricate but invisible methods, the startling effects, and the luminous insights of Alice Munro's stories that they recall, yet in their own ways redirect, not only the bold, gothic moments and style of Poe but also the restrained, everyday moments and style of Chekhov. Metaphorically, Alice Munro's "black room"—of which the kitchen, "the closed hot room" (*Friend* 71) where Almeda Joynt Roth sits all day long one Sunday in "Meneseteung," is another vivid example—is identical to the "black chamber" of Poe's "The Masque of the Red Death" (605) and the "dark room" of Chekhov's "The Kiss" (56). In each case, for protagonists and narrators, for authors and readers, our visits to these sites of transfiguration force us into a wholly new and very intense experience of the terrifying, the soul-shattering, the tragic. But at least as importantly, our visits to Poe's "black chamber," Chekhov's "dark room," and Munro's "black room" also force us into a wholly new and very intense experience of the astonishing, the soul-transforming, the comic.

IV

The basis on which writers have built the great stories that form what I, extending earlier designations by Charles E. May, propose to call the "Tradition of Poe," the "Tradition of Chekhov," and the "Tradition of Alice Munro" does not in any sense consist of simple acts of plot; rather, it consists of complex acts of style, language, and what Northrop Frye in the title of another essay calls "The Expanding World of Metaphor" (*Myth* 108–23). Charles E. May states that ultimately, as readers of the short story, we end up finding answers to our biggest questions "not . . . in a similitude of the real world, but rather by being caught up within the role that the story demands and being therefore metaphorically transformed" ("Metaphoric" 73). May argues that the only way to understand the nineteenth-century American works that he is considering, Edgar Allan Poe's "The Fall of the House of Usher" (1839) and Herman Melville's "Bartleby, the Scrivener" (1853), is "by rhetorical structure and by metaphor" (71). As Louis K. MacKendrick stressed in his prefatory comments to, and by his choice of contributions for, the very first book of criticism on Munro, *Probable Fictions: Alice Munro's Narrative Acts* (1983), the matters that are of paramount importance when reading Munro are "form, language, style, genre, and narrative technique" (1).

Alice Munro's stories must be understood, read, and interpreted not only literally but, far more importantly, metaphorically; not only for plot but, far more importantly, for style; not only realistically but, far more importantly, aesthetically; not only, as critics now often say, materially but, as I would say, transcendentally. Or, to phrase this conclusion another way, Alice Munro's stories must be understood, read, and interpreted not only in terms of what some contemporaries, following theorist Jacques Derrida, would call "the discourse of absence" but in terms of what I, following theorist Northrop Frye, would call "the poetics of presence."

Reading and rereading particular stories, poems, and essays, writing criticism, editing, perhaps running a small press as I do—these are all ways of defining the directions we want our lives to take. At the center of this process is the demanding yet fulfilling challenge, for both those who are young in fact and those who are young at heart, of finding the perfect metaphor, whether for understanding a particular writer's work or for orienting ourselves. The perfect metaphor: some soul-transfiguring word or phrase or aphorism that permits us to try to gather in, to process, to communicate whatever will best serve to enlighten and to direct ourselves and those around us.

Our work as "joint-labourers" (I say here and now to you as William Wordsworth said in his final address to his friend and fellow poet Samuel Taylor Coleridge at the close of *The Prelude*, 13.439) always profoundly involves what Northrop Frye, in the title of another of his essays, calls "The Search for Acceptable Words" (*Spiritus* 3–26). It is a matter of learning the right language, a process that may well require us to relinquish a language (description, metonymy) we have been trained to use and have grown fond of using in favor of a language (metaphor, proclamation) we still need to learn. At this point, as Frye writes, language "becomes a single gigantic metaphor, the uniting of consciousness with what it is conscious of . . . , the transfiguring of consciousness as it merges with articulated meaning" (*Myth* 115). That is one very special reason why I so enjoy talking with writers, in my imagination or in person; much more often than not, it is the writers I have read, interviewed, written about, edited, or published who have raised the most important questions for, and of, me, not the other way around. And it is the writers you choose to read and to reread, like Alice Munro, who will raise the most important questions for, and of, you.

Notes

1. See John W. Pattison's piece about the "Wingham Outrage" (Pattison 246–47).
2. To my mind, Alice Munro's stories need to be reckoned as one of a group of major literary descendants of the book of Job, which I believe can be viewed as the ur-form of the modern short story. Together in this group with Alice Munro's stories I would put the important (and for Munro, I would say, influential) work of her literary precursor Thomas Hardy. His first story collection, *Wessex Tales*, published in 1888, possesses a subtitle that strikes me as perfect for describing our sense of several main qualities of Alice Munro's writing: *Strange, Lively, and Commonplace*.
3. For making me aware of the existence and the importance of Wroth, I am indebted to Marianne Micros; see her article "'For Him What Countless Tears I Must Have Shed': Identity, Subjection, and Subjectivity in the Poems of Mary Stuart and Mary Wroth." For a major study of Wroth, see Margaret P. Hannay's *Mary Sidney, Lady Wroth*.
4. A copy of a portrait of Eloise A. Skimings by the Goderich-based photographer Reuben R. Sallows appears on the time line of local history at the Huron County Museum in Goderich, where Munro may well have seen it displayed. The portrait is reproduced as a frontispiece to the 1904 edition of Skimings's book of poems, *Offerings*.
5. Catherine Sheldrick Ross, in a discussion of Munro's early reading in her brief but very astute biography, *Alice Munro: A Double Life* (1992), directs our attention to Munro's enormous admiration for, indeed intoxication with, Emily Brontë's novel *Wuthering Heights*, beginning at the age of fourteen. As Munro explains to Ross, "*Wuthering Heights* really excited me beyond *anything* that was happening in my real life. I think I probably read it thereafter constantly for four or five years. I was really reading it all the time" (44; italics in orig.). For a version of "The Gondal Saga," see Emily Brontë, *Gondal's Queen: A Novel in Verse* (1955).
6. Additional pairings of theoretical terms that I believe can be of interest and of use, to different degrees for different readers, include the distinction between what American literary theorist Harold Bloom, Canadian poet, novelist, and essayist Daphne Marlatt, and I term *ficticity* versus *facticity*. Or the distinction

that Charles E. May, in the essay from which I have been quoting, characterizes as "metaphoric motivation" or "artistic motivation" in contrast to "story motivation" or "realistic motivation" ("Metaphoric" 68). Or the distinction that Seymour Chatman, Charles E. May, and Ajay Heble make between *discourse* and *story*. Or the opposition between what I term and, I believe justifiably, consider very important, *transfiguration*, and what many contemporaries term and, I believe unjustifiably, consider very important, *representation*.

7. See, for example, Rohrberger's essays "Between Shadow and Act: Where Do We Go from Here?" and "Origins, Development, Substance, and Design of the Short Story: How I Got Hooked on the Short Story and Where It Led Me"; May's essays "Chekhov and the Modern Short Story" and "Metaphoric Motivation in Short Fiction"; New's "Pronouns and Propositions: Alice Munro's *Something I've Been Meaning to Tell You*" (*Dreams* 201–10) and his introduction to his anthology *Canadian Short Fiction* (1986); and my own essays "Once More to the Lake: Towards a Poetics of Receptivity" and "Endings and Beginnings: Reading Clark Blaise's 'A Fish Like a Buzzard.'"

8. Although James Carscallen makes no mention in his major study *The Other Country: Patterns in the Writing of Alice Munro* of her coining and application of the metaphor of the black room, he rightly recognizes Munro's ability to present "an underworld divided into compartments" (142). Insightfully, and poetically, Carscallen suggests that in stories like "Images," Munro "often shows us not just a single space . . . but a whole sequence of rooms and passages—suggesting its own miniature story" (142).

Works Cited

Blaise, Clark. "The Craft of the Short Story." *Selected Essays*. Ed. John Metcalf and J. R. (Tim) Struthers. Emeryville, ON: Biblioasis, 2008. 181–90.

Bloom, Harold. "Criticism, Canon-Formation, and Prophecy: The Sorrows of Facticity." *Poetics of Influence: New and Selected Criticism*. Ed. John Hollander. New Haven, CT: Schwab, 1988. 405–24.

Brontë, Emily. *Gondal's Queen: A Novel in Verse*. Ed. Fannie E. Ratchford. New York: AMS, 1973.

Burke, Kenneth. *A Grammar of Motives*. 1945. Berkeley: U of California P, 1969.

Butt, William. "Southwestern Ontario, the Narrator, and 'Words with Power' in Alice Munro's 'Meneseteung.'" N.d. TS.

Carscallen, James. *The Other Country: Patterns in the Writing of Alice Munro*. Toronto: ECW, 1993.

Chatman, Seymour. *Story and Discourse: Narrative Structure in Fiction and Film*. Ithaca, NY: Cornell UP, 1978.

Chekhov, Anton. "The Kiss." *The Essential Tales of Chekhov*. Ed. Richard Ford. Trans. Constance Garnett. Hopewell, NJ: Ecco, 1998. 51–66.

Frye, Northrop. *The Great Code: The Bible and Literature*. Toronto: Academic, 1982.

_____. *Myth and Metaphor: Selected Essays, 1974–1988*. Ed. Robert D. Denham. Charlottesville: UP of Virginia, 1990.

_____. *Spiritus Mundi: Essays on Literature, Myth, and Society.* Bloomington: Indiana UP, 1976.

_____. *Words with Power: Being a Second Study of "The Bible and Literature."* San Diego, CA: Harcourt, 1990.

Hannay, Margaret P. *Mary Sidney, Lady Wroth.* Farnham, Eng.: Ashgate, 2010.

Heble, Ajay. *The Tumble of Reason: Alice Munro's Discourse of Absence.* Toronto: U of Toronto P, 1994.

Heble, Ajay, Donna Palmateer Pennee, and J. R. (Tim) Struthers, eds. *New Contexts of Canadian Criticism.* Peterborough, ON: Broadview, 1997.

Howells, Coral Ann. *Alice Munro.* Manchester: Manchester UP, 1998.

Johnston, Basil H. "How Do We Learn Language? What Do We Learn?" *Talking on the Page: Editing Aboriginal Oral Texts.* Ed. Laura J. Murray and Keren Rice. Toronto: U of Toronto P, 1999. 43–51.

_____. "Is That All There Is? Tribal Literature." Heble, Pennee, and Struthers 346–54.

Joyce, James. *Ulysses: The Corrected Text.* Ed. Hans Walter Gabler, Wolfhard Steppe, and Claus Melchior. Harmondsworth, Eng.: Penguin, 1986.

Lohafer, Susan, and Jo Ellyn Clarey, eds. *Short Story Theory at a Crossroads.* Baton Rouge: Louisiana State UP, 1989.

MacKendrick, Louis K. "Giving Tongue: Scorings of Voice, Verse, and Flesh in 'Meneseteung.'" N.d. TS.

_____, ed. *Probable Fictions: Alice Munro's Narrative Acts.* Downsview, ON: ECW, 1983.

Marlatt, Daphne. *Readings from the Labyrinth.* Edmonton, AB: NeWest, 1998. The Writ. as Critic 6.

May, Charles E. "Chekhov and the Modern Short Story." May, *New Short Story* 199–217.

_____. "Metaphoric Motivation in Short Fiction: 'In the Beginning Was the Story.'" Lohafer and Clarey 62–73.

_____, ed. *The New Short Story Theories.* Athens: Ohio UP, 1994.

_____. Preface. May, *New Short Story* xi–xii.

Micros, Marianne. "'For Him What Countless Tears I Must Have Shed': Identity, Subjection, and Subjectivity in the Poems of Mary Stuart and Mary Wroth." *Sidney Journal* 27.2 (2009): 53–70.

Munro, Alice. *Friend of My Youth.* Toronto: McClelland, 1990.

_____. *The Progress of Love.* Toronto: McClelland, 1986.

_____. "The Real Material: An Interview with Alice Munro." By J. R. (Tim) Struthers. MacKendrick, *Probable Fictions* 5–36.

_____. *Too Much Happiness.* Toronto: McClelland, 2009.

_____. "What Is Real?" *How Stories Mean.* Ed. John Metcalf and J. R. (Tim) Struthers. Erin, ON: Porcupine's Quill, 1993. 331–34.

New, W. H. *Dreams of Speech and Violence: The Art of the Short Story in Canada and New Zealand.* Toronto: U of Toronto P, 1987.

_____. Introduction. *Canadian Short Fiction*. Ed. New. 2nd ed. Scarborough, ON: Prentice, 1997. 1–14.

O'Connor, Flannery. *Everything That Rises Must Converge*. New York: Farrar, 1965.

Page, P. K. "Kaleidoscope." *Kaleidoscope: Selected Poems*. Ed. Zailig Pollock. Erin, ON: Porcupine's Quill, 2010. 174–76.

Pattison, John W. *Museum Musings: Brief Glimpses of Wingham's Past*. [Wingham, ON]: n.p., [1982].

Poe, Edgar Allan. "The Masque of the Red Death." *The Complete Stories*. Introd. John Seelye. New York: Knopf, 1992. 604–9. Everyman's Library 99.

_____. "Poe on Short Fiction." May, *New Short Story* 59–72.

Prince, Gerald. *A Dictionary of Narratology*. 1987. 2nd ed. Lincoln: U of Nebraska P, 2003.

Redekop, Magdalene. *Mothers and Other Clowns: The Stories of Alice Munro*. London: Routledge, 1992.

Rohrberger, Mary. "Between Shadow and Act: Where Do We Go from Here?" Lohafer and Clarey 32–45.

_____. "Origins, Development, Substance, and Design of the Short Story: How I Got Hooked on the Short Story and Where It Led Me." *The Art of Brevity: Excursions in Short Fiction Theory and Analysis*. Ed. Per Winther, Jakob Lothe, and Hans H. Skei. Columbia: U of South Carolina P, 2004. 1–13.

Ross, Catherine Sheldrick. *Alice Munro: A Double Life*. Toronto: ECW, 1992. Canadian Biog. Ser. 1.

Shakespeare, William. *Hamlet*. Ed. Harold Jenkins. London: Methuen, 1982.

Skimings, Eloise A. *Golden Leaves*. Goderich, ON: Signal, 1904.

Struthers, J. R. (Tim). "Alice Munro (July 10, 1931–)." *A Reader's Companion to the Short Story in English*. Ed. Erin Fallon et al. Westport, CT: Greenwood, 2001. 288–99.

_____. "Endings and Beginnings: Reading Clark Blaise's 'A Fish Like a Buzzard.'" *Short Fiction in Theory and Practice* 1.1 (2011): 7–23.

_____. "Once More to the Lake: Towards a Poetics of Receptivity." Heble, Pennee, and Struthers 319–45.

White, Hayden. *Metahistory: The Historical Imagination in Nineteenth-Century Europe*. Baltimore: Johns Hopkins UP, 1973.

Wordsworth, William. *The Prelude; or, Growth of a Poet's Mind*. Ed. Ernest de Selincourt. Rev. Helen Darbishire. 2nd ed. London: Oxford UP, 1960.

The Complex Tangle of Secrets in Alice Munro's
Open Secrets———————————————————

Michael Toolan

A recurring theme in Alice Munro's *Open Secrets* (1994), which came at what must be roughly halfway through her writing career, is the paradox, shame, and mystery of the open secret: the thing that everyone in the community sort of knows, or thinks they know, but that no one is quite able or willing to state openly, confront, or resolve. Those things, which are almost impossible to tell, are often the most aesthetically and culturally important to tell, including open secrets about desire, fantasy, frustration, loneliness, sex, class, and gender. In this essay, and inevitably referring to some of the eight stories more than others, I will discuss how those inert abstractions come alive in *Open Secrets*.

The very fact that there are only eight stories in this book leads to an initial observation: Munro is at this point in her career writing longer short stories than previously, with accordingly more texture, more complex situations, and a denser interplay of characters and narrative trajectories in each. But while we associate the canonical novel with a "complete" presentation of a specific story world, even Munro's long stories eschew thus "satisfying" the reader. Touching on many times and places across characters' entire life spans, they prefer to present selectively and indicatively, incorporating gaps and unknowns that the reader must negotiate, so that along with other applications here of the phrase *open secrets*, the stories themselves are very open and contain many secrets. Shunning the simplicity of the slice-of-life or single-crisis short story, these stories have the ambition of novels in their psychological depth, complexity of plot, and narrative technique, even while they build on such core characteristics of the short story as brevity, density, and intensity.

Voices and Witnesses, Direct or Refracted: "Carried Away"

Subtlety of modes of narration, which interweave a range of times and places and viewpoints worthy of a novel, is a feature of all these stories. In "Carried Away," which begins in the small town of Carstairs during World War I, we learn of Louisa, the town's librarian, who lives in the anonymity of a commercial hotel, and the letters she exchanges (at his initiation) with a soldier from the town, named Jack Agnew. Munro presents their epistolary dialogue with a minimum of fuss: hers well written but a little self-focused, his less sophisticated but more engaging. Most of this is focalized from Louisa's point of view, and the sense of possibility and even "addictive excitement" (Munro, *Open* 11) is intimated with restraint. However, all is undercut at the end of the section when, from a neutral narratorial position, we learn that Jack was engaged to a local girl even before going overseas.

Two years later (the elapse of time is not immediately apparent), still living at the commercial hotel, Louisa "confesses" to the traveling salesman Jim Frarey the story of her strange, aborted relationship with Jack Agnew, and how she once had (or thought she had) a sweetheart over in France. In contrast to the verbatim presentation in the first telling of Louisa and Jack's letters, printed in italics, the retelling is in the distancing style of indirect discourse. None of the actual words of the characters, in the first person, are presented in this first recounting: "She began to tell him about a soldier who had started writing letters to her from overseas. The soldier remembered her from when he used to go into the Library" (Munro, *Open* 15). The distancing and detaching effect of indirect discourse continues. Louisa tells Jim how she scanned the newspapers for word about Jack while he was away at the war, how she learned he was unhurt and coming home to Carstairs, and how she waited and waited for him to appear at the library. The text continues: "She had to be forgiven, didn't she, she had to be forgiven for thinking, after such letters, that the one thing that could never happen was that he wouldn't approach her, wouldn't get in touch with her at all?" (17). We cannot be entirely sure, in the context, whether these words are simply thought by Louisa to herself (free indirect thought) or actually voiced to Jim (free indirect speech). Overly familiar though she is with Jim— her tongue loosened by whiskey, she says— the free indirect narration may be disclosing to us rather more detail than she shares with him. This is the kind of uncertainty about who gets told what that abounds in these stories, capturing the shifting degrees of understanding that people have of themselves and each other. Louisa then reads a newspaper notice of Jack's marriage to Grace Horne, having also found a scrap of paper on her desk carrying the words "*I was engaged before I went overseas*" as well as her photograph, returned. Jim Frarey's explanation is that Agnew was sincere but "got a little carried away" (18); this is only one of numerous situations in these stories where, to their own or others' detriment or not, someone seems to get carried away.

But why does Louisa tell Frarey (him only, it seems) these humiliating facts in the first place, we might ask? When she is on the point of doing so, Frarey assures her that he is not a gossip: "She gave him a hard laughing look and said that when a person announced they weren't a gossip, they almost invariably were. The same when they promised never to tell a soul" (Munro, *Open* 15). This does not stop her telling, however. The situation embodies one of Munro's enduring interests: the unpredictable ways in which we choose to tell our secrets to one person and not to another, and the complex reasons, sometimes hidden even from ourselves, why we do so. Part of Louisa's motivation here is a bid for intimacy with Frarey, and her confessions lead to them sleeping together (they jointly get "carried away"), an involvement from which Jim rapidly retreats.

The complexity of this opening story is indicative of those that follow. Any ordinary short story would end at this point, but there is a great deal more to come in this one, beginning with Jack Agnew's gruesome death in a factory accident in the early 1920s and ending in the 1950s, by which time Louisa is widowed and suffering from a heart condition. What links these is a typical *but-for* Munro twist: but for Arthur Doud, the factory owner and manager, undertaking to return Jack's purloined library books, he would not have met and, in time, married Louisa. Now, near the story's close, we observe Louisa visiting the city and experiencing something like a transient ischemic attack (a mini-stroke), during which she is drawn into confused imaginary dialogues with people long dead. This final section also features a fantasized rambling conversation with a trade unionist, speaking at a commemoration of the Tolpuddle Martyrs, who just happens to have the same name as Louisa's one-time epistolary sweetheart, Jack Agnew, who seems to have returned to her as a dream or ideal lover (this whole section is a chaos of voices and viewpoints). The elderly Louisa thinks to herself, in the midst of this fantasy encounter, "Oh, what kind of a trick was being played on her, or what kind of trick was she playing on herself! She would not have it" (Munro, *Open* 49). Through Louisa, Munro reminds us not to assume that all the tricks we fall for are perpetrated by others, that we sometimes fool ourselves. But resisting, that is, "not having it," is often easier said than done.

Among many wonderful moments in "Carried Away," there is one that is chronologically one of the earliest, although in the telling (the discourse) it is one of the last to be reported, a few lines from the end. Working as a commercial traveler, Louisa is visiting Carstairs—not for the first time, it seems—and, having heard that the position of public librarian is vacant, has applied for and been appointed to the post. From her third-floor bedroom ("Never climbed so close to Heaven in this place before!" the opportunist salesman Jim Frarey will later croon to her, as he follows her to her bed), she looks out at the bare winter trees, and the narrative modulates into free indirect thought: "She had never been here when the leaves were on the trees. It must make a great difference. So much that lay open now would be concealed" (Munro, *Open* 51). In this subtlest of ways, we are prompted to think of how the whole panoply of facts, truths, tricks, and humiliations that make and shape a life may be starkly visible at one time from one vantage point but undetectable, as if null and void, at another time and from a different perspective. And, leafing out and leaf fall being what they are, such shifts from openness to concealment and back again may happen regardless of our wishes.

In a 2008 article in *Style*, H. Porter Abbott argues that Munro is one of those contemporary writers who often present us with characters whom we must resist the temptation of naturalizing—that is, subjecting to interpretive reduction and closure. This we may find difficult, since, according to various recent theorists, modern fiction seems to be centrally about (our stimulated desire for) mind reading, in the sense of seeing into and possessing, readably, the minds of characters: "One of Alice Munro's signature gifts as a writer of short stories is the efficiency with which she builds to a moment of insight that allows us at one and the same time to see a character anew and to see that there is more we can't see" (Abbott 455). Abbott's example story is "Fits" from *The Progress of Love* (1986), where, he argues, unreadability and its power to captivate are continuously exploited. Such stories work best, Abbott says, when we simply accept that here are unreadable minds. John Gerlach touches on the same achieved openness when he describes how the "not closing" at the end of so many of Munro's stories reflects the fact that we readers have "reached the limit of what we can know," a "charged incompleteness" in which ultimate issues are left still in the balance, "stunningly irresolvable" (Gerlach 154).

Jokes and Violence, Fantasy and the Absurd

In a radio interview Munro gave at the time of its publication (Munro, interview), she noted that in *Open Secrets* she was attempting riskier things than she had before. Many of the stories skirt the absurd, the fantastic, or the ghostly, things ridiculous but not impossible. "Spaceships Have Landed" is centrally about class, sexuality, and ways in which a woman may, in exceptional circumstances, have the upper hand just as much as a man. But a peripheral narrative thread concerns Eunie, a strong-minded girl who goes missing in the middle of the night and returns with an incoherent explanation of having been briefly adopted—*abducted* would be too strong a word—by a mysterious trio of child strangers in seersucker sun suits. Perhaps Eunie is an "Albanian virgin" in training. (For the story of that name, Munro drew on anthropological reports from the 1920s: if a woman of the Gheg tribe accepted celibacy, solitude, and masculine clothes and appearance, she was allowed to live outside the tribe's primitively restrictive gender roles; in the story, an abducted Canadian woman accordingly does so for a period of time.) At any rate, many years later, she has partnered up with Billy Doud, who is probably secretly gay. Even at the story's close, the picture we have of Eunie is incomplete; she herself remains strange to us. And in "Vandals," a different kind of weirdness surfaces: a young, conservative, good Christian couple, Liza and Warren, comply with a request to check on the rural home of an elderly acquaintance named Bea, now living in the city, where her partner Ladner has recently died. But as soon as they are in the house, Liza sets about trashing the rooms, then tearfully telephones Bea to report that vandals must have broken in. Only after this inexplicable sequence do we learn that years ago, when Liza and her brother Kenny were just children lost within a fractured family, she endowed her neighbor Bea with the expectation that Bea could "rescue" her and keep her whole. But the girl's unreal expectations were bound to fail; Bea was always much too self-absorbed to be a surrogate mother, and Ladner, the ultramasculine eccentric, crosses a line when (we deduce) he uses Liza's body in a brief episode of intense non-penetrative sexual contact. This makes Liza's behavior explicable to a degree, but a sense of unpredictable violence and disequilibrium—sheer craziness—remains.

In "The Jack Randa Hotel," a woman adopts a disguise in order to discipline her straying husband, her goal wavering between revenge and rescue. Like the bookstore owner in "The Albanian Virgin," we first encounter her as a female shopkeeper: Gail, who runs a dress store and dressmaking business. Her husband, Will Thornaby, has dumped her (in Gail's imagining, for "some dewy dollop of womanhood younger than their own children") and left for Brisbane, Australia; now she drinks with Will's mother and recalls how she and Will met and how, when they first got together, everything went fine until, at some point in their life together, she stopped having the upper hand. In free indirect thought, she asks, "Was she a person who believed that somebody had to have the upper hand?" (Munro, *Open* 167), and we can hardly avoid soberly wondering if Munro thinks that as well, at least about "normal" long-term marital relationships. Soon, we find Gail, whose original name was Galya, writing letters to her ex-husband in which she passes herself off as the elderly Catherine Thornaby, actually a recently deceased resident of Brisbane. Gail does this after intercepting a letter that Will had written to Catherine on the strength of the shared surname, unaware of her death. Reading between the lines of his replies to "Ms. Thornaby," Gail surmises that Will's relations with bright young Sandy are strained, his wit not sufficiently appreciated by her and her young friends; in short, he has lost that important upper hand. And traces of thoughts on Gail's part of how Will's former life and habits in Canada may inflect his present circumstances slip deftly and cruelly into her letters to him from Catherine Thornaby. In these respects, her makeover is not total but rather a Shakespearean disguise; we are told that she is not too troubled that she may look ridiculous, with her change of hairstyle and hair color and her inappropriate jacket dress: "It is a disguise" (169). Gail, writing as Catherine, mocks "these 'May-December' relationships and how invigorating they are" (177), censuring the men who abandon their erstwhile partners to lives of loneliness, knowing these blows will hit home.

But on sober reflection, we readers realize the situation is preposterous and theatrical, suitable fare for comedy or farce but not commensurate with real life. We question whether Gail would reduce herself to this mere playing of a role rather than living her life, functioning chiefly as a fabrication—part agony aunt, part Brontë-esque relative, part Circean temptress—with a life so inauthentic and so fictionally thin, her evenings spent reading one book at a time borrowed from a meager lending library run out of a neighbor's front room. Nor do we believe it likely that Will, for all his sense of exclusion and dislocation, would choose to relieve this by mining the Brisbane telephone book for other bearers of his family name and promptly writing to them (Why not phone? Why single out Thornabys at all?). In truth, Gail's fabrication is imperfect, the tone uneven. On the one hand, "Catherine" tells Will that she is younger than he is by several years and a globe-trotting "fashion buyer" (Munro, *Open* 177); on the other, she began in a formal style verging on the archaic: "I am at present [the name Thornaby's] only representative in the Brisbane phone book," one of "the true, armigerous Thornabys" (172–73). It is as if Gail herself sees that this is all nonsense when ten days have elapsed and she has still received no letter in response to her last; it takes just one sentence for us to see that for all his failings, she still loves him: "She shivers in the heat—most fearful, most desirous, of seeing Will's utterly familiar figure, that one rather small and jaunty, free-striding package, of all that could pain or appease her, in the world" (180). Thus another relationship by letter writing develops, one of many in the Munro oeuvre ("Carried Away" and "A Wilderness Station" in the present collection, and elsewhere in such stories as "Hateship, Friendship, Courtship, Loveship, Marriage"), but here with the twist that both correspondents already know each other intimately. We know that this fantasy play-acting cannot last; the narrative machinery creaks a little when two "elders" die, Will's mother and the older man of the gay couple down-stairs, and these intimations of mortality serve to hint that Gail must put away such childish things as spying, revenge, and disguise. Some critics have suggested that Gail's fantasy sojourn in Australia, writing what are in effect masterful anonymous letters to Will in a "fine nasty style," amounts to "(re)discovering a possible space for the feminine imaginary" (Howells 130–34, invoking ideas from Irigaray). If so, it means she is caught in a double bind all too familiar to women: Gail is diminished if she persists with it, reduced to fakery and playacting, and she is diminished if she abandons it, losing her power position, her female-honoring space.

Of course, it is not entirely up to her; she does not have a free choice. Before long, Gail's cover is blown, but with Will returned to the kind of unsatisfying sanity witnessed at the close of a Shakespearean comedy—through the door of the apartment he offers her the old familiar language: *love, need, forgive, forever*—she runs home "so as not to honor [those words] out of habit" (Munro, *Open* 188). At least she has not abandoned her upper hand. As she writes to Will in a final spitball-sized message as she heads back to Canada, *"Now it's up to you to follow me"* (189).

Class, Sex, and Marriage in "A Real Life"

There has been so much focus on Munro's gifts for psychological analysis of the lives of girls, women, and mothers, and of the men and boys who rub along beside them, that her treatments of class and social stratification have been perhaps underappreciated. In "A Real Life," class is much on Millicent's mind; she thinks her friend Dorrie Beck won her husband by the way she used her knife and fork, a skill acquired long ago at Whitby Ladies College, where she was sent on "a last spurt of the Becks' money" (Munro, *Open* 53). Millicent herself is acutely aware that, despite her good works in the Women's Auxiliary, she will never be invited to the tea parties in the homes of the town's professionals, because her husband Porter is a farmer and always will be a farmer, "no matter how many farms he owned" (57).

But the impact of class in Munro's stories runs much deeper than table manners and social invitations; it informs ways of seeing all the big issues, including death, sex, family, illness, and work. Wherever death and bereavement come to working-class people, for example, there is a striking matter-of-factness in the reporting, even of a dramatic death such as Jack Agnew's. The telling is spare and pragmatic, with melodrama only injected in the newspaper's lurid retelling, at some imaginative distance from more indulgent representations of these events— enabled by a secure margin of comparative affluence—in Western societies today. The unadorned directness extends to sex as well. Not that it is described in any detail, or with any great erotic charge in these stories, but simply that its occurrence, its chiefly functional procreative role in those days, is reported without decoration. Thus we are told, in "A Real Life," how Millicent's husband warned her on their wedding night, "not unkindly," that she must "take what's coming to you" and how after three children in rapid succession she "developed some problems" but "Porter was decent—mostly, after that, he left her alone" (Munro, *Open* 53). On the other hand, when Millicent and Muriel are making a wedding dress for Dorrie, who has surprised everyone by belatedly finding herself a husband, we are told that Dorrie draws the line at wearing a wedding veil: "She could not stand to have that draped over her, it would feel like cobwebs. Her use of the word 'cobwebs' gave Muriel and Millicent a start, because there were jokes being made about cobwebs in other places" (71). There is a lighthearted intimacy about such innocently aggressive sexual humor, to be set alongside the limited pleasure or fulfillment these women derive from sex.

The familiar wedding-preparation story nearly founders, however, when Dorrie decides that she cannot leave her ramshackle pioneer life of hunting and trapping, of selling muskrat skins, of rough fry-up meals and tending her brother's grave and keeping her own company. Millicent tries to convince her, using a variety of claims she scarcely even half-believes, beginning with the claim that "marriage takes you out of yourself and gives you a real life," to which Dorrie reasonably replies, "I have a life" (Munro, *Open* 75). Dorrie has been living a ruggedly independent life, removed from sex and gender, until this suitor appeared; her life, too, has approximated that of an Albanian virgin.

Millicent browbeats Dorrie into relenting, bullying her with the idea, quite untrue, that she and Porter have already sold Dorrie's house, which they own, so she will have to move on. Yet at the crisis point, it is Millicent, not Dorrie, who bursts into tears and must be comforted: "Then Dorrie had to do the comforting, patting and soothing in a magisterial way, while Millicent wept and repeated some words that did not hang together. *Happy. Help. Ridiculous*" (Munro, *Open*

76). Belatedly, Millicent sees Dorrie—"mulish, obedient, childish, female" (77)—as a person she has conquered in sending her away, but
at greater cost to Millicent herself: a painful glimpse of the damage
women do unto women in the name of men and the institution of a
traditional marriage. The traditional marriage, with its fixed, distinct,
hierarchized roles for wife and husband, was then, and perhaps still
is, the most powerful framework enforcing class and gender expectations on men and women. Decades later, Dorrie and her husband having enjoyed fulfillment and prosperity in Australia, Millicent reflects
on how Dorrie might have lived out a life of "manageable loneliness"
as her neighbor, except that Millicent had not allowed it: "She would
not allow it, and surely she was right" (80), the narrative comments.
Likewise, their mutual friend Muriel leaves town soon after Dorrie and
finds a husband and pious religion in Alberta. So these three women,
once such intimate friends and soul mates, have taken up life's offers,
and in doing so have moved sharply and irrevocably apart, and we are
not at all sure this was right.

"A Real Life" is given depth by another feature of much of Munro's best writing: the insightful portraiture of rural life and small-town
settlements in up-country Ontario in the early and middle decades of
the twentieth century. It is almost sociological documentary, this depiction of ordinary men and women living within a network of tacit
agreements and understandings that enable a limited set of said things
to maintain or enact a wider set of unsaid sequels. For sentences at a
time, we forget that everything here is fictional. For example, we are
told of how, mindful of her own father's terminal alcoholism, Millicent
extracts from Porter a prenuptial promise that he will never drink. The
text continues: "Of course he did—he kept a bottle in the granary—but
when he drank he kept his distance and she truly believed the promise
had been kept. This was a fairly common pattern at that time, at least
among farmers—drinking in the barn, abstinence in the house. Most
men would have felt there was something the matter with a woman
who didn't lay down such a law" (Munro, *Open* 61). More revealing

---

than the hypocrisy here is the power of gender: less the power of women to lay down the law, where it is implied that farmers would follow this pattern anyway, and more the power of men to hold women to account if they fail to impose this empty rule.

Telling Secrets

All of the stories in *Open Secrets* concern secrets: why we have them, how they have power over us, their role in our emotional, psychological, and sexual identities. Secrets can dominate our lives if we let them, as the behavior of many of the characters in this collection attests. We think that telling a secret will vanquish it, but may find on the contrary that its disclosure brings disaster, so we half-tell it and end up with the worst of both worlds. Or, for our whole lives, we are unable or unwilling to tell, while the power of what is secret or underlying continues to harm or comfort us. By the same token, from the point of view of the fiction writer, those things really worth writing about are the things that are almost impossible to express in language.

Nowhere is this more apparent than in the title story of the collection, arguably the most memorable, which presents an assortment of women—Maureen Stephens (née Coulter), Mary Johnstone, Marian Slater (née Hubbert), and Frances Wall—drawn together by the tragic disappearance of young Heather Bell. The story begins with the annual weekend hike of the Canadian Girls in Training, the troop on this occasion reduced to the seven pubescent girls who, for one reason or another, cannot get out of it. The hike is led, as it has been for more than twenty years, by the "wonderful" Mary Johnstone, a spinster with her own story to tell, of a life-threatening attack of polio in her teens and recovery after a visit from Jesus. Every year, Mary tells the girls all this around the campfire before delivering her "plain talk" (Munro, *Open* 158) about boys and urges. But this year the hike goes horribly wrong when Heather Bell, the most forward of the girls, goes missing, never to be found.

The story has a number of the familiar Munro hallmarks. It appears to be about one thing (Heather's disappearance) but gradually enlarges to include a number of other things, especially why Lawyer Stephens has turned so sexually abusive in his old age, and how and why his wife Maureen should cope with this. Again, the story is partly about class and opportunity and gender, and how these things can turn a girl who is a bold and giddy shrieker in adolescence (as Maureen remembers she once was) into a quiet, deferring subject, a woman who, the text sharply notes, had developed "the qualities [Maureen's] husband would see and value when hiring and proposing" (Munro, *Open* 139).

The story is shaped by at least two secrets, only one of which is partially open within the story's world, and a powerful narrative surprise. The open secret, which requires a degree of close and careful reading to recover, is Maureen's conviction that Theo Slater, married in middle age to Marian Hubbert, the corset-sales lady, is probably involved in the disappearance and likely killing of Heather Bell. Against this, the Slaters' only known connection with the girls on their hike is that when they were heading out, Marian gave them sodas, while Theo let them use a hose to spray themselves to get cool. We suspect that he probably watched when Heather was the "worst" and "boldest," "shooting water on the rest of them in all the bad places" (Munro, *Open* 130). Two days after Heather's disappearance, the couple have made the trip to town to interrupt retired Lawyer Stephens's breakfast with possibly relevant circumstantial information. Marian does not merely narrate but grotesquely performs her account of how Mr. Siddicup, speech impaired following throat cancer and possibly suffering dementia, came to her back door and tried to tell her of some unspecified event that seemingly involved copious amounts of water. If this is some sort of diversionary strategy on Marian's part, it is good enough for the town, on whose behalf we are told that "they" (the police, we assume) searched Mr. Siddicup's house and dug up his garden but found nothing, although he is committed to the Mental Health Centre as a result.

While Marian makes her report, the accompanying Theo, seen from Maureen's point of view, is described as "tall and boyish-looking, in a cheap, cream-coloured jacket with too much padding in the shoulders" (Munro, *Open* 140). Little more is said about him at this point, except that when "answering for his wife in regard to sugar for her coffee, he almost giggled when he said *lumps*" (144). All the talking is done by Marian, while Theo "said please and thank you as often as possible" (142). When their visit with the lawyer is over, Maureen continues to watch the Slaters as they sit and rest on a low stone wall across the street. There, Marian takes off her ridiculous hat of brown feathers, which Theo begins to stroke "as if he were pacifying a little scared hen" (153). Maureen sees Marian stop him, say something to him, and clamp a hand down on his—a scene whose implications leave Maureen in shock, with a shrinking in her bones. We hardly have time to reflect on this before we are assailed by another kind of shock: Maureen is ordered into her husband's downstairs office and subjected to what amounts to marital rape, a physical and mental onslaught toward the close of which Stephens commands her in his stroke-affected speech to "ta' dirty!" When his "rampage" is over, stifling the whimper of self-pity that would make her sound "like a beaten dog" (156), Maureen turns to the activity she had planned even during her husband's assault, a trope of domestic feminism of those times and that place: making a custard. A custard is emblematic on several counts. It is traditionally, quintessentially "women's work," everyday kitchen work; it involves products of female animal reproduction, milk and eggs; and making one enacts a gradual change in the viscosity of the ingredients, so that there is a narrative element, an affirming of the possibility of change, in which the cook stirring the mixture continuously plays a critical role that is absent from other kinds of cooking (boiling vegetables, grilling meat).

What makes this section near the story's close exceptional is the way it interweaves the sexual assault on Maureen, her custard making, and her thoughts about the possible role of Theo Slater in Heather

Bell's disappearance. Throughout her husband's rampage, we are told, Maureen "thought of the fingers moving in the feathers, the wife's hand laid on top of the husband's, pressing down" (Munro, *Open* 156), a simple, vivid recollection of what, it is implied, Maureen can only see as Marian's disciplining of the wayward, boyishly immature Theo. But this glimpsed disciplining is imagined a second time during the custard making, as a punishment. Maureen thinks of Mary Johnstone claiming to have seen Jesus and wonders what to make of things you might see that might reveal someone else's life, or your own, in an alternative future—but then again, might be nothing more than fantasies and lurid imaginings. The first of these of which we are told is of Maureen "sitting on stone steps eating cherries and watching a man coming up the steps carrying a parcel" (158); we scarcely need psychoanalytic theory to interpret this as an alternative imagined life of leisure and respectful male attention, in which a baby arrives for Maureen, whose tubes have been tied. The passage that is arguably the narrative high point of the story, in which the reader is most immersed and caught up in the complex and uncertain tangle of secrets, imaginings, desires, and compulsions of the narrative situation we have absorbed, now occurs:

> What she sees now isn't in any life of her own. She sees one of those thick-fingered hands that pressed into her tablecloth and that had worked among the feathers, and it is pressed down, unresistingly, but by somebody else's will—it is pressed down on the open burner of the stove where she is stirring the custard in the double boiler, and held there just for a second or two, just long enough to scorch the flesh on the red coil, to scorch but not to maim. In silence this is done, and by agreement—a brief and barbaric and necessary act. So it seems. The punished hand dark as a glove or a hand's shadow, the fingers spread. Still in the same clothes. The cream-colored sleeve, the dull blue. (158–59)

Without naming Theo outright, Maureen has articulated to herself, and to us, her conviction that Theo has done something terrible to Heather

Bell and will now, and into the future, accept some kind of private punishment meted out by his wife, in place of the public shame and rupture of community that an open trial would entail. Or so it seems to Maureen, for all these ideas are Maureen's imaginings and interpretations. However, we in turn believe they are not only imaginings but memories of the kinds of half-glimpsed acts that shape a life but are removed from evidentiary confirmation.

Freud once famously asked, what do women want? Munro's every story jerks its chin disapprovingly at such a question—such a *man's* question, seeking a once-and-for-all answer for all times and circumstances. Every woman likely wants something different, these stories show, although some factors are frequently implied desiderata: fulfillment, opportunities to be creative, respect and attention, affection, good sex. But which of the above are not equally what men want too? That is to say, our deepest desires ultimately are not limited by our gender. In addition, most women are not sure what they want. Or what women want changes as they grow older. Their detailed desires are infinitely varied and endlessly interesting, a thesis that these stories do not assert but rather perform, presenting a variety of individuals whom we can visualize and who are absorbing to us in their credibility and their incredibility, their ingenuity, deviousness, perceptiveness, and frustration, their submissions and their defiance, their endurance and their humor. Do not try to pin these individuals down, reader, says Munro; do not presume you know them to be women (they are individuals first), even if their womanliness is an intrinsic part of them. What goes for gender applies to genre here too: we should not be too quick to class these stories as either clearly realist, leading us through a consistently familiar everyday terrain, or clearly fantasy, likely to take us to some alien world—but one that comforts us by virtue of being *utterly* alien. What is true of these stories, Munro implicitly argues, is true of our lives, regardless of our so-called defining characteristics of gender, race, nationality, geography, religion, family, et cetera. Origins are not destiny; ends are not dictated by beginnings, or even by middles, although everything that has gone before may return, in memory or response, and shape our future.

Works Cited

Abbot, H. Porter. "Unreadable Minds and the Captive Reader." *Style* 42.4 (2008): 448–67.

Gerlach, John C. "To Close or Not to Close: Alice Munro's 'The Love of a Good Woman.'" *Journal of Narrative Theory* 37.1 (2007): 146–58.

Howells, Coral Ann. *Alice Munro*. Manchester: Manchester UP, 1998.

Irigaray, Luce. *Je, tu, nous: Towards a Culture of Difference*. Trans. Alison Martin. New York: Routledge, 1993. 29–36.

Munro, Alice. Interview by Peter Gzowski. *Morningside*. CBC Radio. 30 Sept. 1994. Radio.

_____. *Open Secrets*. London: Vintage, 1995.

The Houses That Alice Munro Built: The Community of *The Love of a Good Woman*_____

Jeff Birkenstein

> Then I bought another notebook and started the whole process once more. The same cycle—excitement and despair, excitement and despair. It was like having a secret pregnancy and miscarriage every week.
>
> (Alice Munro, "Cortes Island")

Reading Alice Munro is exciting, because we, as readers, are so clearly in the hands of a master short-story writer. Charles E. May believes that "if there is any justice and judgment in matters literary, she should redeem the short story from its second-class status single-handedly" (27). And yet our understanding of Munro's craft remains elusive. Perhaps this is in part because, as fellow Canadian Robert Thacker observes,

> critics have tried to keep up to Munro yet largely have not . . . the ability of critics to encompass her and her work within an overarching rationale has been paltry. . . . Indeed, owing to the shape and the scope of Munro's art—story following upon story, reconnecting, redefining—the critical monograph is not really up to Munro at all. Rather, individual articles on individual stories or connected groups of them now seem, to me at least, to offer the better critical course. (5)

Taking up Thacker's suggestion, I argue in this essay that by reading Munro's *The Love of a Good Woman* (1998) as a late-twentieth-century version of what Sandra A. Zagarell terms the "narrative of community," more insight about, and appreciation for, these stories emerges than would be possible if we just examined, as is more typical, a single story in the collection.

Zagarell argues that the narrative of community evolved in the nineteenth century when white middle-class women, the form's primary authors and subjects, were learning how to react to the changes of the

---

212   Critical Insights

Industrial Revolution. The form, of which Sarah Orne Jewett's *The Country of the Pointed Firs* (1896) is a prime example, "portray[s] the minute and quite ordinary processes through which the community maintains itself as an entity. The self exists here as part of the interdependent network of the community rather than as an individualistic unit" (Zagarell 499). Unlike in *Pointed Firs*, however, the community in Munro's collection *The Love of a Good Woman* does not involve extra-story interpersonal relationships between the characters (that is, they do not know each other), there is no consistent narrator, there are no significant overlapping characters, and temporality does not exist on a book-length continuum. Yet despite being eight separate stories, as a whole, *Love* explores the individualized yet universal searches for meaning by women unified only in their desire to escape the bonds of isolation and deprivation created by their prescribed gender roles in middle Canada. Further, unlike the books on which Zagarell focuses, *Love*'s predominant conflicts concern a time when evolving female autonomy sought not to maintain the community at any cost but to push back against the limiting demands of home and domesticity in a world where the "everyday . . . *is* ritualized" (Zagarell 518; italics in orig.).

Munro's female protagonists reinterpret this domestic space by (re)examining traditional gender roles. To the other characters in the stories, it might appear that these protagonists challenge tradition without caring about the destruction of family or community that might result. But there is the uncomfortable sense here, often barely glimpsed, that the destruction has already occurred before the stories begin, and that an impending explosion is waiting just for a spark, after which will come banishment: exclusion from family, friends, and communities who do not understand. Zagarell explains the challenge: "Whatever women's attitude, their need to negotiate made them highly adept at balancing divergent, often contradictory systems of value and discourse and gave them special skill in the kinds of mediation that . . . are fundamental to narrative of community" (509). Despite these balancing acts, Munro's women do not challenge convention for its own sake; they do not set out to change societal mores. No, they are women just trying to live their own lives. In fact, because of their isolation within a supposed community, they often lack a foundation on which they can build what they desire: love, emancipation, and release.

Examining the architecture of Munro's stories and how they interact becomes helpful in gleaning ever more meaning from them. Writing specifically about Munro, Beverly J. Rasporich argues that "if sexuality is for the female contiguous and relative, then for Alice Munro as a female author writing the body, fictional 'novelistic' structures built on correspondences and juxtapositions without ends and closure are much more natural texts than the traditional narratives of linear logic extended into climax" (162). Munro herself has famously compared the structure of a short story to a house with interconnecting rooms (Ross 788). Catherine Sheldrick Ross argues that in *Love*, we are better able to find the patterns and connections throughout if we employ a type of "scaffolding" built around previous Munro texts (786). Thomas Leitch seeks out such meaning when reading: "The unity of the stories was not a unity of action, available at the level of agents and incidents, but a unity of hermeneutic sequence, available only at the level of the transaction between writer and reader" (48). Thus, reading Munro's book as a whole—though not as a novel or even a short-story sequence or cycle (two names for a subgenre in which stories are typically deliberately linked) per se—where each story represents one house in a larger community, we see that she builds layer of story upon layer, palimpsests of meaning that communicate with the reader in ways wholly unavailable to the stories' characters. Yes, plot creates meaning within each story, as does the form of the short story. But this is also true across the stories of the entire book.

Throughout her oeuvre generally, but specifically in *Love*, Munro is concerned with the repetitive and stultifying demands that middle-class rural Canadian society makes of its women. From story to story, Munro's women are ritually and repeatedly required to nurse the broken bodies and lives of those around them, which creates difficult choices; they must decide between the community, in which they sacrifice the self in order to take on the role of nurse and nurturer, and the wilderness, wherein they might pursue their own desires of autonomy and self-knowledge, usually at the expense of family. It is an ugly choice, made more difficult to negotiate because the terms of the decision are rarely explicit, mentionable, or even wholly knowable. Reading Munro's book as a whole, with an eye to a larger narrative than may be present in any one story, is productive because it encourages the reader to celebrate the uniqueness and independence of each story, even as extra-story connections and themes emerge that, looking both forward and backward, help illuminate the individual stories. If each story in *Love* represents what Frank O'Connor calls the "unearthly glow" (21) of the short story, then to approach the book as a narrative of community is to witness multiple lights on the dark Canadian prairie. Thus, O'Connor's "submerged population group" (17) does, in fact, emerge right before our eyes in the form of white middle-of-the-road Canadian women.

Though there are many articles on the title story, what Thacker calls a "central Munro text" (Ross 786), there is scant criticism that considers the entire book. Even a cursory reading of *The Love of a Good Woman* reveals dramatic and myriad extra-story connections, even if Munro does not make these connections explicit, as does James Joyce in *Dubliners* (1914) or Sherwood Anderson in *Winesburg, Ohio* (1919). Nevertheless, there is precedent here; collections of interconnected stories are well known within the English Canadian literary tradition, and the genre "continues to be well suited to the concerns of Canadian writers intent on portraying a particular region or community, its history, its characters, its communal concerns," as represented by a "unique balancing of the one and the many" (Lynch 92–93). At multiple levels, then, Munro's book engages with this tension between the individual and the community.

Before looking at the stories, I must speak briefly to the concerns that Charles E. May has expressed regarding searching for links between stories in a collection. May is interested primarily in the co-hesiveness—purity?—of the short story and short-story form and not in "forcing" connections onto groups of short stories. He decries the impulse that, early in Munro's career, led critics to attempt "to dignify Munro's short stories by highlighting their linked nature, thus attribut-ing to them the dignity of the novel" (May 18). Though this desire on behalf of the critic or the publisher is understandable, if regrettable, given the long hegemony of the novel in the West, I agree with May that this also points to a lack of understanding of the short-story form, or at the very least a devaluing of it. This confusion stretches well into Munro's career. James Carscallen writes, "Alice Munro is a writer of 'short stories'—in fact even her novels are sequences of 'linked short stories,' as she herself has said. The term 'short story' can, of course, mean different things" (13),[1] while Ajay Heble notes that Munro of-ten "returns to the story-cycle format she employed in *Lives of Girls and Women*" (96), which in turn "forces us to reconsider our notion of genre" (196n1). Addressing this devaluation, May asks a simple question without a simple answer: "Why does Alice Munro write short stories?" The heart of his answer, I think, is that Munro sees things in a "short-story way" (May 16), a phrase suggested in a 1986 Munro interview in which she said, "I got used to writing stories, so I saw my material that way, and now I don't think I'll ever write a novel" (Rothstein).

It is because of what May argues that I proceed with some caution. While *Love* is certainly not a novel, it is also something more than a haphazard collection of stories. While I do not in any way want to sug-gest the inferiority of the short story as a single entity, connections in *Love* led me both forward and backward, similar to Ross, who, upon reading the title story, found herself "digging down through layers and following threads backward through to earlier handlings of the same material" (Ross 786). May writes, "Munro has said that when she reads a story she does not take it up at the beginning and follow it like a road 'with views and neat diversions along the way.' Rather, for her, reading a story is like moving through a house, making connections between one enclosed space and another" (18). Working with this apt metaphor, these different houses (stories), when taken together, create a community, if not for the characters within the stories then certainly for the reader, the foundation of which is the title story.

Additionally, Munro herself addresses the continuity of her stories in *Love*, if indirectly, in her prefatory author's note, explaining that "stories included in this collection that were previously published in the *New Yorker* appeared there in very different form." I wondered about this claim and read those stories originally in periodical form ("The Love of a Good Woman," "Cortes Island," "Save the Reaper," "The Children Stay," and "Before the Change").[2] As Munro claims, many textual differences exist, but in details and not narrative or plot elements per se; even some minor names have been changed to enigmatically overlap with characters from other stories. I have come to believe, then, that "very different form" is better understood to refer not to the stories in and of themselves but rather to their placement within a cohesive volume. Before *Love*, they were truly autonomous; they existed without prequel, without sequel. But once in the book, set among other stories of similar disposition, connections are readily apparent.[3]

In but one example that represents the changes occurring throughout the stories, the added details are copious. In this scene from "Before the Change," the narrator speaks with her father, who, she comes to learn, provides illegal abortions. Text without underlining is from both the *New Yorker* (Munro, "Before" 132) and *Love* (256–7); underlined material represents text added to the book, as do bracketed commas:

What did he think about Kennedy and Nixon?

"Aw, they're just a couple of Americans."

I tried to open the conversation up a bit.

"How do you mean?"

When you ask him to go into subjects that he thinks don't need to be talked about, or take up an argument that doesn't need proving, he has a way of lifting his upper lip at one side, showing a pair of big tobacco-stained teeth.

"Just a couple of Americans," he said, as if the words might have got by me the first time.

So we sit there not talking but not in silence[,] because[,] as you may recall[,] he is a noisy breather. His breath gets dragged down stony alleys and through creaky gates. Then takes off into a bit of tweeting and gurgling as if there was some inhuman apparatus shut up in his chest. Plastic pipes and colored bubbles. You're not supposed to take any notice, and I'll soon be used to it. But it takes up a lot of space in a room . . .

Immediately following, there are an additional ninety-five new words not found in the *New Yorker*. On the surface—through sheer amount of words, for instance—the difference between the two versions is dramatic and would appear to represent Munro's "very different form." However, this additional material does not fundamentally alter the story. In both versions, after this beginning, the story transpires in more or less the same fashion. Yet it is not superfluous either, for this additional material not only foreshadows the story's events but also relates to other women in the book in terms of their relationships with men and the dark spaces they inhabit. The father's breath suggests the dark alleys of illicit abortions; the plastic pipes and the bubbling prepare the reader for the abortion with which the narrator will assist. When the narrator later announces that she knows what is going on and that others in the community "must know," the father replies indignantly, "Must they? There's a difference between knowing and yapping. Get that through your head once and for all" (Munro, *Love* 270). The expanded passage above presages this crucial moment of intentionally not knowing. Thus, my sentence-level comparison of these two versions of the same story, and of all the stories from the *New Yorker*, indicates that there are no significant plot-related changes. Though the added detail is important, it largely does not force us to reconsider the story plots or conclusions, as, for instance, we must do with different versions of Raymond Carver's stories.

E. D. Blodgett argues that Munro chooses her titles carefully and, "as an indication of the collection as a whole, these meanings multiply" (14), a phenomenon altogether different in a magazine. *The Love of a Good Woman*, a slightly sardonic title (the book's cover gives no indication that it does not encompass the whole volume), and the eponymous story represent Munro's search for "a way of saying the unsayable" (Ross 804). At six words, neither particularly short nor long, the title is wonderfully ambiguous. What is the nature of this love? Is it conditional? Who is receiving it? Why and how is such a woman good? As the reader progresses through the volume, the woman becomes women, the loves at once varied and singular.

The title story, broken into five parts, begins like a movie, with initial credits rolling. Munro's camera—her pen—pans across an exhibit in the small Walley, Ontario, museum, focusing on a red optometrist's box, imprinted with the name D. M. Willens. Questions arise. Why is the box in the museum? At first glance, this appears to be nothing more than a mundane local mystery. But over the course of both the title story and the book, this mystery speaks universally, if quietly, to the plight of all the book's women. Leaving opening credits behind, in section 1, "Jutland," we meet three boys on the prowl. They find a car submerged in the Peregrine River—Mr. Willens's car, his body inside. They are excited to find the body, yes, but they sense that this trauma heralds unknown change. In the countryside, they are free (Munro, *Love* 10), whereas in town, constricting expectations are placed upon them.

In section 2, "Heart Failure" (another Munro title with multiple layers), we meet Enid. Enid's father, from his deathbed, urges her not to become a nurse. Her mother follows along, apologetically and pathetically, unwittingly revealing the tension between women of different generations. Nursing, the father believes, makes women "coarse," because of "the familiarity nurses had with men's bodies" (Munro, *Love* 39–40). Enid initially protests, but she does promise, if only for the "noble perversity" of it (40). Sensing this rebellion even in Enid's defeat, her mother says, "Well, I hope that makes you happy." Enid withdraws from nursing school, acquiescing to her father's misogyny and her mother's fear that Enid might have chances she did not. Becoming a nurse, her parents believe, would affect her marriage prospects: "It would spoil her good chances and give her a lot of other chances that were not so good." To some extent, Enid's parents are right, but for all the wrong reasons. Ironically, Enid remains unmarried and, though not officially a nurse, becomes a long-term caregiver: "'Do you think I haven't seen any bottom parts before?' she would say. 'Bottom parts, top parts, it's pretty boring after a while. You know, there's just the two ways we're made'" (35). She learns to compartmentalize: "No bodily smell—even the smell of semen—was unfamiliar to her" (77). However, such work brings Enid into contact not only with patients' bodies but also with their broken lives behind their illnesses.

Enid nurses the infirm Mrs. Quinn, who is dying of kidney failure, but who has been bitter since before her illness. Bedridden, Mrs. Quinn knows she has lost her husband, Rupert. Even his supposed marital duty of nursing her has been outsourced to Enid. Speaking about her own husband's rejection of her, Mrs. Quinn says to Enid, in her husband's voice and directed back upon herself, "Why don't we take her out and throw her out on the manure pile?" (Munro, *Love* 35). Mrs. Quinn asks this particular question for a reason; she tells Enid, who is not sure what to believe and wonders how she is being manipulated, that Mr. Quinn has once before discarded a human body. It was, she claims, due to burning the evidence of this act that Mrs. Quinn's sickness began. Weighed down by Mrs. Quinn's story, Enid excavates her past choices and confronts her own life's failures, even as she senses she is becoming detritus in Mrs. Quinn's story: "Of course, an event was coming, something momentous at least in this family. Mrs. Quinn was going to die, at the age of twenty-seven" (32). Though perhaps as trivial as Willens's box in a small museum, this pain will not remain within this family. Family tragedy radiates outward; houses cannot contain the messiness of life within, the decaying of bodies and marriages. Mrs. Quinn's deathbed secret, slowly revealed, is this: Mrs. Quinn believes that her husband killed Willens after the optometrist raped her during examinations. And because Mrs. Quinn is correct that Enid and her husband are forming a bond, Enid must decide if Mrs. Quinn's story is true.

In section 4, "Lies," Enid wonders: should Rupert be punished? For acquiescing to her father's request and all that has come afterward, should she be punished? The story ends ambiguously, with Enid testing Rupert by putting her life in jeopardy. Enid gets into a rowboat with Rupert—she cannot swim—and waits to be thrown overboard. We never see the concluding action of the story, but the story's epiphany comes a few pages earlier, when Enid decides to give Rupert this chance to kill her and thus silence the last person aware of the murder. As long as his violent past remains a mere possibility, "this room and this house and her life held a different possibility, an entirely different possibility from the one she had been living with (or glorying in—however you want to put it) for the last few days" (Munro, *Love* 75). Enid may have sacrificed her own dreams, but she takes the ultimate risk at the story's conclusion in order to pursue, not an accepted female life, but one of immense possibility. Were she to remain silent, she would be complicit, both in terms of the crime and in terms of her feelings for Rupert: "This was what most people knew. A simple thing that it had taken her so long to understand. This was how to keep the world habitable" (76). But to keep the world habitable as it is (or was, in 1950s Canada) requires the supplication of women like Enid. Yet she will act, come what may: "She would make this house into a place that had no secrets from her and where all order was as she decreed" (77). Or she will die trying.

These macro-themes found in "The Love of a Good Woman" repeat in story after story in Munro's collection. As Allan Weiss argues in a conference presentation on Canadian mini-cycles, it generally takes more than thematic overlap to justify the claim of cycle (or short-story sequence or narrative of community). However, with Munro's stories gathered in a single volume, various patterns of meaning bubble to the surface. For instance, myriad details overlap, including the smell and excretion of bodily fluids as a metaphor for the breakdown of community; multiple female journals, secret or otherwise; and repeated physical characteristics relating to place, in this case the plains of Ontario. Stories feature interconnecting narrative strategies, such as characters whose faulty memories mean that the truth, as viewed from many perspectives, is always suspect; temporal incongruities; explicit references to past writers interested in similar themes, including Virginia Woolf and Katherine Mansfield; and the use of foreboding exclamations without immediate meaning. So masterful is Munro's use of repetition in seemingly completely separate stories, some material of which has been altered from the original stories in order to more clearly overlap, that connections become inescapable. As the reader progresses through the book, he or she comes to see that Enid's revelation sets the stage for what every woman in the book must face. For Enid, and all of Munro's protagonists in *Love*, what matters is not the end result but the moment of decisiveness, of action, of rebellion, of epiphany, which has at least the promise of possibility, even if rarely fulfilled and usually unseen.

Although "The Love of a Good Woman" is the collection's dominant story, it is crucial to examine some key connections in the remaining stories in order to tease out the narrative of community. Recalling Woolf's *A Room of One's Own* (1929), the first line of the second story, "Jakarta," highlights what we do not see Enid attain, but what we know she desires: "Kath and Sonje have a place of their own on the beach, behind some large logs" (Munro, *Love* 79). In contrast, the nearby so-called Monicas seem to be trapped with their gaggle of children, having "reached a stage in life that Kath and Sonje dread" (80). By going on a beach holiday, Kath and Sonje attempt to escape the future they think awaits them because they both have too-perfect, and thus imperfect, marriages. Just as this temporary move did not work for Linda, or indeed any of the Burnells, in Katherine Mansfield's "At the Bay"

(1922), it proves fruitless for Kath and Sonje, though in very different ways. For example, Kath cannot understand how Sonje can say "My happiness depends on Cottar" (85). The stage is set; rebellion will occur. Or not. But true to the "short-story way," we witness the moment of (in)decision in these women's lives.

"Cortes Island" begins in the voice of the narrator: "Some people . . . referred to me as a little bride" (Munro, *Love* 117). Old Mrs. Gorrie nurses her husband, Mr. Gorrie, who is wheelchair bound. Though the narrator considers herself mature and independent, she and her husband, Chess, live in the Gorries' basement. Needing money, she takes a job nursing Mr. Gorrie; the narrator and Mr. Gorrie become a peculiar sort of couple, garnering Mrs. Gorrie's distrust. Over time, the narrator learns the Gorries' secret, which, enigmatically, mirrors a coming change in her own life: "We were right at the end of the time of looking at things that way, though we didn't know it" (123). The narrator, at Mr. Gorrie's urging, reads old newspaper clippings, learning that a man died in a house fire on an island but his wife survived. Troubled by the story, which she believes explains the Gorries' past—that is, Mr. Gorrie killed Mrs. Gorrie's first husband in the fire—the narrator ends "Cortes Island" with menacing dreams. The young bride narrator senses that her life will force her to choose between nurturing either Chess or herself, but not both.

In "Save the Reaper," Eve and her grandchildren take a drive and stumble upon a group of potential misfits, but unlike the Misfit in Flannery O'Connor's story "A Good Man Is Hard to Find" (1953), they are largely without philosophy. They are just men without women, drunk, living in a dilapidated house, and already bored with the prostitute they bring home. They have no overtly evil plans, but still they block Eve's car, and she realizes this is a decisive moment; a palpable threat lingers in the air, with even the "smell of semen in the room" (Munro, *Love* 170, the second mention of such a smell in the book). Eve also knows that the owner of the house, Mary, has been put away in a "Home" (166) and is thus unable to intervene. Unlike women in *Love*, men choose or reject the burden of caregiving without repercussive stigma. What Eve says and does in this house at this moment is connected directly to the relationship she shares with her own daughter, who was conceived on a train with a man from India.

In "The Children Stay," Pauline leaves her husband and young children for a man she meets while performing in the play *Eurydice*. Many years later, Pauline discusses the time with her now-grown daughter. She pretends to fill narrative gaps casually, but "acute pain" remains (Munro, *Love* 213). Pauline, it turns out, did not run away with this first lover, as her ex-husband always claimed, but with another man; the original fling, with the man playing Orphée, was just someone "that I lived with for a while" (214). Her life changed forever all those years ago, but she now realizes that that moment was only a prelude to her other new life.

We meet a complicated mix of people divorcing and remarrying each other in "Rich as Stink." But the sense of victory for Karin at story's end lies not in any community found but in the fact, which must remain hidden, that she exists now autonomously: "Nobody knew the sober, victorious feeling she had sometimes, when she knew how much she was on her own" (Munro, *Love* 253). In "Before the Change," the narrator writes to her former lover, with whom she lost a baby, explaining how she became involved with her father and his illicit abortion business. Though initially traumatized, by both her own life and her father's business, she begins to learn that helping other women with their illegal abortions is, in fact, *helping* other women—and herself.

Every story following "The Love of a Good Woman" involves beach vacations or other types of escape, and in the final story, "My Mother's Dream," the protagonist reminisces about visiting her aunts as a child, in a small community that knows too much. She finally comes to a conclusion about that time long ago that can speak for all the female leads in the book, even if details differ:

To me it seems that it was only then that I became female. I know that the matter was decided long before I was born and was plain to everybody else since the beginning of my life, but I believe that it was only at the moment when I decided to come back, when I gave up the fight against my mother (which must have been a fight for something like her total surrender) and when in fact I chose survival over victory (death would have been victory), that I took on my female nature. (Munro, *Love* 337)

By now, Munro fans and critics alike know her territory—a place in the imagination and of the world that Munro revisits in *The Love of a Good Woman*, an expansive place that paradoxically threatens to confine the women who live there. William Faulkner has Yoknapatawpha County; Munro, her ethereal, rural southwestern Ontario. Munro's location is as expansive for the author as it is isolating for her characters. That is, "her fiction is tangibly rooted in the social realism of the rural and small-town world of her own experience, but it insistently explores what lies beyond the bounds of empirical reality" (Dahlie 5). Similar to Raymond Carver's non-distinct so-called Carver Country, in rural, down-and-out Northern California and Washington, Munro inscribes her peculiar worldview on her territory even as this perspective encompasses a certain kind of universality. Ultimately, however, physical verisimilitude is not as important for Munro as psychological veracity. As when Carver argues that "commonplace things" can be endowed "with immense, even startling power" (275), Munro, too, transforms "ordinary objects . . . [that] can, at any moment, become sinister or threatening" (Heble 4) into something much greater than themselves. As readers, we, too, can benefit by reading Munro's entire book and searching for the many clues laid out for us across traditional story boundaries.

Notes

1. It is unclear whether or not Munro has even written a novel. Her second book, *Lives of Girls and Women* (1971), does have "A Novel" on the cover, but it might be better described as a short-story sequence or cycle. *The Beggar Maid* (1979; released as *Who Do You Think You Are?* in Canada, 1978), also a book of linked stories, is billed as being "Stories of Flo and Rose."

2. Carol Beran asks the question, "What does publication in the *New Yorker* mean to the art of a serious yet widely read writer such as Alice Munro?" (204). Beran chronicles the long history of Munro's work in the magazine, the different editors she has used, and the subsequent effects on her work. While she "found no evidence" (209) that such factors have affected Munro's work significantly, she does address an alternative way of viewing the "very different form" that Munro claims for her stories in *Love*. Beran hypothesizes that "reading experiences are affected by what is outside a story" (211). That is, the writer does not have, as Poe desired, the full attention of the reader of a Munro story (or any story) in the *New Yorker*, for the pages of the *New Yorker* are loaded with side ads, graphics, cartoons, and a host of other items, and "the initial effect of this clutter is to prevent the concentration that stories printed in books with blank margins evoke in readers" (211). Ultimately, whatever Munro's intent, there are clearly significant and multiple changes for the reader from periodical to book, both on the page and off.

3. Critics appear little interested in these differences. For example, Ildikó de Papp Carrington writes in a footnote that "Munro has slightly revised the original *New Yorker* version of this story" (159n2) and leaves it at that. About the stories in the *New Yorker*, Randall Curb notes only that, "if memory serves, most of them were a little leaner there" (618).

Works Cited

Beran, Carol L. "The Luxury of Excellence: Alice Munro in the *New Yorker*." *Essays on Canadian Writing* 66 (1998): 204–31.

Blodgett, E. D. *Alice Munro*. Boston: Twayne, 1988.

Carrington, Ildikó de Papp. "'Don't Tell (on) Daddy': Narrative Complexity in Alice Munro's 'The Love of a Good Woman.'" *Studies in Short Fiction* 34.2 (1997): 159–70.

Carscallen, James. *The Other Country: Patterns in the Writing of Alice Munro*. Toronto: ECW, 1993.

Carver, Raymond. "On Writing." *The New Short Story Theories*. Ed. Charles E. May. Athens: Ohio UP, 1994. 272–77.

Curb, Randall. "When Is a Story More Than a Story? A Fiction Chronicle." *Southern Review* 35.3 (1999): 608–20.

Dahlie, Hallvard. *Alice Munro and Her Works*. Toronto: ECW, 1985.

Heble, Ajay. *The Tumble of Reason: Alice Munro's Discourse of Absence*. Toronto: U of Toronto P, 1994.

Leitch, Thomas M. *What Stories Are: Narrative Theory and Interpretation*. University Park: Pennsylvania State UP, 1986.

Lynch, Gerald. "The One and the Many: English-Canadian Short Story Cycles." *Canadian Literature* 130 (1991): 91–104.

May, Charles E. "Why Does Alice Munro Write Short Stories?" *Wascana Review* 38.1 (2003): 16–28.

Munro, Alice. "Before the Change." *New Yorker* 24 Aug. 1988: 132–43.

_____. *The Love of a Good Woman*. New York: Vintage, 1998.

O'Connor, Frank. *The Lonely Voice: A Study of the Short Story*. Hoboken, NJ: Melville, 2011.

Rasporich, Beverly J. *Dance of the Sexes: Art and Gender in the Fiction of Alice Munro*. Edmonton: U of Alberta P, 1990.

Ross, Catherine Sheldrick. "'Too Many Things': Reading Alice Munro's 'The Love of a Good Woman.'" *University of Toronto Quarterly* 71.3 (2002): 786–810.

Rothstein, Mervyn. "Canada's Alice Munro Finds Excitement in Short-Story Form." *New York Times* 10 Nov. 1986: C17.

Thacker, Robert. "Alice Munro, Writing 'Home': 'Seeing This Trickle in Time.'" *Essays on Canadian Writing* 66 (1998): 1–20.

Weiss, Allan. "Between Collection and Cycle: The Mini-Cycle." Tenth International Conference on the Short Story in English. University College Cork, Cork, Ireland. 19 June 2008. Presentation.

Zagarell, Sandra A. "Narrative of Community: The Identification of a Genre." *Signs* 13.3 (1988): 498–527.

Honest Tricks: Surrogate Authors in Alice Munro's *Hateship, Friendship, Courtship, Loveship, Marriage*

David Crouse

Alice Munro's stories have been classified as miniature novels so often that it has become almost ubiquitous to label her as a short-story writer possessing the stylistic sensibilities of a novelist. *Hateship, Friendship, Courtship, Loveship, Marriage* (2001), her tenth collection of short stories, seems to support this classification before the book is even opened. *Hateship, Friendship, Courtship, Loveship, Marriage* has to be one of the more cumbersome and thorny titles in contemporary literature, and it is exactly this bulky complexity that makes it classic Munro. The title hints at a novelistic sensibility with its gnarled, episodic chain of cause and effect. To some degree, it is a clear sign of what we will be getting in this collection; the stories, and especially the two longest stories bookending the collection, cover vast spans of time, often whole lives, and take as their subject the nature of marriage and romance. But, as with most of Munro's language, the title is also deceptive, more complicated than it first appears.

There is also irony in the title, because the lives of the characters in this collection do not move episodically from one stage of life to the next, and for all their ambition and their sheer scope, the structures of these stories do not follow traditional, novelistic narrative form: *first this, then this, then this.* Perhaps too much has been made of Munro's similarity to a novelist, and not enough of her similarity to a memoirist. Like a memoirist, she is concerned with the distinct flavor of the individual mind and how it shapes human experience. Like a memoirist, she structures her stories to condense a life into unique, lyrical shapes. These stories move from stage to stage as much by poetic association as by cause and effect, and taken in that light, the title of the collection can be seen as a comment on the easy categories we make as human beings, the manner in which we divide a life into segments and make simple connections between first one and then the next.

These stories are not traditionally narrative, but they take on narrative as their subject matter, ruminating on the manner in which we use narrative to shape our identities. Munro's characters are always telling themselves tales and telling other people lies. In this way, they are memoirists themselves, surrogate writers honing their own personal narratives—sometimes only in their heads, but more often than not in some other form as well. These stories are littered with letters, half-remembered childhood tales, and other forms of recollection. *How did we get here*, the characters seem to be asking, *and who have we become?*

In *The Art of Description*, Mark Doty discusses an imagistic writing technique in which a mind becomes deeply involved in the act of seeing, so much so that information is weighed and measured, particularized, given meaning, and ultimately cast in a new, transformative light (17). He is talking about poetry here, specifically Elizabeth Bishop's famous poem "The Fish" (1946), but Doty, an accomplished memoirist, could easily be talking about the memoir. It is no accident, he says, that "The Fish" is told in the past tense, because without memory, the material of reality cannot be refashioned. Present tense would simply not work. The images become flat and lifeless, devoid of the meaning that comes only in recollection.

A mind in action, Doty calls it, a mind engaging and transforming experience through language. His use of the word *action* is nicely appropriate, I think, because of the force with which the mind engages the world. In a moment, when a mind is in action, traditional narrative time—the time of Munro's title—falls away and is replaced with a more meditative, free-associative, slow-moving time; but within this moment there is still action, a sort of thrust and parry as the mind embraces some details, dismisses others, and is forced to choose between this meaning and that, just as a person might choose to walk down one road and not another.

When we discuss the way in which Munro's characters "rewrite" the world, we are talking about minds in action, characters who are deeply involved in the act of seeing. Sometimes this seeing takes the form of twisting the truth to suit their own agendas, or looking deeply at their own memories, but it is important to note that this process goes beyond the physical action into a deeper place. Munro deemphasizes physical action in favor of the mind in action. In her stories, the central action is almost always the act of perception itself; other actions, what we might normally consider to be the plot, are subsumed or transformed to this end. The title story of *Hateship* begins and ends with an act of seeing: first, the station agent's confused attempt to figure out Johanna as she buys her train ticket; and then, years later, the young girl Edith's watchful consideration of the woman Johanna has become.

Grant, the protagonist of "The Bear Came over the Mountain," is physically busy throughout that story, rushing from place to place, hatching his schemes for his wife's salvation and his own gratification. But to emphasize this physical action as the central action of the story would be to ignore the distinct and busy nature of his mind. He is constantly involved in the weighing and categorizing of his memories, possibly in order to assuage some deep guilt he feels through the recasting of his own personal narrative. As Edith is the author of Johanna's love story in "Hateship, Friendship, Courtship, Loveship, Marriage," Grant is the author of his own story, and it is a story that has to be constantly revised in order for it to remain romantic. Witness this section of the story, when Grant awakens from a troubling dream:

> He hauled himself out of the dream and set about separating what was real from what was not.
>
> There had been a letter, and the word "rat" had appeared in black paint on his office door, and Fiona, on being told that a girl had suffered from a bad crush on him, had said pretty much what she said in the dream.

The colleague hadn't come into it, the black-robed women had never appeared in his classroom, and nobody had committed suicide. Grant hadn't been disgraced, in fact he had got off easily when you thought of what might have happened just a couple of years later. But word got around. Cold shoulders became conspicuous. They had few Christmas invitations and spent New Year's Eve alone. Grant got drunk, and without its being required of him—also, thank God, without making the error of a confession—he promised Fiona a new life.

The shame he felt then was the shame of being duped, of not having noticed the change that was going on. And not one woman had made him aware of it. There had been the change in the past when so many women so suddenly became available—or it seemed that way to him—and now this new change, when they were saying that what had happened was not what they had had in mind at all. (Munro, *Hateship* 286)

Consider the use of verbs in the first paragraph: *hauled*, *set about*, *separating*. This is a man getting ready for work. This sifting process, separating the real from the not real, pervades the story, and as the plot moves forward to its conclusion, we are also constantly moving backward, weighing information along with Grant. These flashes of memory—they are not really flashbacks per se—are expository, of course, but the information is certainly not static. The passage possesses a certain neurotic dynamism that lends these sections as much of a dramatic cast as the more physical scenes. What is real here? In the dream, Grant moves closest to a true sense of his guilt, and it is only afterward, when waking, that he is able to address this guilt by the careful assemblage of just the right kind of evidence. In his personal narrative, he is the one who has been victimized, and he is also the hero—the man who has protected Fiona from the rude complications of the world. It does not matter much to him that some of those complications happen to be his own affairs.

Fiona's diseased memory and Grant's revision of his own memories stand in parallel to one another. Both characters are engaged in the separating of the real from the unreal, but in both cases, reality and fantasy are difficult to label with any kind of authority. Fiona soon forgets Grant and reimagines herself in a new relationship with Aubrey, a fellow citizen of the rest home. Is this simple dementia, an act of expediency, or revenge on Grant for his infidelities? The reality here becomes as murky and complicated as Grant's guilt-driven dream.

II

It is easy to see Munro's work running in a continuous line from those realistic short-story writers who preceded her, the John Updikes and John Cheevers of the 1960s. And yes, we find in her work the same intense focus on the mundane detail, the internal psychological landscapes laid bare. However, her techniques often run counter to some used by these other realistic writers. Consider what a mind in continuous action does to the notion of how knowledge is arrived at by a character in a work of short fiction.

Charles Baxter, in his essay "Against Epiphanies," remarks, "The logic of unveiling has become a dominant mode in Anglo-American writing, certainly in fiction, particularly short stories" (49). Munro's techniques run counter to this dominant way of telling, which emphasizes a moment of sharp insight—knowledge as a visitation placed at the end of a story—over slower and more complex forms of learning. Baxter does not mention Munro by name, but her stories seem to act as a solution to what he sees as a relatively pervasive problem: the overuse and misuse of the epiphany in contemporary literature.

In Munro's work, and in this collection in particular, small moments of epiphany are scattered throughout the narrative. In fact, it would be inaccurate to call them epiphanies; they are small realizations not so much visited upon a character as generated by that person's attention to the world, his or her careful memoir-style assemblage of memories and details. Sometimes these realizations are contradicted paragraphs later, sometimes even within the same paragraph. The closest we come to the language and flavor of epiphany is in the title story, when Edith glimpses Johanna and her new family, but even that can be seen as almost a reversal of epiphany, an opening up rather than a closing down of possibilities.

For all Munro's realistic concerns, this strikes me as a very important line of demarcation between her work and that of other realistic writers, and it puts her in kinship with another school that might at first seem adversarial to her particular aesthetic; her stories are equally indebted to those metafictional writers of the sixties, such as John Barth and Robert Coover, who took as their subject the process of writing itself and made it their job to disrupt standard narrative conceits. One of Munro's true strengths as a writer of short fiction is her ability to combine these two styles into a compelling whole. It could be argued, in fact, that this combination of stylistic elements results in one of the central conflicts in *Hateship* and in her work in general: the conflict between reality and meta-reality, the authentic and the manufactured.

Of course, these questions of reality versus fantasy are as old as literature itself. But it is Munro's unique structural conceits, strikingly unusual for the short-story form, that allow her to ask these questions— both overtly, through the minds and actions of her characters, and also more subtly and more viscerally, through the very design of her stories. The narratives stop and start, double back, change perspectives, and argue with each other, just as the language does at the sentence level. These are narratives in conflict with themselves, possessed of a designed messiness that asks the reader to assemble them, jigsaw-like.

One of the most vivid illustrations of this dynamic occurs in the middle section of the collection's title story, where we see the creation of the first draft of the first false letter by Edith and Sabitha. We have already received an abundance of information by this point, including the buying of a wedding dress and the purchase of a train ticket to exit the town, but we are unsure about the exact reasons why these events are unfolding in such a manner. We do get conjecture from outsiders—the man who sells the train ticket to Johanna, Mr. McCauley as he assembles his own take on events—but Munro holds us outside the event, as spectators. Even the small section told from Johanna's perspective focuses on the anxiety of buying the wedding dress and all but ignores the context, offering up only hints about the impending marriage.

So we are deep into the story when Munro moves backward in time, to that first letter. But the episode is not simply offered up as an explanation of Johanna's behavior; what we get is far richer. In a conversation between the two girls, we are given a critique of letter writing and a lesson in the art of fabrication. Edith rejects suggestions from her writing partner as being unconvincing in their adolescent romantic tone, and then quickly moves from parody to a kind of deep, sincere involvement, "her voice becoming increasingly solemn and tender" (Munro, *Hateship* 32) as she reads her own words aloud.

To some degree, Edith is the surrogate author of Johanna's story, but she only becomes this author by growing deeply involved in Johanna's psychology. The letters, of course, are an act of cruelty, but their success as art, as a convincing lie, depends on Edith's deepening empathy for their subject. When Sabitha offers up the word *rapture* for the next letter in the series, Edith rejects it as being too syrupy. The word *gregarious*, chosen by Edith, stays in the letter despite Sabitha's counter-protests, because it is a word that Johanna would use. This debate over the minutiae of language results in Edith granting intelligence to her "character," an intelligence we have seen already when encountering the real Johanna in the dress shop.

Edith acts as the surrogate author of Johanna's story, but her power as puppet master is limited. The story resolves with Edith seeing the results of her fabrication. "It seemed fantastical, but dull," she comments as she ruminates over the sight of Johanna and Mr. Boudreau with a baby. She is perplexed by her own power as a creator of Johanna's narrative: "For where, on the list of things she planned to achieve in her life, was there any mention of her being responsible for the existence on earth of a person named Omar?" (Munro, *Hateship* 54). But she is also perplexed by the opposite realization, her very lack of power in the face of life's strange complexity. "You must not ask, it is forbidden for us to know," she writes at the story's close, "what fate has in store for me, or for you" (54).

The question here centers on the autonomy of the individual, and it is to the story's credit that Johanna is fashioned as such a forceful personality. Her fate is both created by her and created for her, and the first image we see of her in the piece is of a willful and pragmatic person, someone capable of making clear-eyed decisions, a woman who will, much later in the story, save the life of her future husband. And yet her life is also a meta construction, an art object created by a precocious child, and her lack of knowledge about this important fact robs her of some autonomy. She is saved by Edith's story, but also victimized by it, and her lack of awareness of this victimization makes it no less true.

III

We have seen this type of surrogate authorship before in Munro's work, most obviously in her early story "Material," from *Something I've Been Meaning to Tell You* (1974). That story ends with its protagonist considering her husband, who has gone on to be an actual short-story writer: "I was thinking I would tell him how strange it was for me to realize that we shared, still shared, the same bank of memory, and that what was all scraps and oddments, useless baggage, for me, was ripe and usable, a paying investment, for him" (Munro, *Selected* 95). This story, like other earlier work by Munro, acts as a more obvious confrontation of the issues at work in *Hateship*. The argument between the protagonist and her ex-husband is one of interpretation. There are two minds in action present in "Material": that of the figurative author, the protagonist, as she remembers her marriage, and that of the literal author, her ex-husband, who has fashioned this memory into the actual short story the protagonist now holds in her hands. Both have validity, and it is important to note that the ex-husband's story is artful and sensitive, but the protagonist is finally able to dismiss it as "not enough" (95).

What separates "Material" and other earlier work from the stories in *Hateship* is the extent of the control these narratives have over the lives of Munro's characters. In stories such as "Hateship" and "The Bear Came over the Mountain," the narratives often succeed in supplanting reality, so that by story's end, reality has been reshaped to fit the fictions told by the principal characters. This, I believe, is where the meta element in Munro's work can be seen mostly strongly. In these mid-period stories, that element cannot be dismissed in the manner of the protagonist of "Material"; it has real force in the world. Edith, the young girl who writes fake letters in the title story, manages to fabricate the voice of an older woman with a lightness of touch that is startlingly convincing, and this skill changes the lives of everybody around her. Alfrida, the newspaper writer in "Family Furnishings," is able to remember—and most likely manufacture—details from her past in minute detail. These characters share a certain kinship with the dying woman from the title story of Munro's previous collection, *The Love of a Good Woman* (1998), absorbed in their own private inner worlds but skilled enough communicators to convince others of the veracity of those worlds.

"The Bear Came over the Mountain" opens with descriptions of Fiona's early-onset dementia. The memory loss associated with the dementia, specifically an incident involving the misplacement of a fur coat, is described as being "unintentionally on purpose," a way to take a seemingly negative experience and turn it into something more positive, "like a sin she was leaving behind" (Munro, *Hateship* 278). This is an appropriate metaphor, then, for the way these stories unfold, in that it captures the strange way people are influenced by these surrogate authors and their stories. And strangely, just as in the case of the lost fur coat, these changes often have a strongly positive element to them. Edith's fabricated love letters in "Hateship" result in a real love relationship and eventually a child. Grant, the protagonist of "The Bear Came over the Mountain," is a serial adulterer, but his final act of adultery becomes a sort of gift to his rest home–bound wife, a gift that validates her own dementia-produced waking dream and brings her an odd kind of happiness.

The phrase *unintentionally on purpose*, then, could also describe the way the narratives these surrogate authors bring into existence move beyond their control and take on an independent force within the real world, often resulting in happy endings. It could also reference a completely different set of characters—people like Fiona and Johanna, characters who have based their lives on other people's lies but are nonetheless content. Are they active, autonomous characters, blessed with true agency, or victims of forces larger than themselves?

Johanna's marriage is exactly such an act of unintentional purposefulness, and Edith's puzzlement at that act involves the extrapolation of Johanna's situation to herself, because if Johanna could be the victim of such a manipulation, what does it mean for everybody else? In one of the more subtle and interesting passages in the story, Edith splits herself into several personas as well: the past self who wrote the letters, her present self, and "the real self that she expected would take over once she got out of this town and away from all the people who thought they knew her" (Munro, *Hateship* 54). But her awareness of Johanna's story casts doubt on her own, on the story she has written for herself. The authenticity of that future self is now debatable; it could be as much a construction as Johanna's future self, the self with baby and husband in tow. Strangely, her sureness at ever reaching that "real" self is undermined by her own power over Johanna. Both characters are an interestingly complex mix of strength and weakness.

The counterpoint here, of course, is Sabitha, who is "now self-contained and pretty and remarkably, unexpectedly slim" (Munro, *Hateship* 53). She has grown into a strong young woman, and it is precisely her insensitivity and lack of intelligence that seem to give her power. While Edith remembers everything, Sabitha seems to remember nothing, and moves through the crowd of former friends like a stranger. She seems to have remade herself as a new person, untroubled and undefined by her past. She is Edith's longing made actual, a reminder of her failure to do the same. She is also an example of one of Munro's favorite character types: the person who gains power through her insensitivity. Sabitha seems to be resilient precisely because she does not possess a mind in action; she remains unengaged with the world around her, as if suffering a kind of blissful amnesia.

What targets these concepts most effectively, though, is not the language of the story itself, which is precise and intensely visual, but the unusual structure. We begin in medias res, watching Johanna through the eyes of the train clerk and unsure as to what is actually happening. Each new point of view, including Johanna's own, offers up a new, sometimes slightly contradictory portrait of the story's protagonist, and the movements in time place the reader into a state of hyperattentiveness. Even before Edith and Sabitha construct their version of Johanna, we are already constructing her ourselves, placing this information next to that and questioning the veracity of this or that perspective. This particular example might be the best illustration of Munro's memoirist thinking toward her subject matter, the stitching used not so much to generate narrative force as to create a way of seeing her subject matter.

Munro has used this technique to even greater extremes before, of course, most notably in *Friend of My Youth* (1990), although here it is somewhat more accessible than in those stories. Part of its artfulness lies in this accessibility; for such a challenging story, "Hateship" is remarkably visceral. I would argue that it is precisely this double quality of immediacy and complexity that gives these stories their unique power. Because as much as Munro seems intent on disrupting the traditional narrative line, she also gives us moments of physical intensity when we simply ask the question, what is going to happen next? When Johanna finds the prone body of her future husband in a destroyed room, previous meta-based questions are replaced with the immediacy of the situation, and we become deeply involved in the cleaning of a room and the efficient saving of a human life. In the final scene of "Floating Bridge," the strange confrontation between a man and a woman in a remote swamp generates a very traditional kind of drama from a sense of palpable, possibly life-threatening danger.

In later collections, such as *Runaway* (2004) and *Too Much Happiness* (2009), these moments of traditional drama become even more abundant, some might argue to the detriment of Munro's work. In *Hateship, Friendship, Courtship, Loveship, Marriage*, we see a fascinating middle ground between the more memoiristic work of *Friend of My Youth* and Munro's later stories.

IV

As in many of Munro's stories, the relationship between art and lies is a complex one. Like Edith in "Hateship," Grant is given the opportunity to shape and reformulate another person's story, and he does so using the same skills that allowed him to be duplicitous in his own marriage. His gift to his wife is a gift of corroboration: he decides to cease contradicting her reality and embraces his role as manipulator, conniving to play matchmaker for Aubrey and Fiona. It is an act of deep love and sacrifice, of course, but it is also Grant's latest act of infidelity, because it involves the seduction of Aubrey's wife. At the story's end, he considers "the practical sensuality of her cat's tongue" (Munro, *Hateship* 322) as he dials her number. The irony of his situation is not lost on Grant, who is a remarkably self-aware character, and it could even be said that part of his gratification comes from that knowledge. So his physical satisfaction is mixed with another, more intellectual pleasure. It might even be said that this pleasure might be similar to the pleasure a writer takes in the completion of a perfectly constructed, slightly funny story.

It is difficult to know how to judge a character like Grant. He is a striking mix of selfishness and selflessness. The last image in the story is of him embracing Fiona, her "sweetly shaped skull" (Munro, *Hateship* 323). It is a rare sentimental moment in the collection, but an earned one. As with the title story, we are left to consider the autonomy of the individual and the nature of our own constructed realities, but here the final note is tender. We are not brought into an act of seeing, but rather the pure physicality of two bodies touching, the smell of her skin "like that of the stems of cut flowers left too long in their water" (323).

There is a simplicity and clarity to the detail here that feels at odds with much of the rest of the collection—except that it is unclear, really, exactly whom Fiona is embracing. On first reading, it seems clearly to be Grant, but Aubrey is present too, and the dialogue attributions are vague. Could Grant be simply standing, watching Aubrey and Fiona embrace? If so, we are left with another writer/character acting as witness to the strangeness of his handiwork. There seems to be a conscious attempt on Munro's part to play with the idea of epiphany here, to flirt with the notion of Grant having the psychological and spiritual breakthrough we have come to expect in short fiction. As readers, we are most likely desperate for a moment like this, driven in that desire by our disgust with Grant—if anyone needs a spiritual revelation, it is he—but also by his charisma. For all his faults, he is a likable sort, and maybe he deserves a breakthrough.

It is to her credit that Munro does not give us this feeling, of course, but rather offers a simulacrum of it, something that looks and feels like that kind of moment at first glance. To some degree, it is another meta occurrence, slightly mannered because of the intentional vagueness of the language but still emotionally powerful. That it only reveals this double-sidedness upon closer examination is a kind of trick, but one that pays intellectual rewards.

Charles Baxter states that stories without epiphanies can be of "real consequence"—stories "in which no discursive insight appears, or in which the insights are shown to be false. . . . What if, as Raymond Carver argued, insights don't help and only make things worse? We can still see people acting meaningfully or stewing in their own juices or acting out of the depths of their bewilderment, and we can make of that what we will" (54). Munro, by engaging us with a mind in action, gives us all of this and more, a mess of contradictions and confusion in which some insight still might be gleaned, even if it is through an act of fabrication. At the end of her story "Material," the narrator ruminates over her husband's manuscript and her own memories and offers up an opinion that stands as a good summation of my own thoughts on the subject:

> What matters is that this story of Hugo's is a very good story, as far as I can tell, and I think I can tell. How honest this is and how lovely, I had to say as I read. I had to admit. I was moved by Hugo's story; I was, I am, glad of it, and I am not moved by tricks. Or if I am, they have to be good tricks. Lovely tricks, honest tricks. There is Dotty, lifted out of life and held in light, suspended in the marvelous clear jelly that Hugo has spent all his life learning how to make. It is an act of magic, there is no getting around it; it is an act, you might say, of a special, unsparing, unsentimental love. A fine and lucky benevolence. Dotty was a lucky person, people who understand and value this act might say (not everybody, of course, does understand and value this act); she was lucky to live in that basement for a few months and eventually to have this done to her, though she doesn't know what has been done and wouldn't care for it, probably, if she did know. She has passed into Art. (Munro, *Selected* 95)

Works Cited

Baxter, Charles. *Burning Down the House: Essays on Fiction*. Saint Paul, MN: Graywolf, 2008.

Doty, Mark. *The Art of Description: World into Word*. Saint Paul, MN: Graywolf, 2010.

Munro, Alice. *Hateship, Friendship, Courtship, Loveship, Marriage*. New York: Vintage, 2001.

_____. *Selected Stories*. New York: Knopf, 1996.

Narrative, Memory, and Contingency in Alice Munro's *Runaway*

Michael Trussler

Although the stories in *Runaway* (2004) function as independent texts, they are carefully linked together. The book resembles Munro's earlier work in that some of its stories share a cast of characters; however, *Runaway* is a new kind of collection for Munro, because it is not primarily organized around a fictional small town with recurring characters. Instead, *Runaway* acts as a kind of extended narrative that is neither a novel nor a novella, but rather a grouping of eight separate stories that reflect each other along a continuum, embodying, among other things, the primary worldviews constituting Western culture: the ancient Greek and the Judeo-Christian. The short-story sequence featuring Juliet at various parts of her life—"Chance," "Soon," "Silence"—is the most openly interconnected cluster of stories in the book, setting up several thematic problems (such as the possibility of having control over one's life) and structural motifs (such as the journey) that move through the entire collection.

More specifically, the Juliet sequence investigates the numerous ways people use various kinds of representation and discourse, including visual art, personal letters, and narrative in general, as a means of understanding and providing shape for their lives. If Munro's major female characters typically find themselves struggling to create their own individuality distinct from powerful social narratives inherited from the past—Christianity and small-town ideology, for example—they also often spend their lives seeking out the precise person who, as an ideal audience, will be receptive to the particular narrative, often a life story, that one human being may offer to another. Munro's characters ultimately find themselves in situations in which their desire for individual autonomy and their need to create cohesive personal narratives are often thwarted by unpredictable circumstances and events beyond their control. *Runaway* is also deeply interested in how human beings depend upon narrative to shape the experience of time and off-set the frailties of memory, both personal and cultural. An additional component of the book's examination of narrative and representation is Munro's technique of subtly rewriting specific scenes and situations derived from a variety of other texts, some taken from her own previous collections, others from the work of such writers as Leo Tolstoy, Henry James, and Raymond Carver, to name only a few.

In what follows, individual stories will be analyzed as independent texts as well as with some attention paid to how they contribute to the entire collection. Given space constraints, this essay cannot do justice to any of the stories; therefore, instead of attempting to provide extensive interpretations, the essay tries to illuminate as many of the book's numerous artistic techniques and themes as possible.

"Chance"

Introducing an important character and a prevalent thematic concern in *Runaway* for the ancient Greek emphasis on the irrational in human experience, "Chance" depicts the twenty-one-year-old Juliet traveling from southern Ontario to a temporary job and the beginning of a sexual relationship in British Columbia. Munro once made some remarks in an interview useful to an understanding of all her work, but especially helpful for interpreting the story "Chance" and the Juliet sequence: "I like looking at people's lives over a number of years, without continuity. Like catching them in snapshots. . . . I think this is why I'm not drawn to writing novels. Because I don't see that people develop and arrive somewhere. I just see people living in flashes" (Munro, "Interview" 89).

As is often the case with Munro's stories, "Chance" juxtaposes two discrete moments in time. The narrative's first snapshot details Juliet making her way by ferry to Eric's house shortly after his wife has died, though he is not expecting her arrival; the story then spirals back to Eric and Juliet's initial encounter on a train heading west from Ontario the previous year, when a man committed suicide, and concludes by picking up the strands left at the beginning, establishing that Juliet seems to have made the right decision in risking the visit. Munro links these two periods in Juliet's life together almost seamlessly, leaving the reader to fill in the subsequent temporal gaps. It appears to be a logical progression of events that transports the young PhD candidate studying the classics into the arms of an older fisherman on the Pacific coast, a situation that promises to alter Juliet's life irrevocably, as one infers that she does not return to the University of Toronto to complete her degree; however, the story pivots on contingency. Without the suicide of the man on the train, Juliet probably would not have met Eric, and despite Juliet's initial feelings of guilt, this man's death presumably has occurred because of a personal history that has nothing to do with anyone else making the trip. Though she makes decisions, Juliet's life has utterly shifted because of chaotic events completely beyond her control.

That the eventual suicide has interrupted Juliet's reading of *The Greeks and the Irrational* by E. R. Dodds is a key to Munro's technique in both this story and the collection as a whole, which is the use of realist details to open up larger thematic issues that go far beyond verisimilitude. Juliet is reading about maenadism (appendix 1 in Dodds) because, as a devoted scholar, she is paying attention to a relatively current study (this part of the story takes place in 1964; the Dodds book came out in 1951). Munro cites Dodds almost verbatim when she describes women in a Dionysian frenzy being overtaken by a snowstorm and having to be rescued from Mount Parnassus, which "seemed rather like contemporary behavior to Juliet" (*Runaway* 59). One of Dodds's central concerns is how some stages of Greek thought are foreign to twentieth-century experience, and Munro often questions whether universals exist by having her characters ponder the Greeks; see, for example, "The Children Stay" in *The Love of a Good Woman* (1998), which self-consciously responds to the modernist fascination with the Eurydice and Orpheus myth. Munro includes the Dodds reference in order to insist quietly on the power of the irrational and the omnipresent demands of the body in one image: people eagerly jump to the absurd conclusion that the blood in one of the train's toilets be-longed to the dead man—an impossibility, considering how train toi-lets work—when in fact Juliet has been menstruating. The other direct allusion to Dodds occurs when Juliet randomly opens her book and reads a passage she once underlined, which she now finds "obscure and unsettling": "*What to the partial vision of the living appears as the act of a fiend, is perceived by the wider insight of the dead to be an aspect of cosmic justice*" (Munro, *Runaway* 65, quoting Dodds 39; italics in orig.). Munro knows that readers are trained to pick up on signals like this one to interpret the text as a whole; recognizing the chasm between life and death, and the difference between reading a book and interact-ing with others on a train, we will make the critical assumption that "Chance" revolves around these mysterious boundaries. Further, we can use Dodds's description of Greek thought to better perceive how "Chance" dramatizes a struggle between the irrational, the contingent, and the urge to gain control over one's life by seeking to understand it rationally from within the perspective of ordinary human experience.

In the next sentence, when Munro shows us Juliet dropping the book, falling asleep, and having a dream, she requires her readers to operate on several different levels simultaneously. If we read about Ju-liet reading, we need, by extension, to have some sense of what Juliet is herself reading before she falls asleep. We can do this easily enough; however, when we follow Dodds trying to demarcate the complicated transitions between what he terms "shame-culture" and "guilt-culture" in Greek history, we become aware that Juliet seems incapable of un-derstanding her own experiences of shame and guilt thrust upon her by the man's suicide. Not only does she feel distant and estranged from the former self who wrote the marginalia, but further, as a living per-son, she cannot have the enormous perspective Dodds accords "the wider insight of the dead" (Dodds 39). Munro's gambit here is to im-ply ironically that her reader may mirror Juliet because, according to Dodds's analysis of Greek theology, no mortal can achieve the meta-physical scope necessary to understand reality.

A minor realistic detail that suggests Munro's complicated response to historicity occurs when Eric gets off the train in Regina. It is worth noting that the train no longer passed through Regina when the book was published in 2004. That changes occur over time is less important than Munro's use of ordinary details to explore how everything is subject to forgetfulness. Recall how Munro's narrator describes Juliet looking at what she once thought important in the Dodds book: reading in the present, Juliet notices those passages she scored earlier with "an orgy of underlining"; however, "what she had pounced on with such satisfaction at one time now seemed obscure and unsettling" (*Runaway* 65). If a treasured book that one has read often does not seem to provide genuine continuity and coherence over time, Munro hints at the possibility that we do not have the ability to sustain any significant degree of self-knowledge. Just as the individual self finds it impossible to maintain a stable attentiveness to personal identity, perhaps an analogous sort of amnesia extends to culture as a whole. Through its often-understated realist details, "Chance" implies that the passing of time slowly eradicates conscious awareness, whether at the level of private existential experience or the level of cultural memory; for example, Eric knows "the names [of the constellations] but not the history" (72), so it is up to Juliet to inform him of the original Greek myths. "Chance" suggests that human reality is a largely imperceptible gathering of experience that evaporates into oblivion. A nameless man commits suicide, and only Juliet will remember his slightly peculiar phrase of wishing to "chum around" (56) with her, though Munro deliberately shows Juliet keeping this information to herself.

Juliet's somewhat idiosyncratic reading style—she opens up the book "just anywhere" rather than where she presumably left off—gains complexity when one recognizes this particular habit as belonging to Munro herself. In both the frequently cited essay "What Is Real?" and the introduction to *Selected Stories* (1996), Munro describes this reading practice of hers; thus, she can presumably depend on many of her readers catching on to this self-conscious moment. What is of considerable importance to "Chance" is how Munro ties her reading style to her sense of aesthetic form; rejecting linear narrative, she says, "I don't take up a story and follow it as if it were a road. . . . It's more like a house . . . it encloses space and makes connections . . . and presents what is outside in a new way" ("What Is Real?" 1072). A Munro story is not simply a realist representation; art "presents what is outside in a new way." According to Munro, being inside such a structure creates a certain "feeling." Upon entering the "house" that is "Chance," readers thus are immersed in a predominant mood. While different readers will sense the quality of this mood variously, the story's subtle, though recurrent, emphasis on the irrational, death, and the accidental becomes highly dislocating. Before moving to an analysis of the next story in the Juliet sequence, "Soon," it is important to note that Juliet imagines "herself as a young woman in a Russian novel" (Munro, *Runaway* 54) when she gazes at the landscape. This comparison signifies Juliet's romanticized notions of reality, which are seemingly at odds with the bleak worldview she encounters in Dodds, but Munro's choice to include a reference to Russian literature in the same story that features a man throwing himself beneath a train also, of course, alludes to the famous scene in Leo Tolstoy's *Anna Karenina* (1877) in which Anna kills herself in the same way. What occurs in "Chance" as a minor allusion takes on greater depth and complexity in "Passion," a story that includes two suicides and a character who continuously rereads Tolstoy's novel. This technique of connecting two entirely independent stories by recurrent images and allusions occurs numerous times in *Runaway*, giving its autonomous stories permeable borders.

"Soon"

The second story in the sequence, "Soon," begins with a description that is quite bizarre: a cow looks at "a green-faced man who is neither young nor old" (Munro, *Runaway* 88). All writers manipulate how readers turn words on the page into mental images; however, Munro's use of ekphrasis (the verbal description of a visual object, such as Marc

Chagall's 1911 painting *I and the Village*) in the opening sentences of "Soon" is unusual because most writers make it immediately apparent when they are writing about an image, whereas Munro requires her reader to imagine something initially that is far from clear. One can easily picture a man with a green face, but to visualize someone whose age is indeterminate is more difficult. Using this technique to describe the work of a painter who was influenced by surrealism allows Munro to expand the collection's examination of the irrational; furthermore, by referring to Chagall, Munro broadens the range of philosophical worldviews explored in *Runaway*. Chagall's Jewish heritage and subject matter in this specific painting invokes the Judeo-Christian tradition, which, along with the classical world, forms the basis of Western culture.

Returning to her hometown several years after she left Ontario, Juliet brings her infant daughter Penelope—a slightly odd name for a classicist to give her child, considering how Odysseus's wife Penelope, though famous for her fidelity, was presumably lonely for the twenty years her husband was away—to visit her parents, Sam and Sara, whose Old Testament names foreshadow the story's engagement with Christianity. Margaret Atwood's observation that the Christianity present in the "society Munro writes about . . . is not often overt; it's merely the general background" (xvii) is accurate enough regarding *Runaway* as a whole, but "Soon" contains a direct conflict between Juliet and the local minister about her lack of faith. The content of their debate is less important than the fact that the minister is diabetic, unknown to Juliet, and has a sudden seizure. If Christianity forms the background narrative of Munro's milieu, the story brutally undercuts its transcendental claims when the minister has his seizure:

> The look in his eyes was not grateful, or forgiving—it was not really personal, it was just the raw look of an astounded animal, hanging on to whatever it could find.

And within a few seconds the eyes, the face, became the face of the man, the minister, who set down his glass and without another word fled out of the house. (*Runaway* 123)

Our primary identity, the text suggests, is that we are finite mammals; what a cultural narrative such as Christianity does is secure us a provisional place within a society in a given historical moment, though a culture often forgets that these narratives, however influential, are artifices.

Another fundamental narrative that Juliet directly encounters in "Soon" is the fairy tale as depicted in popular culture. *Runaway* frequently underscores how popular culture contributes to stereotypical notions of gender. When Sara and Juliet recall the Seven Dwarves statues that once were in a nearby village (transience again), we recognize that Juliet is associated with Snow White: in "Chance," she tidies up just as Snow White did, and both women find a home. We discover in the next story that her prince is unfaithful to her while she is visiting her parents, but during this particular summer, Juliet is in love when she writes her playfully ironic letter to Eric. Because Munro's characters often write letters, it is worthwhile to ponder this one. The letter offers a brief narrative of the visit, accentuating how seemingly natural narrative appears to be (we tell stories without thinking about it); we also learn that, similar to Juliet's perplexing marginalia, she is surprised when she reads the letter years later: "Juliet winced, as anybody does on discovering the preserved and disconcerting voice of some past fabricated self" (Munro, *Runaway* 125). Not only does Juliet in the present "forget" the younger person who wrote the letter, but she understands that to write a letter to a specific addressee is to construct a self that is an artifice. Apart from these psychological and philosophical complexities, Munro inserts an odd detail in Juliet's letter when Irene is described as "a sort of junior Ilse Koch person" (124). This detail functions on the level of realist verisimilitude; the notorious Nazi sadist committed suicide shortly before "Soon" takes place and so might have been in Juliet's mind owing to press coverage. That Munro chose to include this reference that might not be recognized by some of her readers in 2004 points to her ongoing concern for historicity and oblivion. This allusion to Nazism at the story's end brings "Soon" full circle with the Chagall painting, because the Nazis removed Chagall's paintings from German galleries in 1937, considering his work to be a prime example of so-called degenerate modern art. While the story in no way purports that the cultural oppression in small-town southern Ontario during the 1960s was equivalent to Nazi censorship, it is revealing that while Snow White kitsch deserves public display, Chagall's work is banished to an attic because Juliet's parents fear that the indispensable Irene would find it too "modern" and that they would be considered "weird" for owning it.

We should also note that each of these stories contains characters who are often desperately alone. The final snapshot Munro gives of Juliet, in "Silence," shows her deep isolation; she is estranged from Penelope, and Eric has drowned. In his seminal book *The Lonely Voice* (1963), Frank O'Connor argues that short stories emphasize loneliness: "Always in the short story there is this sense of outlawed figures wandering about the fringes of society" (87). The Juliet sequence affirms the validity of O'Connor's observation.

"Passion"

If the Juliet sequence established an ongoing struggle between so-called pagan and Christian worldviews, "Passion" occupies a place on this spectrum that is self-consciously nihilistic. A contemporary and condensed version of *Anna Karenina*, "Passion" uses a dense, often ironic layering of reference to explore the possibility that human experience is without meaning. From the very start of the story, almost every detail points to decay and the futility of human endeavor. Returning to the "Traverses' summer house" after many years have passed, Grace learns that "Highway 7 now avoided towns that it used to go right through, and it went straight in places where, as she remembered, there used to be curves" (Munro, *Runaway* 159). Munro shows the very landscape mirroring a decaying body: the nubile woman who once attracted Maury is, at the time of narration, presumably as angular as the new highway. Given that Maury's summer job was working with "the road gang repairing Highway 7" (171), the story suggests the vanity of human effort; the new highway has rendered the earlier repair work entirely obsolete and irrelevant.

Refusing to rebuke Neil (whose name evokes the Latin *nihil*) for his drinking, Grace intuits that he embodies something her culture not only rejects but cannot begin to fathom: elemental nihilism. Watching Neil, Grace does not believe that living "with a lack of hope" is cynical. Instead, she understands this position to be a sincere and honest judgment of reality; as the narrator remarks, "This lack of hope—genuine, reasonable, and everlasting" (Munro, *Runaway* 192). Comfortable in Grace's presence, Neil falls asleep after she has agreed to "watch over" him. But she then leaves him alone to explore the nearby river, where she encounters southern Ontario's desire to control reality through enforced ethics: at the river, "a sign . . . warned that profanity, obscenity, or vulgar language was forbidden . . . and would be punished" (193). What Grace perceives in Neil is incommensurate with social ideology: "What she had seen was final. As if she was at the edge of a flat dark body of water that stretched on and on. Cold, level water. Looking out at such dark, cold, level water, and knowing it was all there was" (193). Grace's epiphany here is her recognition that existence is grounded in primordial emptiness.

This scene encapsulates much of the metaphysical anxiety that forms the Western tradition. Grace, who is also Aphrodite—when she cuts her foot on the shell, the text recalls Sandro Botticelli's painting *The Birth of Venus* (1486), mentioned in "Soon"—will offer Neil a fundamental boon of Christianity: she will placate his need to be witnessed (though she deserts him). Shortly after this bucolic drive into the country that is also a descent into the underworld, Neil will drive his car into a bridge, thereby paralleling Anna's suicide in Tolstoy's novel. If the retrospective narration of "Passion" recalls other Munro stories (for example,

"Miles City, Montana"), this story departs from the earlier, more somber treatment of memory and loss; "Passion" giddily mixes farce with tragedy. When one considers that the couple takes a lot of time to return to Bailey's Falls, one suspects that Neil, who is a Nietzschean blend of Dionysus and Jesus, may also be James Stewart's character in Frank Capra's holiday classic *It's a Wonderful Life* (1946)—except that unlike the original George Bailey, who listened to a guardian angel, Neil takes his own life. Part of the story's response to nihilism is to gather together the various ways humans create things, from roads to movies, and to treat them ironically. We invest an enormous amount of energy in producing cultural artifacts, but they are as temporary as the jigsaw puzzle (which is a picture of reality) that Mrs. Travers accidentally destroys on the same Thanksgiving weekend that Neil kills himself.

If we recall Munro's assertion that a short story resembles a house with its own special atmosphere, we might ask ourselves a simple question: what happens if this house is haunted? What is the "feeling" inside this structure called "Passion" that contains a woman who continually reads the emotionally wrenching *Anna Karenina* and has to endure the suicides of both a husband and a son? Let us perform the following thought experiment: if Mrs. Travers has read Tolstoy more often than she can remember, what happens if we think of this story as a combination of the two authors? If we read *Anna Karenina* and "Passion" together, we find a powerful anatomy of both human futility and the seductive powers of self-delusion. There is happiness, too, but most of it is in Tolstoy. Ultimately, both texts use form, particularly juxtaposing scenes with unlike elements in them, to portray a reality that is often pitiless and always busy with death.

"Tricks"

Susan Lohafer's belief that the short story "is the most end-conscious of the literary forms" (50) is helpful to an investigation of "Tricks," owing to its surprise ending. For the reader to discover near the story's conclusion, along with the central character, Robin, that a simple error irreversibly altered the bulk of both her and Danilo's lives means that readers must retroactively rethink the various events that make up the story, and in doing so reimagine the forty years of Robin's life that Munro has omitted from her text. If the story's plot is conventional, it is worth considering Jonathan Franzen's announcement in his brilliant review of *Runaway* that in her eleventh book of short fiction, Munro has become a master of the form: "The moments she's pursuing now aren't moments of realization; they're moments of fateful, irrevocable, dramatic action." The genetic accident that severs Robin's desperate yearning for an exact narratee—"She wished she could tell somebody" (Munro, *Runaway* 269)—is an unnecessary cruelty that would not be out of place in *King Lear*, which is, of course, the first play of many that she sees at Stratford as a young woman.

In a collection whose central characters' devotion to the arts often makes them internal exiles in the largely philistine mainstream of southern Ontario society, "Tricks" is the story that most openly celebrates the mystery of aesthetic experience. Aware of "how different she herself must be from most people," Robin revels in what Shakespeare's plays offer her: "Yet those few hours filled her with an assurance that the life she was going back to, which seemed so . . . unsatisfactory, was only temporary. . . . And there was a radiance behind it, behind that life, behind everything, expressed by the sunlight seen through the train windows. The sunlight and long shadows on the summer fields, like the remains of the play in her head" (Munro, *Runaway* 239). As Munro explains with her house analogy, art alters perception. However, the question that sweeps through her oeuvre is, what kind of knowledge does art provide? If art invigorates life and banishes shopworn habits of perception, much as love does in "Tricks," can art also provide wisdom? When Robin discerns the truth about the two brothers, she feels metaphysical rebellion—"This I do not accept" (265)—and the narrator adds, "Shakespeare should have prepared her. Twins are often the reason for mix-ups and disasters. . . . And in the end the mysteries are solved" (268). Tidy and happy closure may resolve comedies, but

Robin is not in a play. Munro does not offer any solution as to art's value; what she does is use Robin to showcase how it feels to live in a culture of rapid change, a consumer society in which even dogs have jobs to do and science can decode genetics, but nothing can assuage a person's need to recognize and negotiate the interiority of another person and then risk telling him or her one's unique story.

"Powers"

Attentive to Munro's "fascination with connectedness," Mark Levene offers a shrewd interpretation of several Munro collections that examines "how the shadings of one volume come to the edge or to the center of another" (841). Levene's perceptive metaphor suggests how Munro's oeuvre grows increasingly subtle in the ways it reflects and comments upon itself. "Powers" stands on its own, but a situation or even a single word from this story, such as "kilter" (Munro, *Runaway* 173, 303) or "radiance" (239, 332), evokes previous instances in this collection, and others as well. Munro's interest in "connectedness" obviously extends to the works of other authors. That "Powers" overtly alludes to a number of writers—Dante, John Milton, and Tolstoy, among others—and implicitly responds to stories such as Henry James's "The Beast in the Jungle" (1903) and James Joyce's "The Dead" (1914), the latter moving through much of *Runaway* as a kind of shadow, makes these "shadings" a crucial part of the collection. If *Runaway* critiques Christianity's transcendental claims by repeatedly investigating how people are exposed to contingency, historicity, and the body's uncompromising physiology, the coda of the volume, "Powers," accentuates the ineluctable importance of ethical choice to human interaction.

"Powers" stretches over several decades, and in using a variety of discursive forms—the diary, letters, various "chapters" with headings, references to music and movies—the story creates a kind of time capsule of mid-to-late-twentieth-century North American experience that nonetheless leans into the present moment. Though never precisely pinpointed, somewhere in the midst of the story, the cultural residue left over from the nineteenth century disappears as a mode of lived experience and becomes strictly a matter for the historical record. The story also makes its references to Ed Sullivan and hippies seem utterly antiquated as social phenomena, even though much of the story takes place in the "early seventies" (Munro, *Runaway* 312). The story's title itself is a compressed history; it partially refers to Tessa's occult talents, but similar to the way "Trespasses" evokes the Lord's Prayer, "Powers" alludes to William Wordsworth's sonnet "The World Is Too Much with Us" (1807). When Nancy loosely quotes the sonnet to Tessa in a letter, we see one effect of literature—it provides a communal code for people to express interiority—though Wordsworth's poem also returns us to the Juliet sequence in that it castigates a tepid modernity, in contrast to the more robust ethos of pagan Greece. Perhaps the most complicated character in the collection, Nancy is emblematic of Munro's fundamental artistic sensibility.

Referring to her husband Wilf's bizarre behavior, owing to what one assumes is dementia, Nancy remarks, "The mind's a weird piece of business" (Munro, *Runaway* 308). Nancy's folksy assessment of the human condition could easily be the philosophical credo of numerous writers, but especially Munro, who has spent a career exploring the various drives, frailties, and delusions that constitute human experience. As always, though, the writer works behind the comments her characters make; the word *weird* has a long history in the English language (recall the Weird Sisters in Shakespeare's *Macbeth*). Of considerable importance to this particular story, and *Runaway* as a collection, is the Old English definition of *wyrd*: "the principle, power, or agency by which events are predetermined" ("Wyrd"). That Nancy's remark inadvertently contains an echo of the Anglo-Saxon world, which had affinities with Homeric Greece, is less important than Munro's suggestions that the mind may in fact be determined by forces over which it possibly has neither knowledge nor control. But we have no foolproof means of assessing the degree to which this determinism may influence us, and Munro's characters are continually required to freely make ethical decisions.

The section "Flies on the Windowsill," a stylistic tour de force, shows the elderly Nancy ruminating on the mysterious events clustered around her life: "What she believes she is doing, what she wants to do if she can get the time to do it, is not so much to live in the past as to open it up and get one good look at it" (Munro, *Runaway* 330). One could do worse than think about all of Munro's work as an extended effort to comprehend not only how we are rarely contemporary to ourselves within our own lives but also that subjective memory and forgetting are intertwined with other people from whose inner lives we are excluded. In the dream vision that follows, Nancy is somehow witness to a scene (that may or may not have actually happened) in which Tessa's "powers" seem revived, and Ollie wavers as to whether to have her committed to an asylum. Tessa's clairvoyant intuition that a previous occupant of their hotel room "has passed the time killing these flies, and has then collected all the little bodies and . . . neatly piled [them] up into a pyramid" (332) certainly confirms the "weird" oddities of the human mind. However, the specter of determinism returns in the same image because dead flies summon Gloucester's famous judgment in *King Lear*: "As flies to wanton boys, are we to th' Gods; / They kill us for their sport" (*Lr.* 4.1.35–36). What is at stake in this overseen exchange between Tessa and Ollie, where Nancy is parallel to the reader, is the possibility of empathy and ethical action. Refusing to face each other, speaking past each other, the couple do not seem to be even in the same room, let alone sharing a life together. Ollie "understands at once what [the return of Tessa's powers] means to her . . . though he cannot quite enter into her joy" (Munro, *Runaway* 333). We can recognize the autonomy of other people but cannot experience them from inside their own perspectives; people can choose to aid another's well being, though earlier parts of the story suggest Ollie decides against doing so.

Munro's concluding paragraph is an astonishing rewriting of the final paragraph of Joyce's "The Dead"; instead of Gabriel Conroy perceiving imminent mortality in the whirling white snow, Nancy finds herself confronting something darker, "something like soot and soft ash" (*Runaway* 335). Munro complicates this Joycean allusion by suggesting that Nancy is a version of Dante being guided by Virgil (recall the first chapter of "Powers" is entitled "Give Dante a Rest") away from the Inferno. The purpose of the hero's journey into the underworld in classical epic poetry is to learn some necessary truths from the dead. What Munro does, unlike authors of the classic epic, is finish her collection with this journey, which is a way of making the reading experience part of the text itself. The reader is invited to be like Nancy, who tries to open up her life "and get one good look at it."

As we have seen, Munro's stories often thematize existential identity and the experience of temporality, explicitly examining the question A. S. Byatt asks in her review of Munro's *The Love of a Good Woman*: "Do we experience life as a continuum or as a series of shocks and accidents?" (D16). While *Runaway* does not ask this question overtly, the collection contains stories whose narrative structures are often constructed like a series of snapshots. Munro's aesthetic would seem to be the result of her observations on how people live their lives, not with a sense of straightforward continuity and eventual arrival at some hoped-for outcome whose consequences can be predicted, but rather, as Munro puts it, "I just see people living in flashes" ("Interview" 89).

Works Cited

Atwood, Margaret. Introduction. *Alice Munro's Best: Selected Stories*. By Alice Munro. Toronto: McClelland, 2006. vi–xviii.

Byatt, A. S. "The Stuff of Life." Rev. of *The Love of a Good Woman*, by Alice Munro. *Globe and Mail* 26 Sept. 1998: D16.

Dodds, E. R. *The Greeks and the Irrational*. Berkeley: U of California P, 2004.

Franzen, Jonathan. "Alice's Wonderland." Rev. of *Runaway*, by Alice Munro. *New York Times*. New York Times, 14 Nov. 2004. Web. 31 Jan. 2012.

Levene, Mark. "'It Was about Vanishing': A Glimpse of Alice Munro's Stories." *University of Toronto Quarterly* 68.4 (1999): 841–60.

Lohafer, Susan. *Coming to Terms with the Short Story.* Baton Rouge: Louisiana State UP, 1983.

Munro, Alice. "An Interview with Alice Munro." By Geoff Hancock. *Canadian Fiction Magazine* 43 (1982): 74–114.

_____. *Runaway.* Toronto: Penguin, 2004.

_____. "What Is Real?" *The Norton Reader: An Anthology of Expository Prose.* Ed. Arthur M. Eastman et al. New York: Norton, 1992. 1071–74.

O'Connor, Frank. *The Lonely Voice: A Study of the Short Story.* Brooklyn, NY: Melville, 2004.

Shakespeare, William. *King Lear.* Ed. Kenneth Muir. London: Routledge, 1989.

"Wyrd." *The Compact Oxford English Dictionary.* 1981.

"Secretly Devoted to Nature": Place Sense in Alice Munro's *The View from Castle Rock*

Caitlin Charman

As Robert Thacker claims, Alice Munro's "imaginative grappling with her 'home place'" plays a crucial role in her work (7–8). And yet, as the word *grappling* suggests, Munro's representations of her birth-place—Huron County, Ontario, now known by many literary critics as "Alice Munro country"—are not without ambivalence. Likewise, many critics have been ambivalent about the role of place in Munro's work. Unwilling to relegate Munro to the status of regional writer, a designation that has all too often been considered dismissive, critics have been inclined, as Robert McGill notes, to praise "the 'universality' of Munro's fiction." According to McGill, the assumption of universality manifests itself in two ways. Some critics claim that Munro's "fictive Southwestern Ontario small towns are familiar to anyone who has experienced small towns"; these critics thus emphasize "the homogeneity of places." For another set of critics, Munro's fiction "appeals to us" not *because* of geography but "*despite* regional geographic differences" (McGill, emphasis added).

Canadian literary criticism has been plagued by a similarly reductive understanding of the role of place. Playing on Hugh MacLennan's notion that English Canada and French Canada are "two solitudes," Lisa Chalykoff contends that critics of "Canadian literary regionalism" may be divided into two camps, or "solitudes" (161). First-solitude critics operate under an assumption known as environmental determinism; according to this understanding, "environmental features directly determine aspects of human behaviour and society," and "differences among people [are] not innate but [are] due to climate, landscape, and other environmental factors" ("Anthropology"). Employing the work of spatial theorist Henri Lefebvre, Chalykoff argues that these critics "tend to overemphasize the materiality of space" and to believe that "society . . . play[s] no role in processes of spatialization" (161). By contrast, second-solitude critics treat landscape as a text; this approach "tends to dematerialize" space and "reduces it to a subjective condition" (162). Chalykoff argues that both conceptions of space are impoverished and contends that the "Canadian literary region . . . is ripe for reassessment" (160).

Munro's literary region is ripe for reassessment as well. Contrary to critical consensus, her universal appeal is neither despite her focus on local geography nor because her work reveals the homogeneity of the Canadian small town or small-town life. Rather, to borrow the words of environmental philosopher Arnold Berleant, "the special accomplishment of writers whose work centers on particular regions," as Munro's does, "lies not just in their ability to convey a sense of the character and distinctiveness of these areas but also in their ability to locate human identity in them. . . . The appeal is universal, for it exemplifies how a person is formed in the human and natural landscape" (*Living* 123). Moreover, as McGill astutely observes, Munro is self-conscious in her examination of the relationship between person and place:

> Munro is practising a geographic metafiction . . . she explores the way we write and read the land, struggling against the difficulties of achieving what Edward Relph calls "the geographic imagination": "a way of thinking that seeks to grasp the connections between one's own experiences of particular landscapes and the larger processes of society and environment, and then seeks to reinterpret these in a manner that makes sense for others."

In "practising a geographic metafiction," Munro's work bridges the gap between the first-solitude perception of space, with its emphasis on materiality, and the second-solitude perception of space, with its emphasis on textuality. An analysis of four pieces from Munro's autobiographical collection *The View from Castle Rock* (2006)— "Lying under the Apple Tree," "Home," "Working for a Living," and "What Do You Want to Know For?"—through the lens of cultural geography and environmental aesthetics will show that the distinction between environment-as-text and environment-as-material does not hold, nor does the critical tendency to subordinate the role of place in Munro's writing. On the contrary, these works show the evolution of Munro's sense of place as she situates her "own experiences of particular landscapes" within the larger environmental history of her home place.

Like a second-solitude critic, the young narrator in Munro's "Lying under the Apple Tree," who is Munro herself, wishes to read the landscape primarily as a text. In relating her adventures bicycling through "the country along the back roads" in Huron County, for example, she reveals that her connection to, and appreciation for, nature initially came not from nature itself but from textual representations of nature: "I was secretly devoted to Nature. The feeling came from books, at first. It came from the girls' stories by the writer L. M. Montgomery, who often inserted some sentences describing a snowy field in moonlight or a pine forest or a still pond mirroring the evening sky" (Munro 198). She compares her desire to lie under the apple tree in Miriam McAlpin's field so she can view the tree's blossoms in full bloom to offering formal worship in church:

> I wanted to look at them when they flowered. And not just to look at them—as you could do from the street—but to get underneath those branches, to lie down on my back with my head against the trunk of the tree and to see how it rose, as if out of my own skull, rose up and lost itself in an upside-down sea of blossom. Also to see if there were bits of sky showing through, so that I could screw up my eyes to make them foreground not background, bright-blue fragments on that puffy white sea. There was a formality about this idea that I longed for. It was almost like kneeling down in church, which in our church we didn't do. (199)

She "ache[s] to offer" "homage" to nature, as though environment were an external force, and she wishes to appreciate landscape with a sense of detachment (199).

The narrator's assumption—that she can view landscape as a detached observer, and that her experience of the landscape will be mainly a visual one—is rooted in the long tradition of Western aesthetics. Such an understanding dates back to classical times, says Berleant, and it was entrenched as the predominant model of aesthetics in the eighteenth century, when it "became . . . the governing metaphor for the explanation of aesthetic experience, which emerged as a contemplative attitude for appreciating an art object for its own sake alone" (*Aesthetics: Variations* 4). According to what Berleant calls the "contemplative model of aesthetic experience," the "art object" is "separate and distinct from whatever surrounds it, isolated from the rest of life," and the observer of such an object is supposed to maintain "a special attitude, an attitude of disinterestedness, that regards the object in the light of its own intrinsic qualities with no concern for ulterior purposes" (4). This understanding of aesthetic experience is tied, says Berleant, to the eighteenth-century physicists' conception, in which space is considered to be "an abstraction, a medium that is universal, objective, and impersonal, independent of the objects that are situated in and move through it" (5).

When Munro actually does lie under the apple tree, however, she finds that the landscape refuses to be a textual "abstraction," and she is surprised—and somewhat dismayed—to find that the experience is not primarily visual but somatic: "There was a root of the tree making a hard ridge under me, so I had to shift around. And there were last year's apples, dark as chunks of dried meat, that I had to get out of the way before I could settle. Even then, when I composed myself, I was aware of my body's being in an odd and unnatural situation." And what she does see is far from the romantic vision she had imagined: "The sky was thinly clouded, and what I could see of it reminded me of dingy bits of china." With rotten apples all around her, and with her body in an uncomfortable position, she is forced to admit that she is "not quite swept into the state of mind, of worship, that [she] had been hoping for," and she is unable to maintain the attitude of a disinterested observer (Munro 200). She finds, rather, that landscape is both text (subject to her own interpretations and imaginings) *and* material (subjecting her to its forces). As Don Mitchell summarizes, "landscape is both a place and a 'way of seeing,' both a sensibility and a lived relation" (99).

Munro's lying under the apple tree illustrates that the contemplative model of aesthetics does not provide an adequate account of how we experience either art or environment. For as she discovers, the "landscape is not generated out of an act of consciousness; it emanates from the perceiving body and is infused by that body with its meanings, force, and feelings." Perhaps more importantly, contends Berleant, "environment is not wholly dependent on the perceiving subject. It also imposes itself in significant ways on the human person, engaging one in a relationship of mutual influence" (*Aesthetics: Variations* 8). In other words, our relationship with environment is "reciprocal" (Berleant, *Living* 14). Munro discovers this reciprocity when she tries to impose her idealized fantasy of nature, gleaned from L. M. Montgomery's stories, on the physical landscape and finds that the landscape also imposes itself on her. And though she is initially disappointed, she realizes that lying under the apple tree "was worth having done. It was along the lines of an acknowledgement, rather than an experience" (Munro 200).

The memoirs in *The View from Castle Rock* also illustrate Munro moving from sentimental, romantic notions of place, like those exemplified in "Lying under the Apple Tree," to what Svetlana Boym calls "reflective nostalgia." Boym argues that there are two kinds of nostalgia, restorative and reflective, and suggests that these "two kinds of nostalgia characterize one's relationship to the past, to the imagined community, to home, to one's own self-perception." Whereas the restorative nostalgic "proposes to rebuild the lost home and patch up the memory gaps" (41) and purports that there is an "original . . . prelapsarian moment" (49) to which we can return, the reflective nostalgic "dwells in . . . longing and loss, the imperfect process of remembrance" (41) and "does not pretend to rebuild the mythical place called home" (50). And whereas "restorative nostalgia takes itself dead seriously," "reflective nostalgia . . . can be ironic and humorous" (49). In short, unlike restorative nostalgia, reflective nostalgia "reveals that longing and critical thinking are not opposed to one another" (50).

The narrator in "Home," also Munro, reveals herself to be a reflective nostalgic, one who is in the midst of reevaluating her home place and her relationship to it. According to Boym, reflective nostalgics "are aware of the gap between identity and resemblance; the home is in ruins or, on the contrary, has just been renovated and gentrified beyond recognition." It is "this defamiliarization and sense of distance," says Boym, that "drives them to tell their story, to narrate the relationship between past, present and future" (50). In Munro's case, her physical proximity to home spurs her to acknowledge, and to narrate, the disjunction between her romanticized memories of home and the home that is before her. She realizes that when she "lived more than a thousand miles away," she viewed her family's farmhouse with a certain amount of maudlin idealism: "I thought of it then as a place I might never see again and I was greatly moved by the memory of it" (Munro 288). But now that she has returned, she sees the family home, and the changes it has undergone, with a more critical, less distorted lens.

Munro returns to discover that her father and his new wife have completely modified the old house, which is now "dissolved, in a way, and lost, inside an ordinary comfortable house of the present time" (289). The narrative thrust of the story is spurred by her inventory of the changes that have taken place and her attempts to make sense of them. She finds the house's interior and its furniture completely altered: "The wooden kitchen table that we always ate from, and the chairs we sat on, have been taken to the barn" (287); the "ceiling is hidden now behind squares of white tiles, and a new metal window frame has replaced the gnawed wooden one" (288); and "the front rooms have been repapered" (289). The landscape, too, is not as she remembered it: "What there is to see, anyway, is not the bush of golden glow that was seldom cut back . . . or the orchard with the scabby apple trees and the two pear trees that never bore much fruit, being too far north. There is now only a long, gray, windowless turkey barn and a turkey yard, for which my father sold off a strip of land" (289). And "even" the house's exterior, says Munro, "the red brick whose crumbling mortar was particularly penetrable by an east wind, is going to be covered up with white metal siding" (289).

Munro "do[es] not lament this loss as [she] would once have done" (289), when she was miles away from home. When her father tells her that the crumbling bricks were hard to repair and that heating the leaky house was expensive, she recognizes the practicality of the changes, even though she is not inclined to be practical, and the veracity of her father's justifications for them: "I know that he speaks the truth, and I know that the house being lost was not a fine or handsome one in any way. A poor man's house, always, with the stairs going up between walls, and bedrooms opening out of one another. A house where people have lived close to the bone for over a hundred years" (289–90). These changes do inspire Munro to reexamine her own identity, however. When her father expects her to respond to the home's changes as she would once have done, she realizes that part of the reason she sees her home differently is that, like the family home, she herself has changed:

In a way my father wants some objections, some foolishness from me. And I feel obliged to hide from him the fact that the house does not mean as much to me as it once did, and that it really does not matter to me now how he changes it.

"I know how you love this place," he says to me, apologetically yet with satisfaction. And I don't tell him that I am not sure now whether I love any place, and that it seems to me it was myself that I loved here—some self that I have finished with, and none too soon. (290)

Munro's own metamorphosis has altered her relationship with and understanding of place, and she returns home to find that she is no longer the restorative nostalgic she was from afar or the hopeless romantic she was as a child. As Boym says, for the reflective nostalgic, "homecoming does not signify a recovery of identity," nor does it "end the journey in the virtual space of imagination" (50). Far from reestablishing her old relationship with place and her old identity, Munro realizes that back in Huron County, she has shed both. It is this discovery that spurs a new imaginative relationship with place.

This discovery also illustrates that who and where one is can profoundly affect one's relationship with, and perception of, place. Summarizing the work of geographers James and Nancy Duncan, Mitchell argues that when considering the extent to which landscapes function as texts, it is important to "understand, through an analysis of relations of power, *how* differently situated people are *able* to read landscapes" (122; italics in orig.). Quoting Linda McDowell, Mitchell argues that "the 'meanings' implicit in a cultural text like landscape are . . . 'multiple and positional, . . . there are many ways of seeing and reading the landscape'" (123; 2nd ellipsis in orig.). The narrator in "Home" explores the influence of subjectivity on people's readings of landscape and illustrates how "differently situated people" read landscapes differently. The rural people of her father's generation and upbringing, says Munro, consider the aesthetic appreciation of nature to be a foolish and unnecessary preoccupation. As she notes in her description of her parents' home, this attitude is exemplified in the design of the region's farmhouses:

> All those rooms are small, and as is usual in old farmhouses, they are not designed to take advantage of the out-of-doors but, if possible, to ignore it. People may not have wanted to spend their time of rest or shelter looking out at the fields they had to work in, or at the snowdrifts they had to shovel their way through in order to feed their stock. People who openly admired nature—or who even went so far as to use that word, *Nature*—were often taken to be slightly soft in the head. (Munro 288)

The residents of Huron County view those who emphasize aesthetics over practical considerations as dim witted. As narrator Munro relates in "Working for a Living," her father's generation sees this attitude as an indulgence that should be reserved for women: "Only women were allowed to care about landscape and not to think always of its subjugation and productivity. My grandmother, for example, was famous for having saved a line of silver maples along the lane. The trees grew beside a crop field and they were getting big and old—their roots interfered with the ploughing and they shaded too much of the crop" (130). This prioritization of beauty over use value is also considered to be a luxury reserved for eccentrics and outsiders. City folk, for example, might be apt to "pay . . . a big price" for the beautiful—and impractical—red bricks that Munro's father has so pragmatically covered (289). But as the story of Munro's grandmother illustrates, prioritizing the aesthetics of landscape over its use value has material consequences, some of which may be destructive: "The trees stayed and spoiled the crop at the edge of the field until the terrible winter of 1935 finished them off" (130).

That differently situated people read landscapes differently is also illustrated in the tension that Munro portrays in "Home" between city folks' understanding of farming and farmers' understanding of their life and work. When she returns home from a long foray in the city, Munro is in a unique position to comprehend this disjunction. Because her father is sick and in the hospital, she finds herself back in the barn, feeding the sheep and doing chores. Whereas a city person might see this as a bucolic scene, for Munro it recalls the physical difficulty and financial hardship of the farming life: "People I know say that work like this is restorative and has a peculiar dignity, but I was born to it and feel it differently. Time and place can close in on me, it can so easily seem as if I have never got away, that I have stayed here my whole life. As if my life as an adult was some kind of dream that never took hold of me" (312). Rather than feeling restored by this work, she feels trapped and panicked. When she recalls this panic later, she realizes that

the very corner of the stable where I was standing, to spread the hay, and where the beginning of panic came on me, is the scene of the first clear memory of my life. There is in that corner a flight of steep wooden steps going up to the hayloft, and in the scene I remember I am sitting on the first or second step watching my father milk the black-and-white cow. I know what year it was—the black-and-white cow died of pneumonia in the worst winter of my childhood, which was 1935. Such an expensive loss is not hard to remember. (314)

As Munro portrays it, the mistake that city people tend to make is not in their impulse to aestheticize nature but rather in their impulse to de-materialize it, to view nature as being separate from work.

This mistake is a common one in landscape art as well. Mitchell maintains that "those who study landscape representations—such as landscape paintings, photographs, and gardens—are repeatedly struck by how effectively they erase or neutralize images of work" (103). And yet, argues Mitchell, "landscape is clearly a work, something made, the product of human labour" (102). Even landscapes themselves, and not just landscape representations, tend to conceal labor: "If landscape is a work of human labour then it is a peculiar work. In many respects it is much like a commodity: it actively hides (or fetishizes) the labour that goes into its making" (103). By contrast, in *Castle Rock*, Munro ac-tively reveals and analyzes the labor that has gone into the landscape's creation. In tracing the environmental history of Huron County, she emphasizes landscape as a work and uncovers the working landscape. Such an understanding forms the basis of her memoir "Working for a Living," for example, which chronicles her father's working life and situates it within the larger agricultural history of the region. In so do-ing, it illustrates the profound impact that human labor has had on the landscape since the nineteenth-century land clearings:

There was no more wild country in Huron County then than there is now. Perhaps there was less. The farms had been cleared in the period between 1830 and 1860, when the Huron Tract was being opened up, and they were cleared thoroughly. Many creeks had been dredged—the progressive thing to do was to straighten them out and make them run like tame canals between the fields. The early farmers hated the very sight of a tree and admired the look of open land. And the masculine approach to the land was managerial, dictatorial. (Munro 130)

This passage illustrates the limitations of the landscape-as-text metaphor. For landscape is not just a mental image but also "an *imposition of power*: power made concrete in the bricks, mortar, stones, tar, and lumber of a city, town, village, or rural setting" (Mitchell 123; italics in orig.). In this case, power is imposed through clear-cut forests, straightened and dredged creeks, and managed agricultural land.

But as "Working for a Living" demonstrates, Munro's understanding—that the landscape is a work, and one that incorporates both aesthetic and use values—takes some time to develop. As mentioned in my discussion of "Lying under the Apple Tree," the young Munro is inclined to view nature purely in aesthetic and idealized terms rather than in practical ones. Thus, in "Working," she initially portrays her father's desire to become a fur trapper (and later a fox farmer) as being motivated by the books "he had read . . . by Fenimore Cooper" and the "myths or half-myths about wilderness" that he found in them (Munro 131). She believes that her father took to the bush "with a Fenimore Cooper–cultivated hunger" and an "extra, inspired or romantic perception," though she acknowledges that he probably "would not have cared for those words" (132).

By contrast, Munro describes her mother as being motivated purely by economics: "She looked at the foxes and she did not see any romantic connection to the wilderness; she saw a new industry, the possibility of riches" (139). Although she admits that her mother's gifts, which "had something to do with taking chances, making money," were "the very gifts (less often mentioned than the hard work, the perseverance) that had built the country" (139), as an adolescent she finds them repugnant. Whereas she sympathizes with her father's supposedly sentimental motivations for fox farming, her mother's economic motivations—and her skill at selling furs to American tourists— inspire a kind of class shame:

For all this, as I grew older, I came to feel something like revulsion. I despised the whole idea of putting yourself to use in that way, making yourself dependent on the response of others, employing flattery so adroitly and naturally that you did not even recognize it as flattery. And all for money. I thought such behaviour shameful, as of course my grandmother did. I took it for granted that my father felt the same way though he did not show it. I believed—or thought I believed—in working hard and being proud, not caring about being poor and indeed having a subtle contempt for those who led easeful lives. (153)

Not only does Munro "despise" her mother putting herself to use so blatantly, but as she matures, she starts to interrogate the commodification of the foxes, "with their beautiful tails and angry golden eyes" (153). This interrogation happens as she starts to distance herself from the farming life: "As I grew older, and more and more aloof from country ways, country necessities, I began for the first time to question their captivity, to feel regret for their killing, their conversion into money" (153), though she recognizes "this feeling to be a luxury" (154). She also admits that her "regret [for] the loss of the foxes" is motivated more by aesthetic appreciation than by a philosophical concern for animal welfare: "I never got so far as feeling anything like this for the mink, who seemed to me mean and rat-like, deserving of their fate" (153–54).

As Munro grows older, however, she realizes that her father's relationship with the fur business is far more complicated, and far closer to her mother's than she imagined. In her father's "later years," she shares her reservations about killing the foxes for their fur with him, and he admits that he has felt similarly:

In the same spirit he said that he believed there was some religion in India that held with all animals getting into Heaven. Think, he said, if that were true—what a pack of snarling foxes he would meet there, not to mention all the other fur-bearers he had trapped, and the mink, and a herd of thundering horses he had butchered for their meat.

Then he said, not so lightly, "You get into things, you know. You sort of don't realize what you're getting into." (Munro 154)

But she also discovers that although her father viewed the foxes in spiritual terms, he viewed them in economic ones as well, and he never felt the revulsion for his wife's moneymaking ability that Munro did. Recalling the summer he and Munro went to retrieve her mother from Muskoka, where she was selling furs to American tourists, her father says that her mother "saved the day," revealing that "he didn't know what he was going to do, at the end of that trip, if it turned out that she hadn't made any money." According to Munro, "the tone in which he said this convinced me that he had never shared those reservations of my grandmother's and mine. Or that he'd resolutely put away such shame, if he'd ever had it." And Munro finds that now she too has put away such shame, "[a] shame that has come full circle, finally being shameful in itself to me" (154).

Her father's relationship with the foxes here is arguably one of "double economics," to borrow Mark Jones's description of the shepherd's relationship with his sheep in pastoral poetry. Jones notes that critics have tended to read pastoral poems, like Wordsworth's "Michael," as "pitting material economics . . . against . . . spiritual economics" (1102) and have been wont to privilege one over the other, or to "rope off" these values "into separate regions of the poem" (1103; see also 1104). But Jones argues that this tension between the sheep as a spiritual symbol and the sheep as commodity is "central" to pastoral poetry and to pastoral societies, and that these values cannot be separated from one another (1104). Likewise, there is a double economics at work in Munro's representations of the rural, agricultural landscape, and this tension, between nature as aesthetic and nature as economic resource, cannot be resolved, nor can one value be separated from the other.

Munro herself comes to realize that in using her home place as material for her writing, she has used it as a resource, and she worries that the resource has run out from overuse: "The town, unlike the house, stays very much the same—nobody is renovating or changing it. Nevertheless it has changed for me. I have written about it and used it up. Here are more or less the same banks and hardware and grocery stores and the barbershop and the Town Hall tower, but all their secret, plentiful messages for me have drained away" (300). As Thacker argues, however, rather than seeking a new source of inspiration, a new place, Munro searches for a new understanding of place: "Munro was looking not so much for new materials as she was for new ways of seeing, of understanding her 'old' material, her home place" (282). Thacker credits Munro's move back to Ontario in the mid-1970s with helping her to find this new vision of home. "There is a qualitative difference, a new-found complexity," he contends, "in the stories Munro wrote after she returned to Huron County" (328). Part of this complexity is a social one: "With Huron's people, Huron's culture, Huron's life staring her full in the face . . . Munro saw social differences even more clearly" (328). Even more striking, though, is that—perhaps as a result of her relationship with geographer Gerry Fremlin, which began with her return home—Munro starts to take a "longer view" (290) of history; "geographical considerations (the Pleistocene era, pre-glacial lakes, drumlins)" begin to enter her writing and to change her perception of place once more (298).

As Thacker suggests, this shift is readily apparent in "What Do You Want to Know For?," a piece in which Munro "interweaves" a breast-cancer scare with "an investigation she and Fremlin undertook to learn about a crypt they spotted in a cemetery on one of their drives" around the countryside (473). According to Thacker, this memoir "is an elaboration of something the narrator in 'Walker Brothers Cowboy' says after she hears her father's explanation of 'how the Great Lakes came to be': 'The tiny share we have of time appalls me, though my father seems to regard it with tranquility'" (473). In this piece, and in later stories, Munro is still connecting her personal experience of the landscape to the "larger processes of society and environment" (Edward Relph, qtd. in McGill), but the environmental processes Munro considers here are far longer and more in depth than in her early work. She moves from an anthropocentric understanding of the region and its timescales to a glacial sense of time and place:

> The landscape here is a record of ancient events. It was formed by the advancing, stationary, and retreating ice. The ice has staged its conquest and retreats here several times, withdrawing for the last time about fifteen thousand years ago.
>
> Quite recently, you might say. Quite recently now that I have got used to a certain way of reckoning history. (Munro 318)

Munro discovers that when you consider history from a geological perspective, the human presence is but a small blip on the radar. From this perspective, "by far the most important influence on the landscape of southern Ontario has been the last glaciation, and the subsequent legacy of water and drainage from the melting ice" (Lee et al. 35).

As Munro illustrates, it is this legacy of glaciation that has left the southern Ontario landscape particularly susceptible to the imprint of human activity, and has shaped the kinds of human economic activities that have been possible: "A glacial landscape such as this is vulnerable. Many of its various contours are made up of gravel, and gravel is easy to get at, easy to scoop out, and always in demand. That's the material that makes these back roads passable. . . . And it's a way for farmers to get hold of some cash" (Munro 318). The landscape is not just acted upon, in other words, it is also an actor: "Just as landscape is a work—a product of the work of people—so too does landscape *do* work" (Mitchell 102; italics in orig.). And as Munro observes, when people stop working the landscape, "nature" starts to reclaim formerly cultivated areas. Such is the case in parts of Huron County where farming is no longer profitable and is on the decline: "The wooded areas—the bush—are making a strong comeback. In country like this the trend is no longer towards a taming of the landscape and a thickening of population, but rather the opposite. The bush will never again take over completely, but it is making a good grab" (Munro 327).

With the decline of farming, new and "unexpected" human "enterprises" also "spring up to replace it," and these enterprises change the aesthetics of the landscape as well (Munro 327). Munro's parents' farm, for instance, becomes a car-wrecking operation, and its agricultural landscape is "swept under a tide of car parts, gutted car bodies, smashed headlights, grilles, and fenders, overturned car seats with rotten bloated stuffing—heaps of painted, rusted, blackened, glittering, whole or twisted, defiant and surviving metal" (332). These changes do not reveal a separation between person and place, however; nor do they reveal environment to be a text or an aesthetic ideal that is distinct from material considerations. Rather, they suggest that landscape is "a realm in which we live as participants, not observers." When we come to understand our role as participants in, and not just observers of, landscape, we also come to realize, as does Munro, that "the consequences are not de-aestheticizing, a confounding with the world of practical purposes and effects, . . . but intensely and inescapably aesthetic" (Berleant, *Aesthetics of Environment* 170).

Works Cited

"Anthropology." *Encyclopaedia Britannica Online*. Encyclopaedia Britannica, 2011. Web. 19 Sept. 2011.

Berleant, Arnold. *Aesthetics and Environment: Variations on a Theme*. Burlington, VT: Ashgate, 2005.

_____. *The Aesthetics of Environment*. Philadelphia: Temple UP, 1992.

_____. *Living in the Landscape: Toward an Aesthetics of Environment*. Lawrence: UP of Kansas, 1997.

Boym, Svetlana. *The Future of Nostalgia*. New York: Basic, 2001.

Chalykoff, Lisa. "Overcoming the Two Solitudes of Canadian Literary Regionalism." *Studies in Canadian Literature* 23.1 (1998): 160–77.

Jones, Mark. "Double Economics: Ambivalence in Wordsworth's Pastoral." *PMLA* 108.5 (1993): 1098–113.

Lee, Harold, et al. *Ecological Land Classification for Southern Ontario: Training Manual*. London, ON: Ministry of Natural Resources, 2001.

McGill, Robert. "Performing Rurality: Tourists and Topology in Alice Munro's *Something I've Been Meaning to Tell You*." *Gradnet*. Gradnet e.V., 25 Nov. 2000. Web. 1 Sept. 2011.

Mitchell, Don. *Cultural Geography: A Critical Introduction*. Oxford: Blackwell, 2001.

Munro, Alice. *The View from Castle Rock*. Toronto: McClelland, 2006.

Thacker, Robert. *Alice Munro: Writing Her Lives; A Biography*. Toronto: Emblem, 2011.

"Age Could Be Her Ally": Late Style in Alice Munro's *Too Much Happiness*

Ailsa Cox

When *Hateship, Friendship, Courtship, Loveship, Marriage* (2001) was published in Munro's seventieth year, she spoke of this book as her last. As described in Robert Thacker's biography, the recurrence of a troubling heart condition coincided with the book's release, and although this was not the first time she had threatened to give up writing, the possibility seemed more likely than ever before. Yet, far from retirement, the next ten years brought not only three further collections but also a more visible public presence and wider global recognition, marked by the bestowal of the Man Booker International Prize in 2009. Munro would seem to be in her prime. In an interview with Canadian broadcaster Peter Gzowski in 2001, she spoke about a clash between social expectations of serenity in old age and the inner sense of an enduring self: "I'm very aware of my advanced age and the propriety it should bring or the calm it should bring and I'm always surprised that I don't feel very different. Ever. You're the same person at nineteen that you are at thirty-nine that you are at sixty that you go on being in a way" (qtd. in Thacker 494).

In *On Late Style: Music and Literature against the Grain* (2006), Edward Said discusses the radical and often unsettling work produced by many artists nearing the end of their lives. Despite cultural expectations of wisdom, maturity, and reconciliation, direct experience of senescence, illness, and bodily decay induces a distinctive idiom that, following Theodor W. Adorno, Said describes as "late style." This idiom "involves a nonharmonious, nonserene tension, and above all, a sort of deliberately unproductive productiveness going *against*" (7; italics in orig.). To what extent might we apply Said's description to Munro's own late style?

In many respects, Munro, born in 1931, is not only the same person but also the same writer that she was at thirty-nine. Her writing has,

276   Critical Insights from the beginning, been marked by an inclination toward disharmony and a resistance to comforting certainties. What we might call Munro's "nonserene" sensibility is simply made more acute as her protagonists follow their author into old age. The confronting of physical and occasionally mental decline in "The Bear Came over the Mountain," "Comfort," and other such stories in *Hateship* and its successors might be seen as a natural extension of those earlier stories, such as "The Ottawa Valley" (*Something I've Been Meaning to Tell You*, 1974), that respond to the debilitating illness suffered by Munro's mother. Munro's approach to her subject matter has remained consistent, chronicling the cruel ironies and absurdity of the human condition. As Margaret Atwood points out, "hidden sexual excesses, outbreaks of violence, lurid crimes, long-held grudges, [and] strange rumours" come with the territory (2). The high murder rate in *Too Much Happiness* (2009), pointed out by many reviewers, indicates a difference in degree rather than substance.

However, along with an authorial standpoint firmly based in old age, there is a changed emphasis in Munro's handling of time. While her work is still marked by a temporal fluidity in which past and present, impressions and memories intermingle, there is a sharpened awareness that time is irreversible and a growing sense of discontinuity between youth and old age. This aspect of Munro's late style provides the focus for my discussion of *Too Much Happiness*. The title piece is a long historical story, based on the life of the nineteenth-century Russian mathematician Sophia Kovalevsky. This is not the first time that Munro has written stories set over a hundred years ago, but previous examples have tended to be based on local or family material. "Too Much Happiness" refers to primary sources, including Sophia's diaries and letters, in a reconstruction of the events leading to her death; Munro also consulted a recent biography. Sophia's life story is recapitulated through a series of "flashbacks," as Munro terms them in the volume's acknowledgments, which take us through Europe and Russia at a breathtaking pace. There is a great deal of fact-based exposition to absorb in this highly condensed narrative, such as the complicated circumstances of Sophia's time in the Paris Commune.

The discourse of conventional historical fiction, giving us an authoritative version of external events, is in dialogue with a more subjective voice, giving us access to Sophia's interior consciousness. Narrative pace slows down considerably in the present-tense account of the long rail journey that culminates in Sophia's illness and subsequent death. The use of dreams, hallucinations, and other altered states is reminiscent of some of Munro's earlier historical fiction, for instance "Meneseteung" (*Friend of My Youth*, 1990) and "Carried Away" (*Open Secrets*, 1994). Yet the closed ending of "Too Much Happiness" is less speculative than either of those stories, a fictional reconstruction that seems to follow the documentary evidence. A series of fragmentary paragraphs describes Sophia's death and burial and the fate of those who survived her, ending with the poignant revelation that her name has been given to a crater on the moon. "Too Much Happiness" contrasts with the opening story, "Dimensions," which is more typical of Munro's work, focusing on intense personal experience and using an elliptical narrative structure that shifts between past and present. Talking about *Too Much Happiness* in an interview for the *New York Times* podcast, Munro says, "In some of my stories the action is given to me . . . then the whole thing is to find out what there is inside this banal action or horrible thing. To find out how it happens, why, and sometimes how people can survive it. That's what takes me into things that are much more mundane or quieter around the central thing" (Munro, "Book Review").

In "Dimensions," the "horrible thing" is the slaughter of Doree's three children at the hands of their own father. The narrative shifts between Doree's current life, in which she works as a chambermaid and attends counseling sessions, and memories of her relationship with Lloyd and the events leading up to the murder, an event that was triggered by a dent in a tin of spaghetti. Using such mundane details and imagining how an ordinary person might live through her worst nightmare, Munro avoids sensationalism and underplays the kind of suspense and dramatic tension expected in conventional crime fiction. She presents time as a continuum, a seamless flow of experience. The philosopher Henri Bergson coined the term *duration* to describe this indivisible flow of time, in contrast with clock time or absolute time, which is marked out and measured. Yet even though Doree's memories are deeply interwoven with her daily life, she has tried to cut herself off from her previous existence. She has changed her appearance and taken a job conducive to anonymity. Many of the other stories in this collection contain radical disjunctions and sudden transitions in the lives of their protagonists; the continuity between past and present is undermined by the brutality with which one time frame supersedes another. The sense of an enduring, essential self, described so well in Munro's 2001 interview with Peter Gzowski, is under threat, especially when her characters reach old age.

"Fiction" is one of the best examples of this tension between continuity and disruption. The story's iterative opening paragraphs are temporally indeterminate, describing habitual actions repeated over an unspecified time period: "It would already be dark," "There was the one special thing Joyce loved to see," et cetera (Munro, *Too Much* 32). We learn about Joyce and Jon's background and how they have come to be living in a forest, and then how Joyce is suddenly ousted by Jon's relationship with his young apprentice, Edie. Jon's passion for Edie defies Joyce's attempts to explain it away, as she finds his preference for "a heavy-striding heavy-witted carpenter's apprentice in baggy pants and flannel shirts" over "Joyce with her long legs and slim waist and long silky braid of dark hair" (38) inexplicable. Joyce's exile is as irreversible as the expulsion from paradise, and Edie's name may be read as an ironic reference to the biblical Eden.

"Fiction" is split into chapters 1 and 2, each one structured as a montage of elliptical passages. Switching from past tense to present, the second section introduces a rapid temporal and spatial dislocation that implicitly redefines the first third of the story as memories from a vanished past, rather than ongoing experience. The reader is forced to reorient herself in a story that delivers a whole series of narrative shocks. A much-older Joyce, "with a mop of pewter-coloured hair and a slight stoop" (Munro, *Too Much* 42), is remarried and living in a large house in North Vancouver. Although there are links with the previous chapter, notably the figure of Joyce herself, this section appears to be self-contained. The opening paragraph sets the scene and introduces the characters as in the beginning of a conventional narrative. When Jon is mentioned, he is introduced as if he were new to the reader: "She herself has no children, though she does have an ex-husband, Jon" (43).

Joyce's husband Matt is holding his sixty-fifth birthday party, an occasion that brings together a large extended family complicated by patterns of serial monogamy, including same-sex relationships. One of Matt's ex-wives, Doris, brings her partner, the biological mother of their new baby, who is younger than Doris's step-grandchildren. The breakdown of the conventional nuclear family and the muddling of generations is another sign of discontinuity. At the fringes of the party, Joyce encounters Christie O'Dell, a young author loosely connected to the family by marriage and friendship. The story's climactic revelation comes when Joyce recognizes a version of her former self in "*Kinder-totenlieder*," one of the stories in Christie's first collection. She gradually realizes that Christie must be Edie's little girl, one of her music pupils at the time of her breakup with Jon.

"Fiction" is one of Munro's characteristic meditations on the interplay between life and art. While Joyce's age and Ontario childhood bring her close to Munro biographically, it is Christie who stands for an authorial presence. Teasingly, Munro records Joyce's disappointment when she discovers Christie has published a collection of stories rather than a novel: "It seems to diminish the book's authority, making the author seem like somebody who is just hanging on to the gates of Literature" (*Too Much* 51–52). Joyce's assumption that Christie's fiction must be directly autobiographical, and therefore subject to verification, aligns her with Munro's early readers in Wingham, Ontario. "*Kinder-totenlieder*" is paraphrased in the text, placing Joyce's reading of the fiction in dialogue with her reconstruction of the events that provided the raw material. The story itself, in Munro-esque fashion, juxtaposes the young child's perceptions with her reevaluation of past experience as she matures into adulthood. Both the reader of "*Kindertotenlieder*" and its protagonist struggle with memory's tendency to edit personal history; Joyce finds it difficult to establish how much of the story might be real events that she has forgotten and how much might be pure invention. Reassuringly, for Joyce, Christie's story ends with an uplifting epiphany that affirms the relationship with the music teacher. But when Joyce takes her book to be signed at the store, Christie fails to recognize her, despite Joyce's hints. This incident is the last of "Fiction"'s many shocks, but the shock is defused when, in a coda that provides the ending, Joyce reflects, "This might even turn into a funny story that she would tell some day. She wouldn't be surprised" (61). In the bookstore, the division between reader and writer is maintained scrupulously. Joyce is hurried away from a taciturn Christie O'Dell when she is seen to overstep the mark. Yet the story's closing sentences narrow that division by restating the message, that we all share the fiction-making impulse. The two separate chapters in "Fiction" are, ultimately, unified by this fiction-making theme, but they also remain disconnected. The pewter-haired Joyce in the second chapter is no more the dark-haired Joyce in the first than she is the fictional teacher in Christie's story. The past cannot be revived, only reconstructed as another variety of fiction.

"Some Women" begins with the assertion "I am amazed sometimes to think how old I am" (Munro, *Too Much* 164); its final sentence, "I grew up, and old" (187), delivers a forceful reminder that the central consciousness is an elderly woman, imagining her earlier self across an immeasurable distance. "Some Women" establishes a more specific period setting than "Fiction," in the late 1940s or early 1950s, following the end of World War II. Like "Face," "Child's Play," and "Wenlock Edge," it uses a first-person narrator to evoke a period that is clearly differentiated from present-day reality. The second sentence, which begins with "I can remember when the streets of the town I lived in were sprinkled with water to lay the dust in summer" (164), mimics oral historical discourse. By framing "Some Women" as historical reminiscence, Munro distances her narrator's experiences from the reader's, and this historical distance is widened by the distinction between the anonymous narrator and her younger self.

This thirteen-year-old self has a holiday job looking after Young Mr. Crozier, the dying stepson of Old Mrs. Crozier. The widowed Mrs. Crozier, a grotesque, mean-minded tyrant, is presented as a witch-like figure, a parodic version of old age. Much of the story is concerned with attempts to break her spell, symbolically rescuing Young Mr. Crozier from his captivity by locking his door against this wicked stepmother and her familiar, the masseuse Roxanne, whose literal and figurative manipulations are finally repelled. Although these events are related retrospectively, they are mostly seen from the perspective of this younger self, without the benefit of hindsight. She is an impressionable girl whose reading of the situation is informed by gossip and hearsay. On the whole, she is a dispassionate observer, witnessing Roxanne massaging the naked body of Old Mrs. Crozier with detached curiosity. However, the sight of Young Mr. Crozier is more disturbing, "not really because he was sick and ugly . . . [but] because he was dying" (Munro, *Too Much* 173). The adolescent girl finds the emotional and sexual psychodrama played out in the Crozier household difficult to understand because of her inability to comprehend that desire may still be housed in a dying body: "The carnality at death's door—or the true love, for that matter—were things I had to shake off like shivers down my spine" (187).

The narrator's youthful squeamishness is an instance of abjection, that mixture of involuntary repulsion, horror, and fascination most frequently induced by a taboo or a personal phobia. Such states are common throughout Munro's work; no other writer has such an ability to evoke the sensations of shame and disgust. In *Too Much Happi-*

ness, examples include "Child's Play," in which the narrator's near-phobic reaction to a girl with learning difficulties leads to an appalling and shameful act, and "Face," in which the central character's facial disfigurement provokes a range of disturbing reactions. In "Wenlock Edge," the virginal young narrator reacts with surprising calm when her elderly host requires her to dine naked and then read poetry in the nude, until "an intimate agitation" (80), caused by the rough fabric of a library chair, subverts her self-protective rationalism.

According to psychoanalytical theory, abjection is rooted in primal experience. Under maternal guidance, the infant is trained to regulate its own body, differentiating between self and other. As part of this process, bodily substances such as feces, blood, and saliva are made to seem disgusting, and in most cultures they remain taboo. Julia Kristeva's book *Powers of Horror* (1982) analyzes the dangerous energy unleashed by summoning images of abjection in literary texts. Young Mr. Crozier is literally wasting away, turning into a corpse, which, Kristeva tells us, "is the utmost of abjection" (4). The narrator tells us that she has avoided looking at him, and yet has watched Roxanne giving him a sponge bath, observing the effects of premature aging. In a telling image, Munro goes on to invert the taboo, invoking its notional opposition, the holy or sacred: "I was aware of an atmosphere of death in the house, growing thicker as you approached this room, and he was at the centre of it, like the host the Catholics kept in the box so powerfully called the Tabernacle" (*Too Much* 173). The abject fascinates and repels. The gaze is averted, and yet we are compelled to watch. Again and again, Munro invokes "what nobody can stand to be reminded of" (28), that "horrible thing" at the center of the story. As we have seen, "Some Women" is framed by reminders of the narrator's age. The cryptic final sentence, "I grew up, and old," omits whatever may have happened in the intervening years, creating an explicit dichotomy between youth and age. In this story, as in "Fiction," life is presented as a succession of disconnected states, or indeed a series of self-contained stories.

The metaphor used in "Deep-Holes" is the island. "Deep-Holes," like the story "Silence" from Munro's 2004 collection, *Runaway*, deals with a mother's estrangement from an adult child. In both stories, the breaking of the maternal bond seems to stand for a rupture in the continuity of identity through the passage of time. This is the final section of "Deep-Holes": "And it was possible, too, that age could be her ally, turning her into somebody she didn't know yet. She has seen the look on the faces of certain old people—marooned on islands of their own choosing, clear sighted, content" (Munro, *Too Much* 115). The figure of the dead child—which, like that of the nurse and the patient, recurs across Munro's oeuvre—makes several appearances in *Too Much Happiness*. Christie O'Dell's title "*Kindertotenlieder*" (Songs on the death of children) in "Fiction" might have been used for several of these stories. Metaphorically speaking, all children die; they grow up, becoming autonomous individuals, separated from both their parents and their childhood selves. In "Deep-Holes" and "Silence," that separation seems as absolute and irreversible as death.

The title story of Munro's earlier collection *The Moons of Jupiter* (1982) makes clear connections between mother-child estrangement, mortality, and bereavement. The imminent death of a parent runs parallel with a daughter's decision to cut herself off from the family. This triggers memories of a health scare when she was a small child; the narrator found herself anticipating Nichola's death by a subtle and, she believes, undetectable withdrawal: "I saw how the forms of love might be maintained with a condemned person but with the love in fact measured and disciplined, because you have to survive" (Munro, *Moons* 230). This pragmatic approach to survival continues in the two later stories.

In "Deep-Holes," Kent becomes a drifter, gradually losing touch, surfacing by chance some years later as an ascetic living the life of a street beggar under the new name of Jonah. The name he says he thought of choosing, Lazarus, is a self-conscious reference to a near-death experience in the caves at Osler Bluff. The possibility of resurrection is further underlined by intertextual references to the New Testament. But the mother-child dyad cannot be restored. Indeed, Kent/ Jonah has appropriated the maternal figure, heading a substitute "family" of the socially excluded. The worlds of mother and child are mutually incomprehensible. Censuring his mother Sally's almost instinctive interrogation of language, Kent/Jonah says, "I don't fuss about my words" (Munro, *Too Much* 114), but he does, in fact, "fuss" about his mother's words, interrupting and censuring her speech and closing down lines of inquiry:

"Why are you trying not to smile?" he said. "Because I said 'relationships'? That's a cant word? I don't fuss about my words."

Sally said, "I was thinking of Jesus. 'Woman, what have I to do with thee?'"

The look that leapt to his face was almost savage.

"Don't you get tired, Sally? Don't you get tired of being clever? I can't go on talking this way, I'm sorry. I've got things to do." (114)

This reproach—"Don't you get tired of being clever?"—echoes an exchange in "Silence" between the rejected mother and the substitute mother, who heads the cult Juliet's daughter has joined:

"The spiritual dimension—I have to say this—was it not altogether lacking in Penelope's life? I take it she did not grow up in a faith-based home."

"Religion was not a banned subject. We could talk about it."

"But perhaps it was the way you talked about it. Your intellectual way? If you know what I mean. You are so clever," she adds, kindly. (Munro, *Runaway* 131–32)

It is useful once again to turn, briefly, to psychoanalytical theory when we examine these accusations of "cleverness." Kristeva distinguishes between a semiotic and a symbolic modality in language. The semiotic indicates the purely rhythmic and sensuous aspects, the maternal, while the symbolic refers to logic, order and positions, the paternal.

When Juliet and Sally are rebuked for being "clever," their speech is relegated to this paternal modality and their maternal status is denied. In the eyes of their accusers, they are not real mothers. The "Silence" of the title refers not only to the breaking off of communication by Juliet's daughter but also to the silencing of Juliet herself, who is unable to speak openly about her situation.

Neither "Deep-Holes" nor "Silence" minimizes the mother's suffering. Yet, ultimately, both mothers are able to see beyond the trauma of rejection by establishing a provisional boundary between past and present, the former self and the living subject. When an old school friend of her daughter's mentions bumping into her, Juliet surmises that Penelope is based somewhere in the Northwest Territories and has five children. She envisages the kind of life she might be living, and then realizes the futility of such speculation:

> The Penelope Juliet sought was gone. The woman Heather had spotted in Edmonton, the mother who had brought her sons to Edmonton to get their school uniforms, who had changed in face and body so that Heather did not recognize her, was nobody Juliet knew.
>   Does Juliet believe this? (Munro, *Runaway* 157)

As I have suggested, this boundary is provisional. The unanswered question voices the tension between transformation and continuity in Munro's late work, a tension between absolute time and Bergsonian duration. What matters here is finding the means to survive: "She keeps on hoping for a word from Penelope, but not in any strenuous way. She hopes as people who know better hope for undeserved blessings, spontaneous remissions, things of that sort" (158)—that is, miracles. By evoking the spiritual in this final paragraph, Munro again ends the story with the faint suggestion that, despite the external split between mother and child, the mother's subjectivity is constructed in dialogue with the child. Sally is striving toward self-sufficiency with her frozen single portions of ready-cooked lasagna, but "Deep-Holes" also ends with less than certainty: "It was possible, too" (Munro, *Too Much* 115). The image of the island stands for isolation, but also, in the wider context of the story, for its opposite, intimacy. Finding out about small islands used to be a private game between Sally and Kent when he was convalescing after the accident at Osler Bluff. Survival, as these two stories show, does not necessarily mean full recovery.

That final line in "Some Women," "I grew up, and old," serves as a reminder that old age in itself signals survival, in contrast with the fate of Young Mr. Crozier, dead "sometime before the leaves were off" (Munro, *Too Much* 187). The theme of survival comes to the fore in "Free Radicals," the story that immediately follows "Deep-Holes." Truly terrifying, but also grimly comic, "Free Radicals" is Munro at her most gothic. It is also a testimony to the fierceness of the will to live, even, or perhaps especially, in a character on the brink of death. Temporarily in remission from cancer, Nita endures her solitary life, deprived of coffee, wine, and, most of all, the company of her husband, who was seemingly in good health but has died unexpectedly. One morning, a figure materializes as a "dark stripe" (122) at the door, cutting out the morning light. The stranger insinuates his way into the house, at first appearing harmless but soon revealing himself as a killer on the run. At first Nita feels she has nothing to lose—her cancer "freed her, put her out of danger" (127)—but as he reveals the grisly details of his crime, she becomes increasingly frightened: "The fact of her cancer was not going to be any help to her at the present moment, none at all. The fact that she was going to die within a year refused to cancel out the fact that she might die now" (131).

Over an illicit glass of wine, Nita manages to unnerve the intruder by improvising an alternative version of the past in which she casts herself in the role of poisoner. The tactic is intended to persuade the stranger that he can ensure Nita's silence through blackmail, rather than by killing her. But the story and the wine have a secondary effect. Spooked by Nita's tale, he speeds off in her late husband's car, killing himself shortly afterward in a traffic accident. Death has come to the door, and has been, at least temporarily, repelled. Nita survives through an act of protective coloration. She turns the tables on the intruder by constructing an alternative identity, one that is paired with his own self-image:

> She said, "I just think you haven't ever done anything like this before."
> "Course I haven't. You think I'm a murderer? Yeah, I killed them but I'm not a murderer."
> "There's a difference," she said.
> "You bet."
> "I know what it's like. I know what it's like to get rid of somebody who has injured you."
> "Yeah?"
> "I have done the same thing you did." (Munro, *Too Much* 132)

In the made-up yarn that follows, Nita masquerades as her husband's first wife, while recasting her own younger self in the lesser role of murder victim, "the girl my husband was in love with . . . this useless whiner who worked in the registrar's office" (133). After the gunman has fled, Nita has a second unheralded visit, from the police. Now she assumes yet another role, the little old lady who has not even noticed that her car has been stolen: "There followed a kindly stern lecture. Leaving keys in the car. Woman living alone. These days you never know" (137).

A certain existential freedom derives from both the social exile of old age and the lack of investment in a long-term future. In a conversation with Diana Athill, broadcast from the International Festival of Authors in Toronto in 2009, Munro spoke about a growing sense of detachment, saying, "I do feel less bothered by things" (Munro and Athill). Some of Munro's stories imply a contrast between the narrow scope of a human lifetime and the larger timescale of the natural world or of historical forces; once again, we might look back to "The Moons of Jupiter" for its use of astronomy. In "Silence" (*Runaway*), this larger timescale is signaled by Juliet's fascination with the classics and the world of ancient history. "Deep-Holes" references geology to the same effect, shifting the perspective away from the limitations of a single lifetime. "Wood," a variation on the sketch or anecdote as practiced by Mark Twain, concerns a misadventure whilst gathering timber. Placed in the timeless setting of the ancient forest, this story also shows human beings dwarfed by the forces of nature. In "Child's Play," the adult Marlene chooses a profession that also engages with broad sweeps of time: she becomes an anthropologist, removing herself from the expected cycle of marriage and motherhood, doing her best to avoid intimacy in her private life.

The historical emphasis in *Too Much Happiness*, in both the title story and the stories that suggest reminiscence, also forces our attention to the long term. In both "Deep-Holes" and "Free Radicals," the elderly protagonist conducts an internal dialogue with her dead partner. While communion with the dead is not an entirely new departure for Munro (see the title story in *Friend of My Youth*), its extensive use in these stories places Sally and Nita in a liminal space, at a distance from current external reality. In "Dimensions," Lloyd's claim to be able to contact the children he has murdered in another "dimension" outside this world offers Doree a small amount of temporary comfort. But she does not, ultimately, join him there; a random event at the end of the story brings her back to the land of the living, where she belongs much more fully than Sally and Nita do.

In his book *On Late Style*, Edward Said discusses the work of several artists he considers exemplars of late style, including Ludwig van Beethoven, Jean Genet, Giuseppe Tomasi di Lampedusa, Benjamin Britten, Wolfgang Amadeus Mozart, and Thomas Mann—all male. Said's model of the artist suits the romantic image of the striving, iconoclastic hero, raging against the dying of the light. Munro's late style does not belong to the same category as theirs, as understood by Said, in that it is a development of earlier forms and techniques rather than a startling new departure. However, Munro's work confirms Said's view that there is often something radical, even transgressive, in the writings of old age. Despite a literary culture that tends to privilege youth over experience, she reminds us of her age and of our own mortality, confronting all those things we would rather not contemplate.

Works Cited

Atwood, Margaret. "Close to Home." *Guardian* 11 Oct. 2008, review sec.: 2.

Gzowski, Peter. "You're the Same Person at 19 That You Are at 60." *Globe and Mail* 29 Sept. 2001: F4–5.

Kristeva, Julia. *Powers of Horror: An Essay on Abjection.* Trans. Léon S. Roudiez. New York: Columbia UP, 1982.

Munro, Alice. "Book Review Podcast: Alice Munro." Interview by Sam Tanenhaus. *ArtsBeat Blog.* New York Times, 27 Nov. 2009. Web. 7 Apr. 2010.

_____. *The Moons of Jupiter.* Toronto: Penguin, 1995.

_____. *Runaway.* London: Chatto, 2004.

_____. *Too Much Happiness.* London: Chatto, 2009.

Munro, Alice, and Diana Athill. "In Conversation: Alice Munro and Diana Athill at IFOA XXX." Interview by Bill Richardson. *Globe and Mail.* Phillip Crawley, 22 Oct. 2009. Web. 10 Feb. 2010.

Said, Edward. *On Late Style: Music and Literature against the Grain.* New York: Pantheon, 2006.

Thacker, Robert. *Alice Munro: Writing Her Lives; A Biography.* Toronto: McClelland, 2005.

RESOURCES

Chronology of Alice Munro's Life _____

1931	Alice Ann Laidlaw is born July 10 in Wingham, Ontario, to Robert Eric Laidlaw and Anne Clarke Chamney Laidlaw
1949	Graduates from Wingham and District High School, Ontario
1949–51	Attends University of Western Ontario on a scholarship
1951	Marries James Munro and moves to Vancouver, British Columbia
1952–53	Works at Vancouver Public Library
1953	Daughter Sheila Margaret is born
1955	Daughter Catherine Alice is born but dies soon after
1957	Daughter Jenny Alison is born
1959	Mother dies of Parkinson's disease
1963	Moves to Victoria, British Columbia, and establishes Munro's Books with her husband
1966	Daughter Andrea Sarah is born
1968	Publishes *Dance of the Happy Shades*; wins Governor General's Literary Award for fiction
1971	Publishes *Lives of Girls and Women*
1971–72	Separates from her husband, returns to Ontario, and becomes writer in residence at University of Western Ontario
1972	*Lives of Girls and Women* receives Canadian Booksellers Association International Book of the Year Award
1974	Publishes *Something I've Been Meaning to Tell You*; shares the Province of Ontario Council for the Arts Award with Hugh Hood

1976	Divorces her husband, marries Gerald Fremlin, and moves to farm near Clinton, Ontario; begins to publish stories in the *New Yorker*
1978	Publishes *Who Do You Think You Are?* (titled *The Beggar Maid* in British and American editions); receives Governor General's Literary Award for fiction
1980	Becomes writer in residence at University of British Columbia and University of Queensland, Brisbane, Australia
1981	Makes official trip to China with other Canadian writers; a conference on her work is held at University of Waterloo
1982	Publishes *The Moons of Jupiter*
1986	Publishes *The Progress of Love*; receives Governor General's Literary Award for fiction and Marian Engel Award
1990	Publishes *Friend of My Youth*; is short-listed for Irish Times/Aer Lingus International Fiction Prize
1994	Publishes *Open Secrets*
1995	*Open Secrets* short-listed for Irish Times International Fiction Prize
1997	Wins PEN/Malamud Award for Excellence in Short Fiction
1998	Publishes *The Love of a Good Woman*; wins National Book Critics Circle Award for fiction and Giller Prize
2001	Publishes *Hateship, Friendship, Courtship, Loveship, Marriage*; wins Rea Award for the Short Story and O. Henry Special Award for Continuing Achievement
2004	Publishes *Runaway*; wins Giller Prize
2005	Is named one of the world's most influential people by *Time* magazine; wins the Terasen Lifetime Achievement Award

2006	Publishes *The View from Castle Rock*
2007	"The Bear Came over the Mountain" is made into the feature film *Away from Her*
2009	Publishes *Too Much Happiness*; wins third Man Booker International Prize

Works by Alice Munro

Dance of the Happy Shades. Toronto: Ryerson, 1968.

Lives of Girls and Women. Toronto: McGraw, 1971.

Something I've Been Meaning to Tell You. Toronto: McGraw, 1974.

Who Do You Think You Are? Toronto: Macmillan, 1978. Published as *The Beggar Maid: Stories of Flo and Rose* in the United States and Great Britain.

The Moons of Jupiter. Toronto: Macmillan, 1982.

The Progress of Love. Toronto: McClelland, 1986.

Friend of My Youth. Toronto: McClelland, 1990.

Open Secrets. Toronto: McClelland, 1994.

Selected Stories. Toronto: McClelland, 1996.

The Love of a Good Woman. Toronto: McClelland, 1998.

Hateship, Friendship, Courtship, Loveship, Marriage. Toronto: McClelland, 2001.

No Love Lost. Comp. Jane Urquhart. Toronto: McClelland, 2003.

Runaway. Toronto: McClelland, 2004.

Alice Munro's Best: Selected Stories. Toronto: McClelland, 2006. Published as *Carried Away: A Selection of Stories* in the United States and Great Britain.

The View from Castle Rock. Toronto: McClelland, 2006.

Too Much Happiness. Toronto: McClelland, 2009.

Bibliography

Beran, Carol. "Thomas Hardy, Alice Munro, and the Question of Influence." *American Review of Canadian Studies* 29.2 (1999): 237–58.

Besner, Neil Kalman. *Introducing Alice Munro's* Lives of Girls and Women: *A Reader's Guide*. Toronto: ECW, 1990.

Blodgett, E. D. *Alice Munro*. Boston: Twayne, 1988.

Carrington, Ildikó de Papp. *Controlling the Uncontrollable: The Fiction of Alice Munro*. De Kalb: Northern Illinois UP, 1989.

Carscallen, James. *The Other Country: Patterns in the Writing of Alice Munro*. Toronto: ECW, 1993.

Charman, Caitlin J. "There's Got to Be Some Wrenching and Slashing: Horror and Retrospection in Alice Munro's 'Fits.'" *Canadian Literature* 191 (2006): 13–30.

Condé, Mary. "Fathers in Alice Munro's 'Fathers.'" *Journal of the Short Story in English* 41 (2003): 93–101.

Cox, Ailsa. *Alice Munro*. Tavistock, Eng.: Northcote, 2004.

Dahlie, Hallvard. *Alice Munro and Her Works*. Toronto: ECW, 1984.

Fowler, Rowena. "The Art of Alice Munro: *The Beggar Maid* and *Lives of Girls and Women*." *Critique: Studies in Contemporary Fiction* 25.4 (1984): 189–98.

Gerlach, John. "To Close or Not to Close: Alice Munro's 'The Love of a Good Woman.'" *Journal of Narrative Theory* 37.1 (2007): 146–58.

Heble, Ajay. *The Tumble of Reason: Alice Munro's Discourse of Absence*. Toronto: U of Toronto P, 1994.

Hooper, Brad. *The Fiction of Alice Munro: An Appreciation*. Westport, CT: Praeger, 2008.

Houston, Pam. "A Hopeful Sign: The Making of Metonymic Meaning in Munro's 'Meneseteung.'" *Kenyon Review* 14.4 (Sept. 1992): 79–92.

Howells, Coral Ann. *Alice Munro*. New York: Manchester UP, 1998.

Hoy, Helen. "'Rose and Janet': Alice Munro's Metafiction." *Canadian Literature* 121 (1989): 59–83.

Lynch, Gerald. "No, Honey, I'm Home: Place over Love in Alice Munro's Short Story Cycle *Who Do You Think You Are?*" *Canadian Literature* 160 (1999): 73–98.

MacKendrick, Louis K., ed. *Probable Fictions: Alice Munro's Narrative Acts*. Toronto: ECW, 1983.

Martin, W. R. *Alice Munro: Paradox and Parallel*. Edmonton: U of Alberta P, 1987.

May, Charles E. "Why Does Alice Munro Write Short Stories?" *Wascana Review* 38.1 (2003): 16–28.

Mayberry, Katherine J. "'Every Last Thing . . . Everlasting': Alice Munro and the Limits of Narrative." *Studies in Short Fiction* 29.4 (1992): 531–41.

McGill, Robert. "Somewhere I've Been Meaning to Tell You: Alice Munro's Fiction of Distance." *Journal of Commonwealth Literature* 37.1 (2002): 9–29.

_____. "Where Do You Think You Are? Alice Munro's Open Houses." *Mosaic* 35.4 (2002): 103–19.

Miller, Judith, ed. *The Art of Alice Munro: Saying the Unsayable*; *Papers from the Waterloo Conference*. Waterloo, ON: U of Waterloo P, 1984.

Morgenstern, Naomi. "The Baby or the Violin? Ethics and Femininity in the Fiction of Alice Munro." *Literature Interpretation Theory* 14.2 (2003): 69–97.

Munro, Sheila. *Lives of Mothers and Daughters: Growing Up with Alice Munro*. Toronto: McClelland, 2001.

Rasporich, Beverly Jean. *Dance of the Sexes: Art and Gender in the Fiction of Alice Munro*. Edmonton: U of Alberta P, 1990.

Redekop, Magdalene. *Mothers and Other Clowns: The Stories of Alice Munro*. New York: Routledge, 1992.

Ross, Catherine Sheldrick. *Alice Munro: A Double Life*. Toronto: ECW, 1992.

Smythe, Karen E. *Figuring Grief: Gallant, Munro, and the Poetics of Elegy*. Montreal: McGill-Queen's UP, 1992.

Thacker, Robert. *Alice Munro: Writing Her Lives; A Biography*. Toronto: McClelland, 2005.

_____, ed. *The Rest of the Story: Critical Essays on Alice Munro*. Toronto: ECW, 1999.

Wachtel, Eleanor. "Alice Munro: A Life in Writing." *Queen's Quarterly* 112.2 (2005): 267–80.

Woodcock, George. "The Plots of Life: The Realism of Alice Munro." *Queen's Quarterly* 93.2 (1986): 235–50.

CRITICAL
INSIGHTS

About the Editor _____

Charles E. May earned his doctorate at Ohio University in 1966 and is professor emeritus at California State University, Long Beach. He is the author of *Edgar Allan Poe: A Study of the Short Fiction* (1991) and *The Short Story: The Reality of Artifice* (1995), and the editor of *Short Story Theories* (1977), *Twentieth-Century European Short Story* (1989), *Fiction's Many Worlds* (1992), and *The New Short Story Theories* (1994). He has published over three hundred articles and reviews on the short story in various scholarly journals, literary quarterlies, books, reference works, and newspapers. In 1996–97, he was a Fulbright Senior Fellow at University College Dublin and Trinity College Dublin. He writes a blog entitled *Reading the Short Story* at http://may-on-the-short-story.blogspot.com/. He has lectured on the short story at international conferences in France, Spain, Portugal, Norway, Ireland, Canada, and the United States.

Contributors

Charles E. May is professor emeritus at California State University, Long Beach. The author and editor of several books on short fiction, he has also written over three hundred articles and reviews on the short story for various publications. He writes a blog entitled *Reading the Short Story* and has lectured on the short story at international conferences throughout Europe, Canada, and the United States.

Robert Thacker is Charles A. Dana Professor of Canadian Studies and English and associate dean for Academic Advising Programs at St. Lawrence University. As a scholar, he has contributed broadly to Canadian literary studies, the study of the North American West in literature, and especially Canada–United States literary comparisons. In particular, he has published many essays on the works of Alice Munro and Willa Cather, and his work *The Great Prairie Fact and Literary Imagination* (1989) remains the only critical examination of the literature of the prairie-plains region in its binational context. He has been both the president and the executive secretary and treasurer of the Western Literature Association, and has also served as editor of the *American Review of Canadian Studies*. His book *Alice Munro: Writing Her Lives; A Biography*, written with the cooperation of its subject, was published in 2005, with an updated paperback edition published in 2011. His chapter on Munro, Margaret Atwood, Mavis Gallant, and Carol Shields appeared in *The Cambridge History of Canadian Literature* (2009).

Timothy McIntyre is a PhD candidate at Queen's University in Kingston, Ontario, writing his dissertation on Alice Munro's fiction. His academic work has been published in *Stirrings Still: The International Journal of Existential Literature*, *J. M. Coetzee: Critical Perspectives*, *Historical Perspectives on Canadian Publishing*, and *Canadian Literature*. His reviews of poetry and nonfiction have appeared in the *Fiddlehead* and *Vallum Magazine.*

Naomi Morgenstern has a PhD in English and American literature from Cornell University and teaches in the English Department at the University of Toronto. She has published essays on feminist, psychoanalytic, and deconstructive critical theory, as well as on a range of nineteenth- and twentieth-century authors, including Toni Morrison, Carson McCullers, E. L. Doctorow, Charles Brockden Brown, Herman Melville, and Alice Munro. She has recently been working on two monographs: *The Resistance to Being*, an account of literary and theoretical approaches to the "right to death," and an extensive psychoanalytic study of Alice Munro's fiction.

Carol L. Beran earned her doctorate in English at the University of California, Berkeley. She is professor of English at Saint Mary's College of California, where she enjoys teaching short fiction, nineteenth-century British literature, children's literature, introduction to literary analysis, and both freshman and advanced composition, as well as Canadian literature. She has published essays on works by many Canadian writers, including Margaret Atwood, Robert Kroetsch, Margaret Laurence, Hugh MacLennan, Alice Munro, Michael Ondaatje, and Aritha Van Herk. Her book *Living over the Abyss* (1993) is about Atwood's *Life Before Man* (1979). She is an associate editor of the *American Review of Canadian Studies*, a member of the editorial board of *Margaret Atwood Studies*, and past president of the Western Canadian Studies Association.

Medrie Purdham is an assistant professor at the University of Regina, where she teaches Canadian literature and creative writing. Her doctoral thesis was entitled *The Encyclopedic Imagination and the Canadian Artist-Figure*. Her poetry has been published in the *New Quarterly*, the *Malahat Review*, the *Fiddlehead*, the *Antigonish Review*, and other Canadian literary journals, and she has recently been working on a poetry manuscript. Her research is focused on Canadian literature at the intersection of modernism and postmodernism, and her particular interests are in prosody, modernist epistemology, the poetics and politics of collecting, and the aesthetics of the miniature.

David Peck received his BA from Colgate University and his PhD from Temple University. He began teaching at California State University, Long Beach in 1967, and has been a Fulbright lecturer in American literature at the University of Ljubljana in Yugoslavia (1984–85) and a visiting professor of American literature at the University of Leeds (1990–91). He has published half a dozen books, including *Novels of Initiation: A Guidebook for Teaching Literature to Adolescents* (1989) and *Teaching American Ethnic Literatures: Nineteen Essays* (1996, edited with John Maitino). He lives and writes in Laguna Beach, California, where he is chairman of the South Orange County Cross-Cultural Council, a nonprofit organization offering job and language skills to recent Latino immigrants.

Mark Levene teaches in the Department of English at the University of Toronto. His graduate seminars cover such wide-ranging subjects as Alice Munro, novelists and terrorists, and long-form reporting. He has written extensively about political fiction, including a study of Arthur Koestler, as well as contemporary literature. He has coedited two collections of essays on the Canadian short story and, with Rosemary Sullivan, *Short Fiction: An Anthology* (2003). He has recently been working on a book, *The Ghostly World of Robert Stone*, and editing Robert Stone's essays.

Philip Coleman is a lecturer in English studies in the School of English, Trinity College Dublin, where he specializes in American writing. He has edited *"After Thirty Falls": New Essays on John Berryman* (2007), *On Literature and Science: Essays, Reflections, Provocations* (2007), and *Reading Pearse Hutchinson: From Findrum to Fisterre* (2011), and has published widely on aspects of American fiction and poetry.

He has recently worked on a book-length study on John Berryman. His published work on short fiction includes essays on William Austin, Sandra Cisneros, Chuck Palahniuk, and David Foster Wallace.

J. R. (Tim) Struthers is a bibliographer, interviewer, critic, editor, and small-press publisher. He has been publishing work on the short story for more than thirty-five years, including the first two scholarly articles on Alice Munro worldwide, published in 1975. He has edited or coedited some twenty volumes of scholarship, criticism, autobiography, fiction, and poetry, including the widely cited anthology *New Contexts of Canadian Criticism* (1997). His first collections about the short story were *The Montreal Story Tellers: Memoirs, Photographs, Critical Essays* (1985), *New Directions from Old* (1991), and *How Stories Mean* (1993). Most recently, he has prepared the creative/critical volume *Clark Blaise, Proprietor* (2007), Clark Blaise's *Selected Essays* (2008), and George Elliott's story cycle *Sand Gardens on First Beach* (2010). He lives in Guelph, Ontario, Canada. In 2010, he celebrated twenty-five years of service to the University of Guelph.

Michael Toolan studied at the Universities of Edinburgh and Oxford and taught at the National University of Singapore and the University of Washington, Seattle before returning to Britain in 1996. He has published several books on stylistics and on narrative, such as *Language in Literature* (1998) and *Narrative: A Critical Linguistic Introduction* (2001). He is professor of English language at the University of Birmingham, where he convenes the MA program in literary linguistics. He is also editor of the *Journal of Literary Semantics*. His book *Narrative Progression in the Short Story: A Corpus Stylistic Approach* was published in 2009.

Jeff Birkenstein is an associate professor of English at Saint Martin's University in Lacey, Washington. He received his MA in English from California State University, Long Beach and his PhD in English from the University of Kentucky in 2003. He has a second MA in TESOL (Teaching English as a Second/Other Language). His major interests lie in American and world short stories, as well as food and cultural criticism. His first book, *Reframing 9/11: Film, Popular Culture, and the "War on Terror,"* coedited with Anna Froula and Karen Randell, was published in 2010.

David Crouse is an award-winning short-story writer and a teacher in the MFA program at the University of Alaska Fairbanks. His short-fiction collection *Copy Cats* (2005) received the Flannery O'Connor Award for Short Fiction in 2005 and was nominated for the PEN/Faulkner Award the following year. A second collection, *The Man Back There* (2008), was awarded the Mary McCarthy Prize in Short Fiction. His short fiction has appeared in a wide variety of top literary magazines.

Michael Trussler is a writer of literary criticism, poetry, and fiction, and has published widely on short fiction, the contemporary novel, and film. His short-story collection *Encounters* (2006) won the Regina Book Award and the Book of the Year

Award from the Saskatchewan Book Awards in 2006. His collection of poetry, *Accidental Animals* (2007), was short-listed for the same awards in 2007. *A Homemade Life*, an experimental chapbook of photographs and text, was published in 2009. He teaches English at the University of Regina and was the editor of *Wascana Review* from 2002 to 2008.

Caitlin Charman completed her PhD at Queen's University with a dissertation entitled *A Littoral Place: Loss and Environment in Contemporary Newfoundland Fiction*. In 2006, she published an article in *Canadian Literature* on Alice Munro's use of horror and retrospection. She works as a research associate at the Conference Board of Canada.

Ailsa Cox is reader in English and writing at Edge Hill University in Lancashire, England. Her books include *Alice Munro* (2004), *Writing Short Stories* (2005), and, as editor, *Teaching the Short Story* (2011). She is also the editor of the journal *Short Fiction in Theory and Practice*. She has published essays on Helen Simpson, Elizabeth Bowen, and Nell Freudenberger, among other short-story writers, and wrote a chapter on the Vancouver stories of Alice Munro and Nancy Lee for *The Postcolonial Short Story* (forthcoming), edited by Paul March-Russell and Maggie Awadalla. Her short-story collection *The Real Louise and Other Stories* was published in 2009.

Index